THE UNIVERSITY OF
WINCHESTER

Martial Rose Library
Tel: 01962 827306

18 DEC 2009

2 5 JAN 2010

2 4 JAN 2011

2 6 JAN 2012

To be returned on or before the day marked above, subject to recall.

THE SCARECROW PRESS, INC.

SCARECROW PRESS, INC.

Published in the United States of America
by Scarecrow Press, Inc.
A wholly owned subsidiary of
The Rowman & Littlefield Publishing Group, Inc.
4501 Forbes Boulevard, Suite 200, Lanham, Maryland 20706
www.scarecrowpress.com

PO Box 317
Oxford
OX2 9RU, UK

British Library Cataloguing in Publication Information Available

Library of Congress Cataloging-in-Publication Data

Koven, Mikel J.
  La dolce morte : vernacular cinema and the Italian giallo film / Mikel J. Koven.
    p. cm.
  Includes bibliographical references and index.
  ISBN-13: 978-0-8108-5870-1 (pbk. : alk. paper)
  ISBN-10: 0-8108-5870-3 (pbk. : alk. paper)
  1. Detective and mystery films—Italy—History and criticism. 2. Horror films—Italy—
History and criticism. I. Title.

PN1995.9.D4K68 2006
791.43'6556—dc22   2006015624

⊗™ The paper used in this publication meets the minimum requirements of
American National Standard for Information Sciences—Permanence of
Paper for Printed Library Materials, ANSI/NISO Z39.48-1992.
Manufactured in the United States of America.

~

Contents

~

Preface

This book has three aims. The first, obviously, is an exploration of the *giallo*, albeit from a synchronic, rather than diachronic, perspective, with particular attention to some of the thematic concerns that arise from a textual study of these films. This book is categorically *not* a review of the films, debating whether or not they are good or bad; nor does it fall into the "cult of the auteur," helping to establish a pantheon of "rediscovered" Italian horror cinema artistes, putting Lucio Fulci, Sergio Martino, and Aldo Lado into the same revered echelons as Dario Argento and Mario Bava.

Second, this book aims to refocus the discussion of genre (particularly "subgenre") into the Italian concept of the *filone*. Seeing the interrelationships between films, how one influences others, how certain filmmakers take ideas and build off of them, and then how those ideas are further transformed by other filmmakers, is an underdeveloped aspect in genre study. And I hope this book contributes to that discussion.

Third, this book situates the discussion of the *giallo* within what I call "vernacular cinema" as a replacement for the term "popular cinema." To look at a film from a vernacular perspective removes the a priori assumptions about what constitutes a "good" film, how a particular film is, in some way, "artistic." Vernacular cinema asks, to paraphrase Tina Turner, "what's art got to do with it?" Vernacular cinema seeks to look at subaltern cinema not for how it might (or might not) conform to the precepts of high-art/modernist cinema, but for what it does in its own right. With the exception of die-hard aficionados of European or Italian horror cinema, I suspect that most people reading this book will not have heard of many of these films. Proper vernacular cinema is below most of our cultural radar. Go to any local video store and take a look at some of the genre films on display—any genre will do, but the best choices are those genres you are not necessarily a big fan of, or where your knowledge is less. How many of these titles have you heard of? Of course, you will be familiar with the more famous examples; if you read the credit listings, maybe you'll know some of the stars or directors. But when you look on these shelves and find yourself saying, "I've never heard of that" or "Who?" the chances are you are entering a vernacular cinema realm. The power of vernacular cinema, in fact what makes it vernacular in the first place, is that these movies are not necessarily for *us*; the filmmakers have their audience and we are not (necessarily) them. Vernacular cinema does not care if we see these movies. These films are an insider's discourse among themselves. We do not matter. And that is what I find particularly liberating about these films.

My academic background is as a folklorist. That may seem like a strange admission to begin a book on the Italian *giallo* film with, but I think it is important. My doctorate is in folklore studies, and although I lecture in film and television, my training as a folklorist permeates my research into film and TV, even if not about explicitly folkloristic topics. I have published dozens of film/television papers in academic journals and edited collections, but still my folklore orientation tends to bleed through, like some twisted academic palimpsest. Throughout the vast majority of my writings, my own intellectual project has been to address popular film and television texts within an academic folklore context and to demonstrate folkloristic ways of reading mass-mediated entertainment within a film and TV context. While I am certainly writing for the film studies academic market, particularly those academics working in cult, horror, and perhaps even European cinema arenas, I am still a folklorist working on popular film, which perhaps explains why I am approaching the topic the way I am. And while I am not entirely sure I would recognize this book within a folklore context, this academic perspective obviously informs what I do. My hope for this book is to not only have it recognized by film scholars as, to my knowledge, the first English-language academic study of the Italian *giallo* film, but also that folklorists, too, would recognize that how I approach these films fits within contemporary folkloristics (beyond the obvious relevance of chapter 7, which is about folklore *in* the *giallo*).

Academic research is a dialogue, not a monologue. One of the problems of writing on an area that has not been as well trodden as others is that such a project must be inherently preliminary. I invite all readers to disagree with me and point out where I am wrong, what I have misinterpreted, and what new ideas are generated when you apply your own pet theories that I should have included here but didn't. I sincerely look forward to reading your work. And perhaps, if the publishing gods are with me, I'll address those issues in the second edition. I do not believe any scholarship is, or should even attempt to be, definitive. If the "last word" on a topic was even possible, then the rest of us would be out of work.

Despite my intended readership of this book being predominantly academic, as a horror movie fan myself, I am very aware that fans of the genre buy, and more importantly *read*, academic books on their favorite subject. While I hope my discussion of the *giallo* is intelligent enough for the academic market, I equally hope that my writing style and approach does not alienate the nonacademic reader. I hate the phrase "dumbing down," and I categorically reject doing that. There is no reason why complex ideas cannot be explained fully and in such a way that those not academically trained in film studies (or folklore) should not still be able to read and understand my discussion. At the same time, I was not about to alienate my academic readership with excessive description at the expense of analysis, or present movie reviews instead of cultural discussion.

The films included in this book are those I could get my hands on. Many are out of print, or very hard to find. It is pointless to whine that I have not discussed *Death Laid an Egg* (*La Morte ha fatto l'uovo*) (Giulio Questi, 1969) or *Strip Nude for Your Killer* (*Nude per l'assassino*) (Andrea Bianchi, 1975). I tried, but I kept getting outbid on eBay for them. So, if your favorite obscure *giallo* is not mentioned in this book, my apologies. If you have a copy, I'd love to take a look at it, and maybe I can include it in a second edition, again depending on the caprices of the publishing gods.

A few comments on the organization of this book: the first chapter, "What Is *Giallo*?" is intended as an introduction to not only the history of the *giallo*, but also the context of Italian popular filmmaking. The second chapter, "Toward an Understanding of Vernacular Cinema," is a methodological chapter: here I discuss the context of the study of Italian cinema and how such studies tend to ignore horror cinema, how journalistic film critics deride these films as "incompetent," and how such criticisms reveal more about the reviewers' own prejudices than any problem with the film. As a counter to the middle-class bias inherent in the *giallo*'s omission from the academic study of Italian cinema and the poor press these films tend to get, I argue for studying these films by approaching them as vernacular cinema. Together the first two chapters are largely contextual; I am trying to lay a cultural foundation for the later chapters' study of the films themselves.

In chapters 3–9, I address various themes, motifs, and tropes in these films: their use of space; the murders; the role of the detective; the identity of the killer; issues of belief, excess, and the set-piece; and the *giallo* as "cinema of poetry." In each of these chapters my intention is to give an overview of the theme discussed with cross-genre examples. Based on these textual analyses, I begin to hypothesize what such moments might mean culturally, specifically for vernacular audiences. In my conclusions to each chapter, I begin to point to where these discussions intersect with the critical theories of our disciplines. I apologize in advance if my analyses tend to be overly descriptive, but due to the unfamiliarity of many of the films under discussion, I felt that such foci were required.

Finally, as a conclusion, I recontextualize the *giallo* in terms of how it influenced the North American slasher movie of the late 1970s and early 1980s. It is also worth noting how the *giallo* influenced the slasher film then reinfluenced some Italian horror films in the mid-1980s.

So, put on your black leather driving gloves, open up your straight razors, pour yourself a highball of J&B, and let's go back to the sleazy seventies.

~

Acknowledgments

I would like to thank my colleagues at the University of Wales, Aberystwyth, who have supported and encouraged my research into this bizarre subject: Ioan Williams and Martin Barker both actually believed I could pull off this book. Thanks also to Mick Mangan, now at the University of Exeter, who came back from Italy with a Mondadori edition of an Ed McBain novel to inspire my work in *gialli*. Thank you to Kevin Donnelly and Kate Egan, who made some useful suggestions early on in this research. Thanks also to Kate Woodward, whose innocence I helped to corrupt by showing her some of these movies, particularly Dario Argento's *Opera*. Thanks should also go out to my colleagues at large, Steven Jay Schneider, Xavier Mendik, and especially my fellow explorer of vernacular cinema, Sheila Nayar. A shy thank you as well to Richard Dyer, who suggested I continue with this research; your encouragement meant a lot to me.

The research for this book has taken several years to complete, but I would not have been able to complete this at all without the support from the University of Wales, Aberystwyth, Department of Theatre, Film and Television, which granted me two semesters sabbatical leave to complete the project; *diolch yn fawr*! I would also like to thank the British Academy, which awarded me an Overseas Conference Grant in 2003 so I could present a preliminary version of chapter 7 at the Perspectives on Contemporary Legend Conference in Corner Brook, Newfoundland. Also a massive thank you to all of the International Society for Contemporary Legend Research (ISCLR), whose support over the years has been a great encouragement to me; a specific thank you to Carl Lindahl, whom I seem to have converted into a Dario Argento fan due to this presentation. The same paper was also presented at the Fifth Annual MeCCSA Conference in Brighton at the University of Sussex, so thank you to all who heard the paper and gave me such useful feedback. Based on these conference papers, an alternative version of this chapter was published in *Midwestern Folklore* 30.2 (2004): 21–29; thanks also to the journal's editor Greg Kelley.

Also, an earlier version of chapter 3 was presented at the 2003 European Cinema Research Forum conference at the University of Bath, and was eventually published in Wendy Everett and Axel Goodbody, eds, *Revisiting Space: Space and Place in European Cinema* (Bern: Peter Lang, 2005), 115–31; thanks to Wendy and Axel for their work on the volume. An even earlier version was first published in the online journal *Kinoeye* 3.12 (2003) as "*La Dolce Morte*: Space, Modernity and the Giallo."

Thank you as well to Sue Cohen at J&B Whiskey and Danilo Vogt at Marketing-Film for the DVD copies of *All the Colors of the Dark* and *Dance of Satan*.

Special thank you to Alan Simpson at the *Sex, Gore, Mutants* website—probably the best horror fan site in cyberspace (www.sexgoremutants .co.uk)—for bringing me on as a DVD reviewer, particularly the *giallo* discs. And to Adele Hartley at Edinburgh's "Dead by Dawn" film festival, the best damn film festival in the world! Special thanks also to Harvey Fenton at FAB Press—probably the best publisher of horror and extreme cinema fan-oriented materials; without FAB's books, this study could not have been done.

Very special thanks to Kelly Jones, whose support, encouragement, coffee, and proofreading skills I could not have done without. Now if I can just get you to watch one of these movies. . . .

And finally to my wife, Gian, and son, Isaac: your support, love, and affection gave me the strength and encouragement to persevere with this work. That my (now) five-year-old can talk intelligently about *Dawn of the Dead* and *The Texas Chainsaw Massacre* is a bit worrying, but I assure Social Services he's never seen one of these movies! He does do a terrific zombie impersonation, however. Gian, my love and best friend, your idea to demand a first draft of this manuscript as a Christmas present was inspired and with only six more hours till midnight—I might just make it! Thank you for everything.

CHAPTER ONE

~

What Is *Giallo*?

Several years ago, I produced a lengthy article on the relationship between contemporary urban legends and the slasher films largely produced in Canada and the United States in the later 1970s and early 1980s. As part of that piece, I characterized three different types of the slasher film: those slashers that are based on urban legends, which I called "terror tales"; "psycho-character studies," those films that attempt to understand the serial killer from the psycho-sociological perspective, using the killer himself (they are usually male) from the inside; and finally what I called "Scooby-Doo movies"—which I characterized thus:

> named after the children's animated television series which deals with a gang of teenagers solving what appear to the adult, outside world as supernatural mysteries, but are ultimately revealed to be non-supernatural in nature, and are usually the result of some adult who uses the supernatural legend to distract other people from discovering his/her own illegal operation. In the "Scooby-Doo" slasher films, however, the killer is revealed to be human and using some kind of killer-legend to distract from their own motives. These slasher films are, in reality, gory murder mysteries, where the "game" for the audience is to attempt a hypothesis as to whom the killer may be out of a set group of people. (2003a: np)

One of the readers for this article queried the relationship between what I was calling the "Scooby-Doo" movies and the Italian *giallo*, and in the final published version of the paper I made a vague and noncommittal connection between the two in a footnote. But almost immediately after submitting that final edit of the paper, I continued thinking about the relationship between the *giallo* and the slasher movie and realized my term "Scooby-Doo" movie was inaccurate: this particular form of slasher was actually (North) American *gialli*.

My intention at the time was to continue my research into the slasher film, and in preparing that research I wanted to firm up the connection between the slasher and the *giallo*. To do this, I sought out an article or two that defined the *giallo*, as genre, and gave some reference to the defining characteristics of these films. The *giallo* at this stage in my research was highly peripheral to my study. Unfortunately, no such articles or pieces of research could be found. Disappointed and discouraged, I decided that I would have to write those articles myself; but as I dug deeper and deeper into this genre of Italian vernacular filmmaking, I identified increasingly significant issues that had not been discussed within film studies—that were not only essential to a discussion of the *giallo*, but to a larger form of cinema language that often falls below the radar of most "serious" film watchers. This was back in 2002, and for the next three years I found myself exploring the labyrinthine world of the Italian vernacular cinema of the 1970s. These are the results of that exploration.

First, before discussing the *giallo* film as vernacular cinema, some definition of the genre itself is required. The word *giallo* simply means "yellow" and is the metonymic term given to a series of mystery novels that the Milanese publisher Mondadori began producing in the late 1920s. These paperback novels, often translations of English-language novels by writers like Arthur Conan Doyle, Ngaio Marsh, Agatha Christie, and Edgar Wallace, were presented with vibrant yellow covers. A few years earlier, Mondadori had achieved success with a series of romance novels published with bright blue covers, and so their "*giallo*" series was an extension of this color-coding of popular literature. The "*giallo*" series is still going strong, with Mondadori continuing to publish *gialli* paperbacks with vibrant yellow covers. Very quickly other Italian publishers joined in on the demand (or at least availability) of mass-market murder mystery novels. Dozens of competing series were produced, all using the term *giallo*, further defining the literary genre within an Italian context. A quick perusal of a list of those books published in the 1930s and early 1940s reveals that Edgar Wallace seems to have been one of the most popular authors—certainly translations of his novels are plentiful in the various series, followed closely by Agatha Christie, Conan Doyle, and Dorothy Sayers. The term *giallo* acts as a metonym for the entire mystery genre: in a British or North American bookstore, if we wanted to find, say, an Agatha Christie novel, we would look for a section called "Mystery"; however, in an Italian bookstore, that section would likely be called "*Giallo.*" So at the most basic level, any murder-mystery narrative *could* be classed as *giallo.*[1]

Despite their popularity during this period, *gialli* were seen as corrupt and decadent by the Italian Fascist government; it viewed the books as advocating the worst kinds of criminal behavior (as opposed to the "right" kinds of criminal behavior, like their Racial Laws). In spite of this, or maybe *because* of it, filmmakers tended to overlook the *giallo* as potential source material. Fascist cinema tended to prefer the facade of sophistication in the so-called "White Telephone" films.[2] Literally the first *giallo* film was made under Mussolini's nose toward the end of Italy's participation in the Second World War. Luchino Visconti's *Ossessione* (1942), although mostly heralded as the first neorealist film, since the film is loosely based on James M. Caine's novel *The Postman Always Rings Twice* (1934), is also the first *giallo* film.[3] Perhaps significantly, Visconti did not read Caine either in the original English or in an Italian translation, but in French; the novel was given to him by Jean Renoir (Liehm 1984: 52). So, whether or not *Ossessione* was literally a *giallo*—that is whether or not an Italian translation published by Mondadori or any of the other competing publishers was then currently available—might be moot; the crime film, based on the popularity of the crime novel (*giallo*) was seen as potentially ideologically subversive, at least under Fascism. That being said, perhaps it is ironic that, although the script for *Ossessione* passed by Mussolini's censors untouched, Vittorio Mussolini, Il Duce's son, was said to have been appalled by the film, and officially it was condemned by the government (Liehm 1984: 57–58). What is significant for this current discussion of *Ossessione* in respect to the *giallo* is that part of the filmmaker's mandate was to "reopen Italian film to foreign influences and to re-establish contacts with the world culture disrupted by the fascist isolationism" (Liehm 1984: 57).[4]

The later *giallo* filmmakers tend to be contextualized within other forms of exploitation horror cinema, although often they worked in as many different genres as were being produced within Italian cinema at the time—mondo documentaries, zombie pictures, police action films (*poliziotto*), and sex comedies. So most histories of *giallo* cinema, such as are available, contextualize the genre within the history of Italian horror cinema, rather than the crime film, with Mario Bava unofficially credited with inventing the *giallo* as a cinematic genre. This invention can be said to have occurred through two specific films. Bava's *The Girl Who Knew Too Much* (*La Ragazza che sapev troppo*) (1962) established the *giallo* films' narrative structure: an innocent person, often a tourist, witnesses a brutal murder that appears to be the work of a serial killer. He or she takes on the role of amateur detective in order to hunt down this killer, and often succeeds where the police fail. Two years later, Bava further developed the genre with *Blood and Black Lace* (*Sei donne per l'assassino*) (1964). This film, although the narrative structure is quite different from *Girl*, introduced to the genre specific visual tropes that would become clichéd. Specifically, the graphic violence was against beautiful women; there were many murders committed (in *Girl*, all the victims are stabbed the same way, but in *Blood and Black Lace* we see stabbings, strangulations, smotherings, burnings, and other violent acts); but most important is the introduction of what was to become the archetypal *giallo* killer's disguise: black leather gloves, black overcoat, wide-brimmed black hat, and often a black stocking over the face. Obviously, at the time these films were being made, Bava thought he was just making entertaining horror/mystery pictures, not that he was establishing a genre as such. Nevertheless, Gary Needham sees the opening sequence of *Girl*, where we are introduced to Nora Davis (Letitia Roman) on an airplane arriving in Rome for a holiday, reading a *giallo* novel, as announcing the arrival of a new self-aware kind of genre, what Needham calls mise en abyme (2003: 136).[5]

The year 1970 is generally considered the key threshold for *giallo* cinema, due to the international success of Dario Argento's *The Bird with the Crystal Plumage* (*L'uccello dale piume di cristallo*) (1970), which takes the innocent eyewitness who becomes an amateur detective through a grisly series of murders from Bava's *Girl* and adds the graphic violence and iconically dressed killer (black hat, gloves, and raincoat) from Bava's *Blood and Black Lace*. It is this combination that really defines the *giallo* film as it is more commonly understood. An avalanche of similar films was quickly brought out by Italian producers looking to cash in on Argento's success, all using combinations and variations on the complexity of the mystery, with the standard *giallo*-killer disguise.[6]

In West Germany at the time, there was a parallel movement in crime cinema, the *krimi*. In many respects, Bava's *The Girl Who Knew Too Much* drew upon the German *krimi* tradition, which predated Bava's first *giallo* by a year: *Dead Eyes of London* (*Die Toten Augen von London*) (Alfred Vohrer, 1961) and *The Green Archer* (*Der Grüne Bogenschütze*) (Jürgen Roland, 1961) were both based on novels by Edgar Wallace, who appears to have had a remarkable popularity in postwar Germany. Likewise, Dario Argento was heavily influenced, not only by Bava, but by these *krimi* films too, as Julian Grainger noted:

Argento drew on the German brand of murder-mystery (or *krimi*), usually based on the works of Edgar Wallace and hugely popular in the 1950s and

1960s. In Wallace's novels the hero was usually a Scotland Yard detective but the cases he was called upon to solve often had something of the bizarre or exotic about them. Both *The Cat O' Nine Tails* and *The Bird with the Crystal Plumage* were sold in Germany as based on novels by Edgar Wallace's son Bryan. The Italian *giallo* mixed the *krimi* with the police procedural and added a twist of its own; an almost fetishistic attention to the murderer and the killings he (and sometimes she) perpetuated. (2000: 118)

As Ken Hanke noted regarding the cross-fertilization between the *gialli* and *krimi*:

> The final film from Rialto, Massimo Dallamano's *Cosa avete fatto a Solange?* . . . , was ultimately less a *krimi* than it was an early *giallo*, the form that took over from the *krimi* in many ways. Old Rialto favourites Joachim Fuchsberger and Arin Baal were in the cast and the film claimed to have been "suggested" by Wallace's *The Clue of the New Pin*, but it was a different sort of film for a different audience and a different time, and might best be viewed as an homage to the *krimis* rather than a true member of the series. (2003: 123)

I point out this parallel tradition to demonstrate that the *giallo* was not entirely an independent phenomenon; these films were heavily influenced by, not to mention funded by and marketed to, international interests beyond Italy.

Filone

Although, in Italian, the word *genere* does literally mean "genre," within the context we are currently discussing genre, the Italian *filone* may be more appropriate. In literary studies, the *giallo*, like crime or detective fiction as genre, would be considered *genere*. *Filone*, on the other hand, would tend to be used primarily in a more scientific context, like geology (where *filone* would refer to a vein of mineral in a rock) or geography (as in the main current in a river). However, rather than the more traditional literary approach, *filone* here tends to be used more idiomatically, as in the phrase "*sullo stesso filone*" ("in the tradition of") or "*seguire il filone*" ("to follow the tradition of"). Even the geological use of *filone* has an English equivalent: to be "in the vein of." Wagstaff defines *filone* as "formula," which in reference to cinema is often "dismissed as *sottoprodotto* (a debased, ersatz product)" (1992: 248). Paul Hoffmann, writing in the *New York Times*, defined *filone* (in the sense I am discussing it) as "streamlet," as in a small stream off a main river (quoted in McDonagh, 1994: 95). Putting these together, if we think of a larger generic pattern as a river, in this context the *giallo* as genre, several smaller "stream-lets" branch off from that genre-river, occasionally reconnecting to the main flow farther "downstream." Perhaps, in some cases, what we think of as a film genre, like the *giallo*, may be a cluster of concurrent streamlets, veins, or traditions—*filone*.

> It should be understood then that the *giallo* is something different to that which is conventionally analysed as a genre. The Italians have the word *filone*, which is often used to refer to both genres and cycles as well as to currents and trends. This points to the limitations of genre theory built primarily on American film genres but also to the need for redefinition concerning how other popular film-producing nations understand and relate to their products. (Needham 2003: 135–36)

On the one hand, as Gary Needham does, we can see the *giallo* as less a distinct genre of film than as a *filone* of the larger horror or crime genres (this latter, of course, in Italian, is *giallo*). On the other hand, from a more conservative literary perspective, if we see the *giallo* as referring to the entire crime genre of literature (which it does, at least in the original language), then it should be possible to identify smaller variations on that genre—the various *filone* that make up the genre, at least in popular cinema. Or, as I am here, we can see *filone* more idiomatically, as a "tradition" to be followed; and, as we shall see below, the *giallo* appears more as a tradition of film narrative than as a genre.

Seeing the generic diversity of the *giallo* in terms of its various *filone* strikes me as more productive than the subordinated term "subgenre." I noted above that Mario Bava introduced the theme of "the unlikely witness becomes amateur detective" in *The Girl Who Knew Too Much*, and then introduced what was to become the sine qua non of *giallo*-killer disguises—black hat, black overcoat, black gloves (sometimes wearing a mask)—in *Blood and Black Lace*, but that it was Dario Argento who brought these two together in *The Bird with the Crystal Plumage*. From *Bird*'s release in 1970, a slew of similar films were produced that likewise featured this archetypal killer disguise and the amateur detective role. Using *filone* in this sense, Argento was *sullo stesso filone* Mario Bava, but then a number of films were produced that were *sullo stesso filone* Dario Argento, that is, in the tradition of first Bava and then Argento. These films make up the central core of the *giallo* film, and perhaps we should designate them as "classic *giallo*." This corpus of films includes, in addition to those already mentioned, Giuliano Carnimeo's *The Case of the Bloody Iris* (*Perche quelle stran gocce di sangue sul corpo di Jennifer?*) (1971), Massimo Dallamano's *Solange* (*Cosa avante fatto a Solange?*) (1972), Aldo

Lado's *Who Saw Her Die?* (*Chi l'ha vista morire?*) (1972), Luciano Ercoli's *Death Walks at Midnight* (*La Morte accarezza a mezzanotte*) (1972), Armando Crispino's *Autopsy* (*Macchie solari*) (1973), Umberto Lenzi's *Eyeball* (*Gatti rossi in un libirinto di verto*) (1975), and Argento's *Deep Red* (*Profondo rosso*) (1975). As can be gleaned from the selection above, the "classic" period of the *giallo* film ran from approximately 1970 until 1975.

If the film takes the narrative perspective of the police in investigating and finally revealing the machinations of the plot, then rightly the film is more of a police procedural thriller than a classic *giallo*. Italian vernacular cinema recognizes the *poliziotto* as a separate *filone*: films where the police are the protagonist. Despite the differences between the *giallo* and the *poliziotto* film, both focus on the hunt for a serial killer or the investigation into some kind of drug or white slavery ring. Often these *filone* are difficult to tell apart, with many *poliziotto* referred to as *giallo* in their marketing (at least in the contemporary marketing of these films on DVD to horror fans). A number of films in this period and under consideration here clearly fall within the cycle of the police procedural. In particular, Paolo Cavara's *The Black Belly of the Tarantula* (*La Tarantula dal ventre nero*) (1972) runs the gamut between both *giallo* and *poliziotto*, privileging the investigative perspectives of both an amateur detective Paolo Zani (Silvano Tranquilli) and police officer, Inspector Tellini (Giancarlo Giannini). Massimo Dallamano's *A Black Veil for Lisa* (*La Morte non ha sesso*) (1968) and *What Have They Done to Our Daughters?* (1974) are much more *poliziotto* than classic *giallo*, with the centrality of the police reflected in the latter's original Italian title (*La Polizia chiede aiuto*, literally, "The police need help"). Flavio Mogherini's *The Pyjama Girl Case* (*La Ragazza dal pigiama giallo*) (1977), despite the use of the word *giallo* in the original Italian title, focuses more on Inspector Thompson's (Ray Milland) investigation than the events leading up to the murder being investigated. Significantly, Dallamano's *Black Veil* was made before the classic *giallo* began to dominate Italian *terza visione* screens (i.e., those films *sullo stesso filone* Argento's *The Bird with the Crystal Plumage*) and Mogherini's *The Pyjama Girl Case* is fairly late in the cycle. So while the classic *giallo* dominated Italian vernacular cinema roughly between 1970 and 1975, this *filone* was topped and tailed by more traditional *poliziotto* films. Stephen Thrower noted "Italy's exploitation directors had, during the seventies, turned from the labyrinthine narrative excesses of the *giallo* to the right-wing law enforcement wet dreams of the *poliziesco* [sic.]" (1999: 109). While Thrower's dismissal of the *poliziotto* is perhaps overly simplistic, films such as Lucio Fulci's *The New York Ripper* (*Lo Squartatore di New York*) (1982) and Argento's *The Stendhal Syndrome* (*La Sindrome di Stendhal*) (1996), both more *poliziotto* than classic *giallo*, seem to support his point. Contemporary *gialli*, like *Occhi di cristallo* (Eros Puglielli, 2004), focus almost exclusively on the police investigation. This suggests to me that the classic *giallo* existed as *filone* in the first half of the 1970s and emerged out of an existing demand for more traditional *poliziotto* films. Once the cycle had run out of steam, the *filone* returned back to the more familiar cop dramas.

Some *gialli* tended to avoid both the police and the amateur detective, coalescing around plot lines that are more akin to suspense thrillers than either of the two *gialli* forms noted previously. As Charles Derry defined it, "The suspense thriller [is] a crime work which presents a generally murderous antagonism in which the protagonist becomes either an innocent victim or a nonprofessional criminal within a structure that is significantly unmediated by a traditional figure of detection" (1988: 62). In the classic *giallo* films, the amateur detective looks for the killer "out there," somewhere in the city; the investigation is *external* to the film's protagonist, even if the killer may be a friend or relative of the amateur detective. Likewise, in the *poliziotto* films, the investigation is externally driven, despite the possibility of uncovering internal corruption within the force. But in the "suspense thriller" *gialli*, the criminal activities (murder, blackmail, adultery, incest) are *internally* driven. These films tend to feature fewer settings and locations, restricting most of the action to one or two locations. For example, in Enzo Castellari's *Cold Eyes of Fear* (*Gli occhi fredda della paura*) (1971), most of the film occurs in the home of a wealthy solicitor whose nephew, Peter Flower (Gianni Garko), has been living there. Two escaped convicts, Welt (Frank Wolff) and Quill (Julian Mateos), break in holding Peter and his girlfriend Anna (Giovanna Ralli) hostage as revenge for Juez Flower's (Fernando Rey) botched defense of Welt. Instead of any *external* investigation in the public spaces of the city, these "suspense thriller" *gialli* are *internalized* within more private and domestic spaces. Aldo Lado's *Night Train Murders* (*L'Ultimo treno della notte*) (1975), an Italian version of Wes Craven's *Last House on the Left* (1972), limits its action to a train compartment and the home of Professor Giulio Stradi (Ernico Maria Salerno). The liminal space of the train compartment is particularly highlighted in this film—while a semipublic space (anyone who has a ticket can occupy the space), it is a *closed* space with doors and curtains. Other films in this *filone* include Mario Bava's *Hatchet for the Honeymoon* (*Il Rosso sego della follia*) (1969), *Five Dolls for an August Moon* (*Cinque bambole per la luna d'agosto*) (1970), and *Bay of Blood* (*Reazione a catena*) (1971); Umberto Lenzi's *Paranoia* (1969); Lucio Fulci's *One on Top of the Other* (*Una sull'altra*) (1969) and *A Lizard in a Woman's Skin* (*Una Lucertola con la pelle di donna*) (1971); Sergio Bergonzelli's *In the Folds of the Flesh* (*Nelle pieghe della carne*)

(1970); Luciano Ercoli's *The Forbidden Photos of a Lady Above Suspicion* (*Le Foto proibite di una signora per bene*) (1970); and Fillippo Walter Ratti's *Crazy Desires of a Murderer* (*I Vizi morbosi di una governante*) (1974). Troy Howarth noted:

> An over-simplification of the codes of the *giallo* would be that the genre focuses on the more unsavoury aspects of crime detective fiction, specifically sexual peccadilloes and gruesome acts of violence. In fact, not all *gialli* dwell on the morbid details of violent death (Lucio Fulci's *Una sull'altra*/*One on Top of the Other*, 1968, and Riccardo Freda's *A doppia faccia*/*Double Face*, 1969, have nary a violent confrontation to their credit), but the threat of violence is always there, and voyeurism, sexual dysfunction and the like are never far behind. The ultimate result is a totally chaotic spectacle which inevitably bends, twists and destroys the (typically naïve) world views of their protagonists. (2002: 71–72)

Again, with a quick perusal of the films in this *filone*, it appears that this was a popular form quite early on in the cycle, to some extent overlapping the move from *poliziotto* to classic *giallo*. Without denying Argento his historical role in developing the *giallo* film with *Bird*, in the same year, 1970, Sergio Martino's *Next!* (*Lo Strano vizio della Signora Wardh*) fused the *internal* suspense thriller plot of deceit and murder, with the *external* investigation of the "Classic *giallo*." Martino's *Torso* (*I Corpi presentano tracce di violenza carnale*) (1973), again begins as a classic *giallo*, but approximately halfway through, moves indoors to the older form of the "suspense thriller"; but this particular fusion of *external* serial killer stalking an *internally* bound group of young women may be the first proper slasher film, a discussion I will return to toward the end of this book.

As crime fiction, the *giallo* must conform to the demands of Cartesian logic, no matter how baroque the solutions to the crimes may be (a topic I discuss in a later chapter). Most of these films intentionally eschew a supernatural explanation in favor of a more rational one. Some supernatural explanations may be used as a cover for the murders (as in Crispino's *Autopsy*), but the murderer is always human. But with their focus on the more exploitative aspects of crime fiction, namely the graphic depiction of violence and murder, these *gialli* films are often linked directly with the horror genre, despite the absence of any supernatural agency. There are, however, a small number of *gialli*-like films, which draw from the visual rhetoric of the *giallo* but situate that rhetoric into the context of a more traditional *supernatural* horror film. Kim Newman refers to these films as *giallo-fantastico* in a quite reasonable coinage (1986a: 23). Perhaps the most explicit of these is Dario

Argento's *Phenomena* (1985), wherein the traditionally dressed *giallo* killer is hunted down by the traditional amateur detective, Jennifer (Jennifer Connelly), but in this film, the young detective also is able to telepathically communicate with insects, and through this conceit is able to track down the killer.[7] Mario Bava's *Kill, Baby . . . Kill!* (*Operazione paura*) (1966) features a traditional Conan Doyle–type murder mystery plot, wherein the detective tries to disprove the belief that a rash of suicides are the result of seeing a ghost, but in fact, the ghost of a young girl is haunting this German village and *is* compelling all who see her to kill themselves. Likewise a killer pussycat is on the loose in Lucio Fulci's *The Black Cat* (*Il Gatto nero*) (1981), despite all the film's *giallo* trappings. Sergio Martino's *All the Colors of the Dark* (*Tutti I colori del buio*) (1972), while availing itself of the tropes of the *giallo*, specifically the killer's disguise and the themes of adultery, blackmail, and murder, contextualizes these within a plot about a witches' coven. Witches' covens and *giallo* killers also appear in José Mariá Elorrieta's *Feast of Satan* (*Las Amantes del diablo*) (1971) and in Riccardo Freda's *The Wailing* (*L'Obsessione che uccide*) (1980), while a Satanic sex-cult is featured in Aldo Lado's *The Short Night of Glass Dolls* (*Malastrana*) (1971). But these *giallo-fantastico* are largely infrequent, worth mentioning in passing but not significant enough to dwell on. However, the *beliefs* these films engender are significant enough to discuss in a later chapter.

Giallo in the Context of Italian Popular Cinema

Exploitation cinema, by its very nature, is derivative. Whether we are talking about horror movies, action films, or even pornography, these movies are rarely taken seriously. Pam Cook noted:

> Exploitation is a derogatory term, implying a process of "ripping off." It also implies an economic imperative—very low budget, tight production schedules, low-paid, inexperienced, non-union personnel, minimal production values, "sensational" selling campaigns and widespread saturation booking aimed at specific markets (predominantly the youth/drive-in audience generally uninterested in critical reviews), all in the interests of making a fast buck. (1985: 367)

Given Cook's characterization of the reception environment of exploitation cinema, it becomes even easier to dismiss certain films if they are "foreign," or someone else's exploitation trash.

Italian popular cinema, particularly horror cinema, is highly derivative. Italian screenwriter and director Luigi Cozzi is quoted as noting: "In Italy . . .

when you bring a script to a producer, the first question he asks is not 'what is your film like?' but 'what *film* is your film like?' That's the way it is, we can only make *Zombie 2*, never *Zombie 1*" (quoted in Newman 1986c: 92).[8] I have already noted that Aldo Lado's *Night Train Murders* is an Italian reworking of Wes Craven's *Last House on the Left*.[9] Sergio Martino's *All the Colors of the Dark* is highly derivative of *Rosemary's Baby* (Roman Polanski, 1968). As Maitland Mc-Donagh noted, "Italian cinema, lacking Hollywood's dense multi-studio structure and with a great deal of power concentrated in a very few hands, is simply more so: a hit unleashes a veritable flood of imitations in record-breaking time" (1994: 95). It is this culture of production that creates the environment of the *filone*. But first we need to contextualize this culture.

When one thinks of Italian cinema one tends to immediately focus on high-art filmmakers and internationally recognized "classics" of world cinema. "Historical surveys of Italian cinema prefer to concentrate on neo-realism, existential angst and Visconti, rather than on films that are every bit as Italian but that tip their hats to Hollywood" (Frayling 1998: xii). Luigi Cozzi noted:

> In that period [the 1960s], only directors like Fellini or Visconti were considered, at least by intellectuals, as representative of Italian cinema, whereas somebody like Bava was primarily ignored, because [of] those low independent companies that often went bankrupt even before the movies came out in theatres (usually third-rate suburban cinemas). Indeed, Bava's films never surfaced in first-class theatres, and were seldom reviewed in newspapers. (2002: 5)

I discuss these "third-rate suburban" movie houses in the next chapter, as well as the dominance of high-art filmmakers like Fellini within the scholarship on Italian cinema. But at this preliminary stage, it is worth noting, at least in passing, that those canonical filmmakers rose to their status on the shoulders of "jobbing" filmmakers, making films for the working-class audiences. As Stephen Thrower noted:

> The success of the industry was not, however, based on the artistic credibility of its emerging international directors. Italy was producing its own specific brand of mainstream entertainment: populist, and keenly attuned to audience demand, it provided a constant whirl of different genre amusements. It was this ingenious mainstream product that accounted for the industry's high level of activity. It also provided for the financial security necessary to make Italy's "art" cinema viable. Producers could afford to gamble on critically lauded but "difficult" directors like Michelangelo Antonioni because the home market provided a steady flow of cash from the less esoteric, more populist entertainments. (1999: 42)

Thrower's point is a significant one and needs highlighting: the only way an intellectual and critically acclaimed film culture can exist, particularly without complex studiolike systems as in Hollywood, is through an exploitation and populist cinema. It is in this context that new filmmakers can gain experience, ideas can be explored (albeit oftentimes quite roughly and crudely), and revenues gained from "lower" films can be used to help finance more "prestige" pictures. And parallel to all of this is the hegemonic domination of Hollywood (see Cook 1985).

In response to Hollywood, Italian filmmakers produced a steady flow of popular films, including the *gialli* discussed here. Certainly the most famous of these popular genres is the "spaghetti western," Italian-made (often in Spain) movies about the American West that were often more violent and grisly than anything Hollywood had produced to date. Equally popular, at least in the early 1960s was the *peplum*, the "sword and sandal" epics, often taking place in a mythical Classical world, that dominated popular cinema in the wake of *Hercules* (*Le Fatiche di Ercole*) (Pietro Francisci, 1958). And by the time the 1970s rolled around, Italy was producing hundreds of horror and spectacle films, cheaply and quickly.[10] Christopher Frayling, in his study on the spaghetti western, noted:

> Italian formula films of the 1960s and early 1970s were certainly popular, and were the product of an industry which seems to have been directly in touch with its audience: toward the end of this period, Italy, with help from co-producers, was producing over 200 feature films a year (a total surpassed only by India, especially Bombay, and Japan), could support nearly 13,000 cinemas (a total surpassed only by the USSR and the USA), and registered over 540 million cinema attendances per annum (a total surpassed only by the USSR and India); perhaps this had something to do with the fact that Italians (mainly Northern and Central Italians) only owned 11 million television sets (a total surpassed by the USA, USSR, Japan, West Germany, the UK and France). (1998: xxi)

Stephen Thrower, writing from a more explicitly British perspective and about the *giallo* specifically, noted similar statistics.

> Figures for the early 1970s illustrate the strength of the Italian film market in comparison to the UK. In 1972, Italy's total population was around 54.8 million. Cinema admissions for that year totalled 553.6 million, meaning that on average each citizen attended the cinema ten times a year! Compare that with the figures for the UK in 1972: the population was approximately 55.7 million, almost the same as Italy; but with cinema admissions reaching a mere 156.6

million, the average number of visits for the year per head of population was only 2.81. . . . Small wonder that the Italian pastiche and parody of whatever was popular, was able to flourish on such a hyperactive scale. (1999: 66)

Although this will be discussed in more detail in the next chapter, it is worth noting here that Italians, particularly in the working-class neighborhoods where *gialli*, as well as spaghetti westerns, *peplum*, and other forms of popular cinema were shown, would, as likely as not, go to the movies *every night*; therefore the demand on a sufficient supply of film product was quite tremendous.

Unlike the Hollywood Studio system, which produced movies within a strong Fordian industrial tradition, the Italian "studio," *Cinecittà*, operated very differently. Christopher Frayling outlined several significant aspects of the Cinecittà way of making movies including

the need to attract co-production money, if possible; the key role played by Spanish producers and audiences (and cheap Spanish labour on location work);[11] the hasty shooting schedules and the necessity of dubbing (more up-market products, by contrast, being shot in various foreign-language versions); the use of pseudonyms (a relatively recent phenomenon—most directors of muscleman epics worked under their own names); the flexibility about scripts, and the strange compulsion to make this film more bizarre than the last one. This system—evidence of the tendency of Cinecittà producers to capture audiences rather than to keep them, to seize on any immediately available consumer potential—has been interpreted by Lino Miccichè as "in many ways typical of the popular cinema of underdeveloped regions—the *comedieta populachera* of Mexico, the Egyptian *song-film*, the Brazilian *chanchada*, the Indian 'picturised song,' the South American *telenovela*, and Italy's film-fumetto." By the time of the Spaghetti Western boom, this "capturing" of audiences (Miccichè calls it "rape"), this pitching of a fresh "genre" at (predominantly Southern) Italian urban audiences when the products of the assembly-line ceased to get top figures on the home market, had been a characteristic of the Cinecittà production system for over ten years. (1998: 70)

Thrower, again, characterizes how this kind of low-budget exploitation film could be produced so quickly, in what within the industry is referred to as the "presale" (150). *Giallo* screenwriter Dardano Sacchetti explains the presale thus:

[Italian exploitation films are] made for foreign investors, because in Italy there's no market for them. Great Britain, Germany, Denmark, France, Japan, and even the USA are very hungry for strong horror movies, thrillers or adventures. The problem is the foreign market is tougher, there is greater competition; at MIFED, in the Cannes market, there are movies from everywhere in the world. So the producers go to the markets with a brochure, a title, a synopsis, saying: "I've got this movie to sell." Actually they sell the idea: when and if they find a buyer, they make him sign a contract promising to buy the movie for a certain amount of money. On the basis of this paper they are able to obtain the financing from the banks. They make the movie, sell it to the buyers and give back the money to the bank. So the budget of the movie depends upon the number of buyers and the amount they are willing to pay. (Fulvia) would go to MIFED with a couple of posters, ten lines of plot and a tentative title: when they found a buyer they would call me from Milano and say: "Dardano, we've sold 'Whatchacallit'—start writing now! You have six days, we're giving them the finished copy in three months!" (quoted in Thrower 1999: 150)

Given the fast turnaround required in producing these films, it is not surprising that so many of these Italian vernacular films are derivative of (often) Hollywood products. While Kim Newman refers to these films as "Rip-Off/Spin-Off" films (1986b: 54), Stephen Thrower coins the phrase "premature emulation" (1999: 193).

We have to thank American movies that give us something to eat! . . . Ob- . viously, it's easier for a producer to get money if he cashes in on the success of another film. So when they call you to make one of these movies, it's up to you to profit from the occasion to make something different and personal, or to chose to make a bad copy of the original; I always try to make something different. It's easier when you work with intelligent people; sometimes you write one way and then the movies comes [sic] out as a copy of the model, and then sometimes not. Take *Zombi 2*, which was based on Romero's *Dawn of the Dead*, *Zombi* in Italy. A producer decided to make a small horror film, although my inspiration came not from the Romero movie, but from the comic-strip hero Tex Miller." (Dardano Sacchetti, quoted in Thrower 1999: 148)

Donato Totaro noted that

the Italian horror industry has continually struggled against cultural stigmatisation, financial constraints, industry apathy and the over bearing presence of American cinema. Because of this latter fact, the industry developed a parasitic relationship with American cinema. Sometimes out of financial necessity, sometimes out of creative laziness, Italian cinema became . . . extremely derivative of popular American cinema. But the Italians, with their spirit of reconciliation and ability to make the best of a bad situation (*"arte di arrangiarsi"*), managed to turn a negative into a positive by adapting their own cultural and artistic temperament to an American model. (Totaro 2003: 161)

Not only were these Italian exploitation films derivatives of American cinema in the first instance, but also since the vast majority of these films were actually produced with a global market in mind, Italian exploitation film producers were often highly successful at *remarketing* these films back to the United States.

> There were plenty more Italian *gialli* released on the American exploitation circuit during the seventies. Hucksterish US distributors soon realised there was money to be made in the wake of home-grown independents like *Night of the Living Dead* and *Last House on the Left*. Cheap, bloodthirsty horror films, though generally despised by Hollywood and the mainstream press, were doing just fine, both in the big cities where high levels of blue-collar custom kept the grind-houses open and down in the southern states where the drive-ins flourished on a smaller basis. Enterprising distributors found the parallel excesses of the Italian horror/thriller genres a handy (and relatively cheap) source of shock-milking revenue. They could be marketed aggressively under lurid new titles, with attention-grabbing ad-copy that promised ever more traumatic sights in store for the curious; and of course the Italian films tended to stir plentiful nudity into the equation too. (Thrower 1999: 67)

Conclusions

So what is the *giallo?* The *giallo* is, on the one hand, a literary genre (*genere*), the Italian equivalent of crime fiction or mystery. But as understood within a filmic context, the *giallo* is a *filone*, or perhaps a series thereof, a short-lived cycle of films "in the vein of" or "in the tradition of" the murder mysteries of Wallace, Poe, Conan-Doyle, and Christie. These *filone* go even further by emulating previously successful films "in the vein of" directors such as Mario Bava and Dario Argento.

And to consider the *giallo* as *filone* is still to cast the net wide: there are several different kinds of *gialli*, or at least of films that have been marketed as such. While the classical *giallo* features a serial killer clad in black gloves, hat, and overcoat being hunted by an amateur detective, the *poliziotto* puts the police investigation front and center in the investigation. Other *gialli* tend to focus on more private and interior settings, creating more of a suspense *giallo*. Still others, embracing the strong connection between the *giallo* and the horror film, offer a more supernatural narrative, the *giallo-fantastico*. What we mean by *giallo*, then is quite a broad spectrum of films, despite their formulaic narratives.

The *giallo* film is a kind of vernacular cinema. Its discourses, while neither subtle nor abstract in presentation, are directed toward a distinct vernacular audience, those predominantly of the *terza visione* theaters of the late 1960s and early 1970s (discussed in the next chapter). As such, by approaching these films as vernacular discourses, we gain insight into the cultures for which these films were predominantly made.

If I am correct in asserting that vernacular cinema depicts the cultural concerns of vernacular culture, then the *giallo* film depicts the cultural concerns of vernacular Italian culture. If there is any single theme that binds the entire genre together, that is, any single discourse that is common across the entire *giallo* cinema, it is that these films display a marked ambivalence toward modernity. The early 1970s was a period of marked change within Italian culture and society—stretching across the entire country—varying by region, but profound throughout. Things were changing, and while it might be academically advantageous to say the Italian "folk" were resistant to such changes, and viewed modernity with suspicion, such an approach is simplistic and only partially true. Modernity is not condemned in these films, but neither is it praised. The changes within Italian culture, across all the different regions of the country, can be seen through the *giallo* film as something to be discussed and debated—issues pertaining to identity, sexuality, increasing levels of violence, women's control over their own lives and bodies, history, the state—all abstract ideas, which are all portrayed situationally as human stories in the *giallo* film.

The *gialli* were not intended for consumption in the first-run theaters in Italy or meant to circulate internationally through film festivals and arthouse theaters. These films circulated on the margins of Italian, European, and International film exhibition—the drive-ins and grind houses, rather than the art houses. They appealed to the most salacious aspects of literary crime fiction, thereby making these films closer in spirit to horror films than to mysteries. And within this context, not only in terms of production but perhaps more importantly consumption, a traditional aesthetic consideration of the *giallo* alongside high-art filmmakers such as Fellini, Bertolucci, and Antonioni cannot work. The *giallo* is not high art; it is *vernacular* in its marketing, consumption, and production. And it is *vernacular cinema* to which I now wish to turn my attention.

Notes

1. See Agnelli, Bartocci, and Rosellini (1998).
2. A "White Telephone" film is the term given to Italian Fascist-era romantic melodramas. These films were set in the contemporary world and filled with elegance and sophistication. White telephones in the décor were seen as indicative of this elegant lifestyle.

3. That being said, when conducting this research and attempting to discover the publishing history of James M. Caine's novel in Italy, I put out an e-mail request on the Italian Cultural Studies listserve e-mail group. Although it was as a result of this query that I was able to confirm the Jean Renoir connection, one respondent in particular was outraged that I was debasing this classic of neorealism by referring to it as a *giallo*. As I discuss below, the attitude of Italian cinema scholars to the *giallo* is marked by such biases.

4. Troy Howarth (2002), while he recognizes Bava's *The Girl Who Knew Too Much* as the first "proper" *giallo* film, suggests that the earliest precursor is not *Ossessione* (which he does not mention), but *Cortocircuito* (Giacomo Gentilomo, 1943).

5. A similar image occurs a few years earlier in George Pollock's *Murder She Said* (1961), based on Agatha Christie's novel, *4:50 from Paddington* (1957). In Pollock's film, Miss Marple (Margaret Rutherford) settles down on the (novel's) titular train with a murder mystery novel (*giallo*, by any other name), just prior to her glancing out the window and seeing, in a passing train, a young woman being murdered by a black gloved, black-overcoat-wearing figure—a disguise Bava will appropriate a few years later in *Blood and Black Lace* (1964), and will become the archetypal *giallo*-killer disguise.

6. Chris Gallant offered the following useful summarization of *giallo*: "*Giallo*, which translates literally as 'yellow' is the Italian term for the whodunit thriller, derived from the yellow covers of detective novels, rather like the French *série noir*. In the Italian language, the word may just as easily refer to an Agatha Christie novel as to an Argento thriller, and applies to whodunit detective fiction in a broad sense. In the vocabulary of English-speaking audiences, its application tends to be restricted to the Italian whodunit-thriller film (one wouldn't refer to an Agatha Christie novel as an example of the 'giallo' in English). The genre as it tends to be categorized by English-speaking audiences has its own conventions and clichés: the visual enigma, which may be solved through the gradual exploration of memory; anxiety over gender confusion; the murder sequences as an elaborate and artistic tableau, and so on. The 'giallo film' draws heavily upon the tradition of Agatha Christie's fiction, hard-boiled American detective novels and film noir. *Blood and Black Lace* is one of the genre's earliest examples, the tale of a series of gruesome murders in a fashion house. Bava's film and *Peeping Tom* must share some of the responsibility for ushering in and popularising the plot that revolves around the murders of a series of young women, with its overtones of misogyny and sexual aggression" (2000a: 19).

7. Maitland McDonagh refers to *Phenomena* as "a *giallo* with paranormal (if not quite supernatural) underpinnings" (1994: 187).

8. While Cozzi's point is well taken, it is not entirely accurate. Lucio Fulci's *Zombie* (1980), known in Italy as *Zombi 2*, seems to be Cozzi's example here; however, George A. Romero's *Dawn of the Dead* (1978) was released in Italy as *Zombi*. So, contra Cozzi, *Zombi 2* did have a precursor, although the two films are not very similar.

9. And, of course, Craven's film is an exploitation reworking of Ingmar Bergman's *The Virgin Spring* (1960).

10. Although never using the word *filone*, Kim Newman produced a series of three articles in the British *Monthly Film Bulletin* (1986) where he defines and discusses a number of these cycles. In these articles, Newman discusses the *peplum* (1986a: 20–22), the Italian Gothic horror film (1986a: 22), the mondo documentaries (1986a: 22–23), the *giallo* (1986a: 23–24), the "Superspy" movies (1986b: 51–52), the spaghetti western (1986b: 52–53), Italian sex and violence movies including the Nazi sexploitation film (1986b: 53–54, also see Koven 2004: 19–31), the tradition of "ripping off" popular Hollywood movies (1986b: 54–55), "The Gothic Revival" (1986c: 88–89), the cannibal films (1986c: 89–90), the return of the *peplum* in the 1980s (1986c: 90–91), and the cycle of "Warriors of the Future" movies (1986c: 91). Taken together, Newman's pieces are a remarkable introduction to Italian vernacular cinema and these articles should be better known than they are.

11. Frayling is discussing Cinecittà's production operations, of course, within the context of the spaghetti western, but several *gialli* were also made in Spain, with Spanish money (as coproducers), and utilizing Iberian actors. *Giallo* regular Susan Scott (born Nieves Navarro) is from Spain, to cite but one famous example, and Umberto Lenzi's *Eyeball* takes place in Barcelona as a handy cover for the Spanish funding of the film.

CHAPTER TWO

~

Toward an Understanding
of Vernacular Cinema

As I argued in chapter 1, approaching the *giallo* as one would other kinds of Italian cinema, such as that of Fellini or Antonioni, is not productive, as this genre was never intended for the art house, but for the grind house. These films were produced for marginalized movie theaters (and people), and for no other reason than immediate enjoyment. This chapter is an attempt to find a method for studying the *giallo*, one that does not displace these films, inappropriately, to some ersatz canon of modernist high art, but looks at the *giallo* on its own terms, at its own level. We need to understand these films as vernacular, as a kind of cinema intended for consumption outside of mainstream, bourgeois cinema culture.

Studying Italian Cinema

One immediate problem in studying Italian horror cinema in particular, and to a lesser extent popular Italian cinema in general, is the absence of published material on Italian film culture. The main textbooks tend to omit references to "low-brow" films in favor of distinctly *auteurist* approaches to modernist, high-art works and/or movements. As Giorgio Bertellini noted, "Because the horror film genre was not germane to Italian film culture, many critics often concluded that films like [these] did not express a national filmic urge" (2004: 214). A significant test of this bias comes from a glance at the British Film Institute's *Companion to Italian Cinema*: an encyclopedic volume with entries on "significant" filmmakers, writers, performers, and movements.

Of the more than twenty-five different directors whose works I discuss in this book, only Mario Bava (Fofi 1996a: 19), Riccardo Freda (Fofi 1996b: 54), and Dario Argento (Canova 1996: 17) are given their own entries. The "Italian Horror Film" also has its own entry, and within this section are the only references to Lucio Fulci, Michele Soavi, and Lamberto Bava (Volpi 1996: 63–65). In addition, what few references there are to Italian horror films and their makers are almost all disparaging—frequently commenting on how Italian horror is merely derivative of American/Hollywood models (see Hay and Nowell-Smith 1996: 6; and Volpi 1996: 63). Perhaps the most condescending comment on Italian horror cinema comes from Morando Morandini, who, discussing Dario Argento's success, noted that "[his graphic horror films] made him a cult director both for the public and for many of the *younger* generation of critics" (1996: 594, my emphasis), implying, not without prejudice, that Argento is popular, particularly with "the kids."

Peter Bondanella (2001) offers the most sustained discussion of Italian horror cinema in these mainstream textbooks (approximately five pages' worth). But the comments are typically derisive:

> The Italian "spaghetti nightmare"[1] film is perhaps condemned to remain as a minor but intriguing variant of the mainstream Hollywood genre. They too often lack the kinds of production values that raise them above the B-movie level. . . . [And] all too often, the "spaghetti nightmare" films . . . emphasize such gore at the expense of coherent plots, complex character development, or subtle themes. (423–24)

I discuss below the problematic approach of critics like Bondanella to Italian horror films, wherein they chastise these films for their lack of a "sophisticated screenplay" in favor of exploitation sequences of gore, sex, and violence, but as a typical comment, it is worth introducing this criterion here first. Significantly, Bondanella seems to be dismissing the majority of Italian horror movies because of their low budgets in a manner that is not only elitist, but also prejudicial. Bondanella includes a few pages on horror cinema, he implies, because some horror filmmakers managed to transcend the genre ghetto into more respectable filmmaking: "While the 'spaghetti nightmare' film was primarily a low budget cinema aimed at commercial distribution and was decidedly low-brow, some mainstream directors, like Pupi Avati, began their careers by making such films" (419). Implied in Bondanella's comment is that the earlier horror films these directors made are to be tolerated, but only when the filmmakers go on to produce films more in keeping with a bourgeois aesthetic that appeals to elite audiences.[2] On the other hand, Pam

Cook suggested that "one reason why exploitation films are deemed unworthy of serious critical attention is their blatant commercialism—they do not aspire to be art, indeed, they seem to revel in their own trashiness and aura of immediate disposability. In exploiting, or capitalising on the success of more up-market, mainstream productions, they parody rather than emulate them" (1985: 367).

Despite no mention of the *giallo* genre at all, Marcia Landy, in her book *Italian Film* (2000), does give approximately three pages to Dario Argento's *Deep Red* (357–59). But Landy's approach is distinctly not contextual: she identifies significant films, including *Deep Red* we can assume, and discusses their significance as *objet d'art*, removing the film from any kind of contextual or cultural consideration. What is particularly problematic about these approaches, despite again being clearly elitist, is that by focusing only on modernist, high-art films, the majority of films produced in Italy and the majority of Italian films consumed by Italians are ignored. We are only getting half the picture of a national film culture (as problematic as such a term may be). Pierre Leprohon, in his book *The Italian Cinema* (1972), noted the importance of examining popular cinema:

> The history of cinema cannot be written in terms of "intellectual" works alone. That is why this digression [into popular cinema] was necessary, even if one does not share certain critics' oneiric ravings at the erotic burlesque of *La Regina delle Amazoni* (1960) or the scarcely concealed sadism of *Il Colosso di Rodi*. The great popular currents are of prime importance in the evolution of the art. (175)

Leprohon concludes that popular Italian films, despite being largely ignored by critics and scholars alike, "are the other side of the medal, with art, unfortunately, conspicuous through its absence" (183).

Richard Dyer and Ginette Vincendeau (1992) also noted the conspicuous absence of discussions about European popular cinema. Like Bondanella and the others quoted above, Dyer and Vincendeau noted that popular European cinema has either been "despised through a comparison with art cinema, [and/or] been judged in relation to Hollywood and found wanting" (11). In particular, they noted the elitist agenda that denigrated popular forms of cinema, specifically in how, at the level of film form, it violated classical Hollywood norms. Dyer and Vincendeau noted:

> [This avenue] of research is into forms that derive from the most "low-brow" types of popular entertainment. . . . These are often discussed in terms of their formal differences from classical narrative cinema: their emphasis on the

"spectacular," their hybrid, disunified, aesthetically as well as ideologically contradictory nature. (12)

Dyer and Vincendeau conclude that "popular European cinema is less subjected to the disciplines of verisimilitude, generic unity, and a rigorous regard for coherence, relating it to the aesthetics of '*primitive*' cinema" (12, emphasis added). While I doubt that Dyer and Vincendeau *intend* to advocate an alternative elitist perspective that assumes cinematic sophistication predicated upon classical narrative norms—as evidenced by the word "primitive" in quotation marks, they do not appear entirely confident about what could take its place. "The specifics of such '*low-brow*' or '*poor*' European cinemas await examination" (Dyer and Vincendeau 1992: 12, emphasis added).

One attempt at examining the specifics of European popular cinema, at least in a cursory way, comes from Pierre Sorlin's work on Italian cinema (1996). In his discussion of Italian "popular" film, Sorlin characterizes the biases noted above thus:

> If "popular" signifies a film which cannot please intellectuals, the label is not appropriate for the [peplum] epics or [spaghetti] westerns, which did very well in various social sectors and were watched, on their opening run, by upper- and middle-class audiences. If "popular" means artless, the label is again ill-suited for there was much sophistication in several of these films. There was no homogeneity in these so-called series. Far from being "mass produced" they were shot in different circumstances, by different crews and aimed at different audiences. Trying to analyse their themes and formulas to specify what is "popular" would be totally misleading. (125)

While I appreciate the attempt at rescuing the study of popular Italian cinema from elitist obscurity, Sorlin's own schemata merely expand the already elitist criteria for artistic inclusion. Sorlin makes explicit that popular Italian film is just as sophisticated as the canon of modernist, high-art cinema. This is a point other writers on Italian popular cinema echo—from Christopher Frayling's *Spaghetti Westerns* (1998) through to Maitland McDonagh's *Broken Mirrors/Broken Minds: The Dark Dreams of Dario Argento* (1994).[3] The argument reaches a ridiculous level of self-justification in Michael Grant's defense of Lucio Fulci's *The Beyond* (*L'aldilà*) (1981) as a modernist text related to T. S. Eliot's *The Waste Land* (see Grant 2000; 2003)!

This is not to say that any of these theoretical approaches are *wrong*, just that the theoretical schemata is misapplied. Certainly there is high quality in some of the films in question, but these scholars are desperately trying to make square pegs fit into round (modernist) holes. In order to truly understand popular cinema, we need an alternative approach that examines the films on their own level, what I am calling "vernacular cinema."

The Text-Audience Relationship

How do we watch movies? This may seem like a self-evident question, but I think it needs consideration. When we enter the darkened cinema, or pop a video or DVD into our machines, we tend to settle quietly and for ninety minutes or two hours sit back and witness the narrative/images presented for us. This is not the place to discuss active and passive audiences, for what is common between all of, say, Hall's (1980) viewing positions is the assumption of a quiet spectator whose entire focus is on the screen. Consider the norms of movie-watching behavior: the film on the screen is supposed to be the focus of our attention; before the feature we are asked, often through a series of comical short films or locally produced slides, to turn our mobile phones off and to refrain from talking or making unnecessary noise while eating our popcorn during the film. Violations of those norms are often met with intrusive and perhaps even louder admonitions to keep quiet—and in extreme cases, staff is called in to eject any disruptive patrons. A distinct picture of acceptable behavior in a movie theater emerges.

But consider the significance of these behavioral norms: through the direction of the audience's attention based on the spatial layout of the theater itself, along with the admonitions to silently give the screen our complete and undivided attention, the filmic text—that which is projected on screen—becomes an object for silent contemplation. At our local cinema, and this phenomenon is observable elsewhere, during the advertisements and coming attractions, which precede the feature film, the lights in the auditorium are only *half* dimmed; the lights are not fully extinguished until the main feature begins. From a semiotic perspective, of sorts, while reasonable social behavior is permissible during the advertisements and trailers, when the feature begins, all eyes should be focused on the screen and any noise kept to a minimum. The normative social behavior of a movie theater audience is keyed and coded through the auditorium's lighting: lights on, the room is a fully social space; dimmed lights mean the audience is required to settle down, although still permitting some low-key social interaction; when the lights are fully extinguished, however, and the movie proper begins, social time is suspended while the film plays.

Likewise within our "home theaters," when we watch a movie on video or DVD, or watch a particularly favorite television show, the televisual text becomes almost our sole focus. Telephone calls, conversations, or other activities are (albeit less so) disruptive to the text-centric activity of watching. Perhaps we have our own normative rules: "I can't talk now, *Desperate Housewives* is on." Or we pause the video in order to get another beer or piece of cake. In both cases, and the infinite number of variations possible, we "pause" so as not to "miss" any of what is important: namely, the text.

By directing our attention in this way, the filmic text becomes a special object: we are expected to shut out the outside world and immerse ourselves totally in the cinematic experience presented for us. Nothing else is expected to matter; the movie should be our total and all-encompassing focus. This text-centric perspective, in part, determines the relative success or failure of the text itself: does it hold our undivided interest for its running time, or not? "I lost myself in the film" might be said if the movie was, in this regard, successful; or "I couldn't get into it" if the film fails to hold our attention. The relative success or failure of the cinematic experience rests almost exclusively with the quality of the filmic text, for that is the object under consideration. We bestow upon the text an idealized significance; all meaning and information is assumed to be there on screen. But what if the text does not *really* matter, particularly to the audience?

Pauline Kael, in her review of the dubbed American version of Georges Franju's *Les yeux sans visage* (1959), released as *The Horror Chamber of Dr. Faustus*, noted the following:

> But the audience seemed to be reacting to a different movie. They were so noisy the dialogue was inaudible; they talked until the screen gave promise of bloody ghastliness. Then the chatter subsided to rise again in noisy approval of the gory scenes. When a girl in the film seemed about to be mutilated, a young man behind me jumped up and down and shouted encouragement. "Somebody's going to *get* it," he sang out gleefully. The audience which was, I'd judge, predominantly between fifteen and twenty-five, and at least a third feminine, was as pleased and excited by the most revolting, obsessive images as that older, mostly male audience is when the nudes appear in *That Immoral Mr. Teas* or *Not Tonight Henry*. They'd gotten what they came for: they hadn't been cheated. But nobody seemed to care what the movie was about or be interested in the logic of the plot—the reasons for the gore. (quoted in Hawkins 2000: 58)

In this excerpt Kael identifies what, for her, is a violation of the normative behaviors of a movie audience. The San Francisco crowd she saw the film with did not share the same "reverence" for the filmic text that she did; it was, in her words, as if they were "reacting to a different movie." And they seemed to be having more fun than she was, regardless of what they were watching. It is this "regardless" dimension that seems to confuse Kael the most: by disavowing the logic between the sensationalistic moments, the film text matters less, or rather differently, than it does to a metropolitan film reviewer. For Kael, a movie is a self-contained world with its own aesthetics and logic that needs to be contemplated on its own merits; whereas for the actual (i.e., *paying*) audience, the "gore" is logic enough.

Bill Landis and Michelle Clifford, in their study of the Times Square grind-house theaters, directly confront the perspective of critics like Kael: "Spending time in those theatres, I grew increasingly irritated by the offhand putdowns and snide comments of cinema snobs like the *New Yorker*'s Pauline Kael and the *New York Times*'s Vincent Canby, who implied that Times Square movies could only entertain low-IQ types, and seemed unable to praise anything beyond the hip new Fellini or Bergman film" (1994: xii). Here, then, a distinction needs to be made between those for whom the filmic text is an object intended for (aesthetic, ideological, narratological) contemplation, and those for whom the filmic text is sensationalist occasion. Christopher Wagstaff makes this point even more clear:

What the audience purchases with its ticket-money is not usually an artistic experience, but a psychological service; it is paying to be made to laugh, to be moved to tears, to feel the tension and release of suspense, to indulge in romantic and erotic fantasies, to witness the playing out of unresolvable conflicts in social life, to experience for two hours the plush luxury of the movie palace, to be momentarily freed from the trials of daily life, and many other things. What the cinema industry is trying to do to get that ticket money and to make a profit from its activities of producing, distributing, and exhibiting films is to supply a homogeneous product that balances the needs and exigencies of the cinema-going public with the capacities of the industry and the motivations of the film makers. The production sector cannot draw on an unlimited supply of creative and inventive talent, nor can it afford the dangerous tactic of constantly innovating. Hence it is engaged in an activity of repetition with variation: finding stories wherever it can (from plays, novels, short stories, newspaper items, and by no means least, from other films); reusing sets, costumes, story-plots, and, of course, performers as much as possible; and striving to produce new films that serve up once again the recipe that most succeeded in appealing to the public's taste the previous year. Films are not sold by the name and artistic reputation of the director or scriptwriter; they are marketed on the basis of the stars performing in the film and the type of story that the film tells, or the type of emotional experience it evokes in the audience. The type of story or emotional experience provoked are described with the notion of "genre." . . . Hence the origin of the majority of films lies in what have been called the "signifying practices" of the cinema industry: the procedures used to give stories clarity and impact, and the stereotyped situations that evoke laughter, fear, suspense, identification with the hero or heroine, and erotic satisfaction, for example. (1996: 221)

While we may be getting slightly ahead of ourselves here, Wagstaff echoes not only what I was saying in the previous chapter about genre and *filone*, but also the inherently escapist nature of vernacular cinema. The aesthetic considerations of a Pauline Kael are largely irrelevant here.

This distinction is further revealed in Anthony Mann's criticism of the Italian spaghetti westerns. In an earlier piece by Christopher Wagstaff (1992), he quotes the Hollywood veteran filmmaker as noting: "The shootouts every five minutes reveal the director's fear that the audiences get bored because they do not have a character to follow. In a tale you may not put more than five or six minutes of 'suspense': the diagram of the emotions must be ascending and not a kind of electrocardiogram for a clinical case" (quoted in Wagstaff 1992: 245). Mann's comments are even more explicit than Kael, at least the Kael quoted above. For mainstream Hollywood filmmakers like Mann, the spaghetti westerns demonstrated what they saw as utter contempt for "the audience," but that audience is conceived of as the kind championed by Kael—sitting quietly in the cinema, absorbing and contemplating the filmic text in front of them. To offer a different audience an alternative pattern, one where quiet contemplation of the filmic text is not the primary concern, results in what Mann likens to an electrocardiogram of a "clinical case."[4] The main thing that neither Mann nor Kael are aware of is cultural variation in cinema spectatorship, and that is what I will turn to now.

Context of Italian Moviegoing

Scholarship on Italian moviegoing practices, especially in English, is sparse. What little reference there is refers to Wagstaff's article "A Forkful of Westerns," wherein he noted three "classes" of cinema in Italy:[5] *prima visione* (first-run theaters, located in the sixteen major Italian cities) "where the big, immediate [box-office] receipts were achieved, because ticket prices were high" (1992: 246); *seconda visione* (second-run houses); and *terza visione* (third-rate movie houses located in the more rural and industrial residential regions). Films would often open at the *prima visione* theaters, trying to maximize their box-office receipts, followed by short runs at the *seconda visione* houses, and only then would be released to the *terza visione* screens. However, as Wagstaff noted, due to the demand for product at the *terza visione* houses, cheap and quick exploitation films would often play *only* there (1992: 274).

But it is the cinematic culture within these *terza visione* movie theaters that needs elaborating. As Wagstaff noted:

> The audience of the *terza visione* cinema was more like the television audience than like a *prima visione* cinema audience. The viewer (generally he) went to the cinema nearest to his house (or in rural areas, the only cinema there was) after dinner, at around ten o'clock in the evening. The programme changed daily or every other day. He would not bother to find out what was showing, nor would he make any particular effort to arrive at the beginning of the film. He would talk to his friends during the showing whenever he felt like it, except during the bits of the film that grabbed his (or his friends') attention (the film would stop anyway at an arbitrary point for an intermission). People would be coming and going and changing seats throughout the performance. (1992: 253)[6]

Within the *terza visione* cinema culture, the film text was of less importance than generally "going to the pictures," a context for social interaction rather than textual contemplation. *What* the *terza visione* audience watched was, if we believe Wagstaff, largely irrelevant. This description has much in common with Kael's description of the audience for *The Torture Chamber of Dr. Faustus*, albeit from a more generous and sympathetic perspective.

Wagstaff goes on to note, much as I have been arguing, that while the *prima visione* audience may indeed desire quiet contemplation of the artistic text as a whole, as "a unit to be studied" (1992: 253), that is not necessarily *always* the case. Wagstaff indicates that Mann's "electrocardiogram" model is perhaps closer to the truth, and not necessarily a negative: "The picture we have seen emerging of the situation in which the spaghetti westerns were produced and marketed (and viewed) explains completely that deliberate seeking after the 'electrocardiogram'" (1992: 254).

None of this, however, needs to dismiss textual analysis from an understanding of the *terza visione*–aimed films; it *does*, however, require us to shift our concerns away from seeing the film's integrity as a whole to seeing what the various electrocardiogram peaks indicate. And how these *terza* marketled practices of filmmaking impact on the text of the film itself.

Consider, for example, Mario Bava's *Bay of Blood*.[7] The film, whose running time is eighty minutes, neatly breaks up into three segments. The film opens with about twenty minutes of people being killed, one-by-one, by an unseen killer, with little narrative context. Following this is about forty minutes of contextual narrative exposition, wherein we are introduced to all the major characters, and are filled in on their backgrounds. The film then concludes with another twenty minutes of further slaughter, where all those still living are killed off. It is easy to project onto *Bay of Blood* the model of the *terza visione* audience Wagstaff outlined above: the lights go down and Bava immediately grabs their attention with his keenly orchestrated death scenes—hangings, slashed throats, machetes to the face, and even a spear impaling two young lovers together. After about twenty minutes, Bava seems to expect the audience's attention to wane, and so he clusters all the exposition as to what is supposedly going on in the film into this central forty minutes. If anyone in the audience actually *cares* what the "logic behind the gore" is, to use Kael's phrase, this is where it comes, such as it is. But Bava appears to be anticipating the *terza visione* audience's reaction, and gives them the space they require to move around and socialize within the cinema space. For the final twenty minutes, Bava calls the audience's attention back to the screen for these last few grisly deaths, before bringing everything to an end.[8] Of course, this analysis is pure speculation, and in none of the other films under consideration here does this pattern seem quite as evident. However, the intention of this speculation is to demonstrate an ideal type of film text for the *terza visione* audience. It is this kind of film text that I am here calling "vernacular cinema."

Vernacular Cinema

The dictionary definition of "vernacular" distinguishes between the noun and adjective: in the former sense, it refers to a localized dialect or language usage, in the latter, more generally to any kind of localized practice or style (again, often in reference to language). Vernacular cinema, clearly using "vernacular" as an adjective, modifies the kinds of cinema we are studying to recognize local cinematic practices, but furthermore, we can speak of a cinema *in the vernacular*—using the word as a noun to specify the localized cinematic *language*. The distinction is slight perhaps, but significant nonetheless: *vernacular cinema* refers to stylistic issues, including narrative and representation, while *cinema in the vernacular* would refer to more formal practices of cinematic language.

The use of *vernacular* I am evoking here comes partially from its use in the study of vernacular architecture. As Richard MacKinnon defines it:

> In much scholarship the term *vernacular* has been used interchangeably with the terms *folk, common, native* or *non-academic* architecture. It is usually placed at the other end of the spectrum from professionally designed architecture, or what is sometimes termed "high-style" architecture. One scholar uses the analogy of a "filter" to define the vernacular in architecture. Kingston Heath argues

that a fixed locale or region with its unique character, cultural mix, values, materials, climate and topography can "filter" conventional ideas about architecture whether they be folk, popular or high style. What results from this filtering process is vernacular architecture—"product of a place, of a people, by a people." (1995: 5)

There are three connotations from this definition, which inform the meaning of "vernacular cinema": one is, in keeping with the dictionary definition, the idea of localized practices, be they linguistic, architectural, or in this case, filmic; second is the idea of a "filtration" process from high-art predecessors (i.e., the *prima visione* films down to films made exclusively for *terza visione* audiences);[9] and third, the intentional opposition to a "high style," much like the "electrocardiogram" filmmaking noted by Mann above, which he read as merely incompetence on the part of the filmmakers. In truth, these connotations are never mutually exclusive in vernacular cinema; they work in unison, often overlapping.

Another evocation of *vernacular* comes from Leonard Primiano's study of vernacular religion. From Primiano, but applied to vernacular cinema, the idea assumes the fullest range possible of cinematic expressions, including those that may violate or contradict the hegemonic norms of filmmaking (and consuming) practices. Vernacular cinema, then, paraphrasing Primiano, privileges not the Platonic ideal of filmic orthodoxy, but the experiential dimension of a people's cinematic lives—that is, with and around cinema. This includes as central, rather than peripheral, the study of Kael's audience for *The Torture Chamber of Dr. Faustus* and Wagstaff's *terza visione* audience. Robin Hardy, the director of the British horror film *The Wicker Man* (1974), noted, in bemoaning the box-office failure of his film in the United States when it was released on the drive-in circuit: "What hope did the film have [in succeeding] with an audience who were fucking themselves silly in the back of their parents' Fords?" (quoted in Brown 2000: 129). Here there was a breakdown between the kind of film *The Wicker Man* was and the distribution strategy that was chosen for it. In other words, the film failed in the United States partially because a *non*-vernacular film was released into a vernacular cinema context.

The reverse also holds true, as when the *giallo* films discussed here are reviewed by the *Monthly Film Bulletin* upon distribution in the United Kingdom. The film reviewers tend to give the films more attention than the filmmakers may have intended. What the MFB reviewers may identify, in their ersatz-Kael way, is oftentimes the entire point of the film. A brief survey of the reviews the *giallo* films received in the United Kingdom reveals the biases that professional film reviewers have toward the kinds of films I have identified as vernacular. First, of the more than fifty films under consideration here, only a tiny handful were reviewed by the *Monthly Film Bulletin*—perhaps the most comprehensive cinema review source in the country. I could only locate fifteen reviews of these films in that publication between 1965 and 1983. There are several potential meanings of this dearth. Published by the British Film Institute (BFI), MFB was a fairly comprehensive collection of reviews, supposedly encompassing everything that received a theatrical release in the United Kingdom,[10] so the small number of *giallo* reviews I was able to find could indicate that the vast majority of the films under consideration here were never released in Britain. Second, it is hypothetically possible that those films not reviewed by the MFB did receive some kind of limited release within the United Kingdom but within markets and to audiences the editors felt would not be of interest to the journal's readers. Third, given the tone of the fifteen *giallo* reviews I found, perhaps editorial decisions were made not to include the bulk of this genre as they were seen to be less interesting films in the first place. Fourth, it is further possible that I may have missed some reviews due to the variants of English-language titles under which these films were released, as I demonstrate below. But regardless of *why* so few *gialli* were reviewed by this esteemed publication, what *was* reviewed, or rather the substance of those reviews, is significant.

The reviews I was able to find in the *Monthly Film Bulletin* are, for the most part, auteur oriented: Mario Bava's *The Girl Who Knew Too Much* had a UK release as *The Evil Eye* (unnamed reviewer 1965), *Blood and Black Lace* also received a review (P.J.D. 1966), as did *Five Dolls for an August Moon* (Milne 1972). Most of Dario Argento's films were reviewed as well, including *The Bird with the Crystal Plumage*, released in the United Kingdom as *The Gallery Murders* (1969) (unnamed reviewer 1970), *The Cat O' Nine Tails* (*Il Gatto a nove code*) (1971) (Combs 1971), *Four Flies on Grey Velvet* (*4 mosche di velluto grigio*) (1971) (Pirie 1973), and *Tenebre* (1982) (Strick 1983: 139). Significantly, Argento's best known *giallo*, *Deep Red*, "received no British cinema release at all and only a patchy release in the United States under the misleading title *The Hatchet Murders*" (Hutchings 2003: 129–30). This accounts for more than half of the *giallo* films reviewed by the journal. The other films reviewed are *A Black Veil for Lisa* (unnamed reviewer 1969); *Paranoia*, released as *Orgasmo* (unnamed reviewer 1970); *The Forbidden Photos of a Lady Above Suspicion* (Combs 1972); *The Black Belly of the Tarantula* (Pirie 1972); *The Case of the Bloody Iris*, released as *Erotic Blue* (Combs 1973); *A Lizard in a Woman's Skin* (Raisbeck 1973); *The Fifth Cord* (*Giornata nera per l'ariete*) (Luigi Bazzoni, 1971), released as *Evil Fingers* (McGillivray 1973); and *Torso* (Rosenbaum 1975).

One distinct theme emerges from these reviews: the films themselves are not very good. The problem for a study of vernacular cinema, however, is that this assessment is predicated upon the film's narrative and screenplay exclusively, for when the reviewers move on to discuss the films' visual styles, they are often praised. David McGillivray's review of Bazzoni's *The Fifth Cord* is a case in point. After an extensive plot summation, McGillivray's assessment consists of two sentences:

> Shoals of red herrings do little to make up for *Evil Fingers'* meager characterisation, the scrambled course of its plot, or its shamefully deceptive ending. Mercifully, Luigi Bazzoni's briskly paced direction . . . contrives to sweep it all under the carpet as quickly as possible. (227)

Most reviewers criticize the *giallo* for its contrivances—the "shoals of red herrings" McGillivray notes in *The Fifth Cord*. But they are often quick to praise the film for its visual style, particularly those by Bava or Argento. David Pirie, in his review of Argento's *Four Flies*, noted on the one hand that "the script remains as flat and predictable as that of the most meager Italian 'B' feature," while then turning around to praise the film for "enough eerie moments to confirm Argento's promise as a director" (1973: 56). Likewise, Richard Combs referred to *Cat O' Nine Tails* as "the sort of thriller where professional expertise and a certain visual elegance struggle to give 'tone' and 'style' to blandly undistinguished material" (Combs 1971: 120). A decade later Philip Strick offers almost the same criticism of Argento: "To do reluctant justice to Argento, it must be admitted that visually the film is seldom boring. . . . One is made all the more aware of the director's inability to match visual flair with anything worth watching" (139).

These reviews give us insight into the criteria the MFB reviewers used in assessing these *gialli*: good writing takes precedence over visual style. Combs, in reviewing Carmineo's *Bloody Iris*, highlights this criterion even more: "[Carmineo] directs the cheap and nasty plot like a poor man's Dario Argento, papering over the cracks with a camped-up surface of luscious wide screen photography, kinky sex, and the occasional close-up of a baleful eye, psychotically attentive amidst the shadows" (Combs 1973: 81). The assumption is that visual style (luscious photography, kinky sex, close-ups, etc.) is a device that *covers up* the holes in the narrative, thereby emphasizing one particular criterion for filmic assessment. In another review by Combs, this time for *Forbidden Photos*, he notes, "Neither the plotting nor the psychology bear much attention [for discussion in this review], however; like two worn gears failing to mesh they spin ponderously round, a vastly inefficient and unnecessary

means of powering the film's standard scenes of exploitive sex" (Combs 1972:
112). Here, with Combs's consistent emphasis on plot, he assumes the film's
exploration of psychology *motivates* the sex, rather than the alternative, that
the psychology is the barest excuse *for* the sex. Cook succinctly suggests that
perhaps the popularity of exploitation cinema is in "the way it scandalises
some of the most hallowed canons of film criticism—the assumption that the
critic knows better than 'unsophisticated' audiences how to judge a good or
bad film, for instance, or that a 'good' film is judged in terms of taste, aesthetic
coherence, serious themes, and so on" (1985: 367).

Jonathan Rosenbaum is the single reviewer in *MFB* during this period
who understands these films, or at least, understands what the films offer. His
full review of *Torso* is worth quoting:

> This well-dubbed, lightweight horror opus supplies us with everything that it
> thinks we need: pretty girls in various states of dress and undress, a steel guitar
> on the soundtrack to establish menace, lectures on Italian sculpture, tastefully
> elliptical dismemberments and mutilations of body parts . . . , a gratuitous
> lesbian sequence, and enough red herrings to keep a German restaurant in
> business for a week. (132)

Rosenbaum understands the popcorn sensibility of these films, whereas
Combs, Pirie, McGillivray, and Strick clearly do not: either they take the
films too seriously or they are too serious in holding the film up to standard
criteria for what they think cinema should be. Rosenbaum's review understands that these films are designed to give the audience a set of "thrills," and
the "plot" is merely a pretext on which to hang those thrills, an alternative
demonstration of Anthony Mann's "electrocardiogram" model of filmmaking.

Fanzines and other forms of vernacular criticism tend to understand the
intended audience for these films better than the BFI (Rosenbaum ex-
cepted). L. A. Morse's *Video Trash & Treasures* (1989), a compendium of
schlock video reviews organized into "at home" film festivals the reader is
invited to program for themselves, is but a single example of the kind of vernacular criticism more appropriate to the *giallo* film than the *Monthly Film
Bulletin*'s reviews. Morse concludes each of his paragraph-long reviews with
an appropriate summary. For example, his summation of Lamberto Bava's *A
Blade in the Dark* (*La casa con la scala nel buio*) (1983) reads "Six bodies;
rather subdued splatter; trace bimbo exposure [i.e., female nudity]; lots and
lots of corridor footage" (233); or his review of Michele Soavi's *Stage Fright*
(*Deliria*) (1987) is summarized as "Ten bodies; a masked killer; no skin, but
an interesting 'fat suit'; good production values; decent dubbing; abundant

blood; a dismemberment; a decapitation" (242). Morse's reviews direct the reader toward the features that he understands his audiences are particularly interested in—the amounts of sex, violence, gore, and "interesting" visual business in a specific film.

Antonio Bido's *The Cat's Victims* (*Il gatto dagli occhi di giada*) (1977), known to Morse under the title *Watch Me When I Kill*, with an apparent release date of 1981, advertises itself as an Italian slasher film. However, it runs against the vernacular cinematic criteria of "video trash" Morse is advocating: "Not a psycho-slasher flick, and the only point of the title is to sucker you into thinking it is one. In fact, this is a wretchedly dubbed, terribly made, thoroughly stupid mystery about revenge for some wartime atrocity. Tedious even at fast-forward" (248). It is a pity that I could not lay my hands on the MFB review of this film, if it was even reviewed, since it is more the carefully plotted, subtly executed kind of film that the BFI privilege.

Setting aside my disagreement with Morse's assessment of Bido's film, it is his last comment I want to pick up on. "Tedious even at fast-forward" suggests a viewing strategy contrary to mainstream moviegoing—of fast-forwarding a videocassette or DVD to get to the "good stuff" summarized by Morse in most of his reviews. Although not about an Italian *giallo* film, Morse's review of *Nightmare* (USA, 1981, Romano Scavolini) gives further evidence of this alternative viewing practice: "Still, there are a few decent splatter effects from Tom Savini . . . so this does catch your attention at least occasionally" (244).[11] Morse identifies a viewing practice akin (not necessarily identical) to that of Wagstaff's *terza visione* audience, who watch these vernacular films with divided attention, distracted until "the good stuff" hits the screen. Where the individual has control over the remote control unit on the video/DVD player at home, in the theater, the *terza visione* (or equivalent) audience members lack that immediate control, and so exert a kind of control by alternative cinematic behaviors—alternative, that is, to the standard, normative behavior in a movie theater of a quiet and contemplative spectator-to-text relationship.

One of the problems in discussing the *giallo* film is the lack of an adequate vocabulary for doing so. This is evidenced, in part, by the genre's omission from books on Italian cinema and in the negative reviews these films tend to receive in the mainstream press. Designating films as vernacular cinema is a way of approaching genres, like the *giallo*, without adhering to the bourgeois criteria of classical narrative, intellectual abstraction, and elitist notions of "the artistic." It is intended to partially replace other, more inchoate, terms like "popular," "mainstream," "mass," or "B-grade" references to cinema. One of the more problematic words frequently cited is "popular." Dimitris Eleft-heriotis (2001) noted: "Some of the confusion around the popular (especially 'popular cinema') arises from the existence of a cluster of terms that are per-ceived and used as more or less interchangeable—crucially the terms 'com-mercial,' 'entertainment,' 'mainstream' and 'genre'" (69). These words are not synonymous with each other; however, in a number of works on "popu-lar" European cinemas, including Eleftheriotis's, they are treated as such.

We need to distinguish between "popular" and "mass" forms of entertain-ment. Raymond Williams, in his *Keywords* (1976), defines "mass," used in ref-erence to forms of entertainment or culture, as directed toward the greatest number of people as possible (236); that is, the "mass media" ensures its prod-ucts are available to a majority audience, creating, essentially, a kind of "main-stream" from which the modernist high-art and the "popular" are diametri-cally opposed offshoots. Italian cultural scholar Vittorio Spinazzola defines the distinction between mass and popular cinemas from a highly Williamsian per-spective: "To the popular cinema belongs works destined to be consumed by the lower classes exclusively; the mass cinema is instead designed to unify the public, bourgeois and proletarian, and therefore appears to have an interclass value" (quoted in Wagstaff 1992: 249). By "lower classes," Spinazzola is refer-ring to Williams's reference to the "popular" as the domain of "the folk"; Williams identified the word "popular" as deriving from Latin legal and polit-ical terminology as "belonging to the people" (236).

But "popular" is just as problematic a term as "mass." Dyer and Vincen-deau attempt to define what "popular" cinema is, recognizing two senses of the term "popular" as "commercially successful" and as "express[ing] the thoughts, values and feelings 'of the people'" (2)—this latter definition de-riving from Williams's *Keywords*. In trying to create a polarized discourse on popular cinema, the authors juxtapose what they term "mass" culture with "folk" culture, that is, commercial success measured in terms of the box of-fice and "audience preferences" (Dyer and Vincendeau 1992: 2). The current study is highly influenced by what Dyer and Vincendeau characterize as an "anthropological" or "folk" approach (2). The problem is that the authors are less confident about how to define such an approach, considering the quite truthful observation that cinema can rarely be truly "of the people," since "the people" rarely have the opportunity to make and display their own films, (3) although this is beginning to change. Dyer and Vincendeau propose that there is only one way an approach to film studies can be "anthropological," or "folk";[12] that is, the focus must be "on the way film uses cultural practices seen as existing prior to or outside the mass media" (3). The authors correctly identify the problematic assumption in this approach of "positing a culture 'of the people' that is either not in fact separable from mass (industrially, centrally produced) culture or is not in reality part of the life of the mass of people" (3). Viewing these films as vernacular cinema, then, is a way forward in this argument: how do we situate these films within the lived experience of the folk for whom they are intended and still maintain some kind of schemata for critically addressing them? Part of the solution may lie in applying Walter Ong's aspects of oral culture to cinematic practices in order to develop a culturally responsive schema for textual analysis—what I am calling vernacular cinema. In other words, we need to find a way, contra Pauline Kael, the majority of Italian film scholars, and the MFB reviewers noted above, to discuss the *giallo* on its own terms, particularly in order to analyze these films' address to their historical, and perhaps more importantly, cultural, audiences.

The Psychodynamics of Vernacular Cinema

In *Orality and Literacy* (1982), Ong includes a lengthy discussion of what he calls the "psychodynamics" of primary orality—that is, those cultures that are not chirographic, who do not have writing. It should not be inferred by this application that I am contrasting *literate* cultures with vernacular cinema audiences, or that Ong's psychodynamics of orality are direct equivalents to vernacular cinema, but in applying those psychodynamics to cinematic expression, the vernacular cinema culture is better understood. So, by "psychodynamics" Ong is referring to those cognitive processes that characterize primarily oral cultures. The terms that we, in our highly literate society, use to describe the world around us—our very "literate" worldview—are often inappropriate to describe the worldview of primary orality cultures. Ong notes that orality in mass-mediated, technological societies such as our own does exist in a secondary capacity (11). But, by conceiving of oral "texts," as well as other linguistic metaphors to describe primary oral cultures, we demonstrate our literacy prejudice (13). Ong noted that primary orality often lacks analytical discourse, that is, the discourse of introspection or self-reflexivity (30). Likewise, vernacular cinema is often criticized for its lack of introspection and self-reflexivity, as I noted in the discussion of the reception of the *giallo* films above.

Part of the problem here is that we are preconditioned to approach films as we do literary texts, that is, through a literary/literate paradigm of consumption. Of course today, having copies of favorite movies on video or DVD is commonplace, allowing the viewer to "review" or reread favorite passages, going back and watching again something that may have been missed the first time. DVD technology is even more chirocentric, insofar as the film is now divided up for ease in consuming the text, no longer necessarily in one sitting. To try and understand the similarities (again, not explicit correlations but merely similarities) between orality and vernacular cinema, we may look at how Ong, in describing the cognitive dimensions of orality, problematizes our chirocentric worldview. Ong noted:

> Fully literate persons can only with great difficulty imagine what a primary oral culture is like, that is, a culture with no knowledge whatsoever of writing or even of the possibility of writing. Try to imagine a culture where no one has ever "looked up" anything. In a primary oral culture, the expression "to look up something" is an empty phrase: it would have no conceivable meaning. Without writing, words as such have no visual presence, even when the objects they represent are visual. They are sounds. You might "call" them back— "recall" them. But there is nowhere to "look" for them. They have no focus and no trace (a visual metaphor, showing dependency on writing), not even a trajectory. They are occurrences, events. (31)

Vernacular cinema too is often highly ephemeral: as noted above in the discussion of the *terza visione* theaters, films would change several times a week, if not every night, and so audiences would have one opportunity to see a specific film.

For Ong, there are several cognitive processes, psychodynamics, which differentiate primary orality from primary literacy cultures. Below is a gloss of a selected few that have particular relevance for vernacular cinema:

- Formulaic narratives: Ong noted that within primary oral cultures "to think through something in non-formulaic, non-patterned . . . terms, even if it were possible, would be a waste of time, for such thought, once worked through, could never be recovered with any effectiveness, as it could be with the aid of writing" (35).
- Redundancy and repetition: As Ong noted in his discussion of this psychodynamic, within a literacy-based culture, should an idea be confusing or obtuse, or even just missed the first time around, it can be reread by glancing back over the text. In an orally based culture, there is nothing to be glanced back at. "Hence, the mind must move ahead more slowly, keeping close to the focus of attention much of what it has already dealt with. Redundancy, repetition of the just-said, keeps both the speaker and hearer surely on the track" (39–40). Ong further noted, and this is particularly relevant for these psychodynamics' application to vernacular

cinema, that redundancy and repetition are essential within "the physical conditions of oral expression before a large audience. . . . Not every one in a large audience understands every word a speaker utters, if only because of acoustical problems. It is advantageous for the speaker to say the same thing, or equivalently the same thing, two or three times" (40).

- Ideologically conservative (traditionalist): perhaps one of the most significant of Ong's psychodynamics to the study of vernacular cinema is understanding the role of conservative ideologies. For Ong, "in a primary oral culture conceptualized knowledge that is not repeated aloud soon vanishes, oral societies must invest great energy in saying over and over again what has been learned arduously over the ages. This need establishes a highly traditionalist or conservative set of mind that with good reason inhibits intellectual experimentation" (41). Intellectual experimentation, although possible without literacy, could not be effectively communicated, for some kind of written-down text is required for any kind of rebuttal.

- Narratives must take place in a recognizable space. Even if in fantasy narratives, wherein the world is not necessarily the world we live in, its features must be immediately recognizable as our own *liebenwelt*[13] (42–43). Furthermore, ideas are expressed situationally, rather than abstractly (49–57).

- "Agonistically toned": Ong noted that only within a literate culture can ideas become abstract and divorced from human experience. Characters, then, become embodiments of gross ideas, in very concrete forms, and those forms need to be in conflict with one another. These conflicts (*agon*) are, within primarily oral cultures, highly physical—violent and (I would add) sexual. Ong notes that as the oral dimension of these narratives give way to literary narratives, the physical gradually gives way to more sophisticated and subtle abstraction. But again, these abstractions are impossible within primary orality (43–45).

- Orality demands empathic and participatory relationships with narratives. The kind of narratives that allow intellectual abstraction and a "distant" reader/viewer is evidence of a literary culture, not a primary oral one. The written text itself tends to distance the reader by the very process of *reading*, that is, as a level of abstraction (from writing to words, from words to ideas/experiences). Orality creates immediately experienced, and as noted above, recognizable sensations. Participation furthers that experience by expressing one's sensations with an immediate and shared context of others (45–46).

Clearly Ong's psychodynamics are "producer" oriented; that is, they are oriented toward the cognitive processes of the orator, not necessarily the audience. He is concerned with how a storyteller like Homer could have *orally* told epic narratives like *The Odyssey* and *The Iliad* without the aid of writing. My concern here is less with the cultural producers of the *giallo* than with their relationship with the cultural consumers through individual filmic texts.

There is perhaps a certain irony in invoking Ong's theories of orality when discussing a filmic genre as explicitly *literary* as the *giallo*: the term does after all refer to a series of *books*, so the literary is invoked from how the genre is known. Beyond that, a number of the *giallo* films discussed here are, to some degree (and this is highly variable), based on novels. Of course, most fiction films are not improvised as narratives in front of the camera but are based on screenplays, and again this presupposes literacy. Unlike most filmic literary adaptations, however, knowledge of the source material, particularly in the *giallo* films, is not assumed. An awareness that Mario Bava's *Five Dolls for an August Moon* is based on Agatha Christie's *And Then There Were None* (1939) or that Dario Argento's *The Bird with the Crystal Plumage* is based on Fredric Brown's book *The Screaming Mimi* (1952) is largely irrelevant. Furthermore, the murder mystery, as a genre, tends to be more literary than the horror film, which tends toward the more oral-like: the former depends on an intricately woven plot, while the latter largely on affect. To discuss the *giallo* as narrative may invoke the genre's dependence upon literary models of murder mysteries, but to sit through most of the films discussed here is to *experience* them as horror films.

Vernacular cinema, then, is largely formulaic cinema: it relies heavily on preexisting formulas that enable the, for example, *terza visione* audiences to transform the movie theater into a social space for a variety of activities, while still enabling the film text in question to be comprehensible. Although the narrative may be of secondary importance to vernacular audiences, the film itself must be comprehensible at the time of its projection. Formulaic narratives enable the story to be followed undemandingly. In addition, due to vernacular cinema's tendency to function as an "attraction"—to draw the vernacular audiences' attention back onto the screen—narrative functions as merely the framework on which hang the spectacle sequences of violence, sex, and graphic gore.

When we read a murder mystery, we tend to look for clues along with the fictional detectives; we scan suspects' testimonies looking for inconsistencies and red herrings, trying to accurately predict "whodunit." The murder mystery as a genre cannot exist within an oral culture, because in such a culture there is no way of "going back over" what has already been said and scrutinizing the testimony for further clues. It is a genre that demands literacy. In the *giallo* films, although certain pieces of evidence need literary-like attention, we cannot simply rewind a film (like we can with video) in order to replay a piece of evidence. Instead, vernacular films like the *giallo* tend to overemphasize clues and red herrings (as evidenced by how many times these were criticized by the MFB critics). Vernacular cinema therefore tends to be an *obvious* cinema—what is important needs to highlighted, often repeatedly, not just through repetition in the script, but also visually through repeated flashbacks. For example, in the denouement of Armando Crispino's *Autopsy*, when the killer is finally revealed, we are presented with a series of flashback images recapping how it was that he could have been the killer. Rather than a lengthy exposition given verbally, from one character to another (as is usually the case, even in *giallo* cinema), the "rereading" occurs visually. Vernacular cinema tends to render visually and without subtlety or abstraction all the important information the audience needs to know. *Gialli* are also filled with sudden and seemingly obvious zoom-ins, particularly on people's eyes, showing concentration, shock, or emotion. Again, such visual devices lack subtlety, but that is exactly the point. Vernacular cinema is an exceptionally obvious cinema.

Ideological discourse in film studies, at its worst, tends toward superficial assumptions about its filmmakers, reading a seemingly conservative ideology as consciously propagandistic or "against the grain" in subsuming potentially counterhegemonic discourse in a seemingly disarming way—Robin Wood's seminal article, "An Introduction to the American Horror Film" (1979) being a key example of this. But what approaches like Wood's fail to recognize is that, within vernacular cinema, conservative, or to use Ong's term, "traditionalist," ideology is essential, not because hegemony needs to be maintained, but because of the cognitive processes required in quasi-orality. "On paper," to use a chirocentric allusion, we can play around with ideas and challenge hegemony, but as we engage in the ephemeral nature of cinema, particularly a vernacular film, those challenges become meaningless without some kind of text to refer back to. This is not to say that cinema cannot experiment with ideas; of course it does, and even some genre films can experiment with ideas and ideologies. But those films tend to be less "vernacular," self-consciously moving into a more literate field of either "mass/mainstream" cinema, such as *The Silence of the Lambs* (Jonathan Demme, 1991) or *Se7en* (David Fincher, 1995), or modernist, high-art films such as *Wes Craven's New Nightmare* (Wes Craven, 1994).

Vernacular cinema also needs to be significantly simplistic, particularly with regard to its settings. The world the film is situated within needs to be

immediately recognizable as the world the audience lives in. I discuss this feature in more detail in chapter 3, but for now let me note provisionally that
despite some foreign and exotic locales chosen for *giallo* film narratives, the
world the characters inhabit is immediately recognizable, even if audience
members have never experienced those places themselves. The characters
have to act like people the audience is familiar with—either in "real life" or
from previous encounters with those character types in other films. So we
find a similarity in character behavior regardless of whether the characters
are the Eastern European diplomats in Dublin in Riccardo Freda's *The Iguana
with a Tongue of Fire* (*L'iguana dalla lingua di fuoco*) (1971) or some artists in
Venice, as in *Who Saw Her Die?* by Aldo Lado.

Also simplistic within vernacular cinema are the characters' actions.
While it is perfectly appropriate (and perhaps even desirable) within a literary culture to have characters embody certain ideas or philosophies, within
vernacular cinema, as within orality, these kinds of abstractions must be represented situationally; that is, not only must we see the characters act according to base categories of behavior, but we define those characters *because*
of those actions. Traits cannot be divorced from the actions we have witnessed characters perform, and as such, any kind of discourse these films offer needs to be represented visually through the interactions of those characters. So, for example, in the *giallo* we see the obsessed amateur detective
hunting down the deranged killer while an apathetic police force goes
through the motions, with an inevitable final battle between good (amateur
detective) and evil (psycho killer). But it is the discourses that *do* open up,
through these base conflicts, that give us some insight into Italian vernacular culture in the early 1970s—and it is these discourses that much of this
book is concerned with identifying.

Finally, and this is perhaps the major distinction between modernist high-
art cinema and vernacular cinema, the former can allow an audience enough
distance to critically examine the ideas presented; vernacular cinema cannot.
Vernacular cinema demands an immediate and personal relationship to the
narrative, and in part, this explains the graphic and exploitive representations of gore, sex, and violence. Vernacular cinema demands that we respond
immediately to the images and not distance ourselves from the film through
abstraction. Perhaps even more significant—and this is a dimension lost
when viewing these films by oneself in the privacy of one's own home on
video—the viewer's relationship with the actions and characters on screen is
heightened when experienced with others in a movie theater. If we are just
watching a film to absorb its narrative and its ideas, then a video version is
quite sufficient; but, as Kael's audience for *The Horror Chamber of Dr. Faus-*

tus demonstrates, and as anyone who has watched a horror movie in a crowded theater can attest, the shared experience is very different.

If we approach the *giallo* film, or indeed any other kind of vernacular cinema, from a literacy bias, a consistent series of criticisms emerges, as noted above. The problem is that vernacular cinema is not made for the critics—be they movie reviewers or scholars (although ironically *giallo* filmmakers like Dario Argento and Lucio Fulci were movie reviewers before making their films). These films are made for vernacular audiences, appealing to vernacular standards and demands. It might be overstating it to say that vernacular filmmakers do not care about outsiders' assessments of their films, but such a sentiment comes close. Vernacular cinema is truly "the people's cinema."[14]

Notes

1. The term coined by Luca Palmerini and Gaetano Mistretta for a horror movie equivalent to the spaghetti western. See Palmerini and Mistretta 1996.

2. Contrast these comments by Bondanella with those of Pam Cook (1985) who, while making almost the same argument, emphasizes the role exploitation cinema offers as a training ground for filmmakers. While it is certainly true that horror filmmakers often develop into world-renown *auteurs*, for example David Cronenberg, Bondanella seems too willing to dismiss a filmmaker's early work, like that of Avati.

3. Although not specifically on *Italian* exploitation horror, but making the same argument that popular cinema can be seen as high-art cinema, see Hawkins 2000.

4. The flip side to the denigration of exploitation cinema, at least within an Anglo-North American context, is the elevation of these films as cult films. As Kirstin Thompson and David Bordwell noted in their *Film History*, "Since the 1970s, exploitation movies have become cult items. Some fans find hilarity in the overblown dialogue, stiff performances, and awkward technique. This so-bad-it's-good attitude was popularized in Harry and Michael Medved, *The Golden Turkey Awards*. . . . Other aficionados consider the exploitation films a direct challenge to the idea of normality presented by the Hollywood mainstream. Arising at the time of Punk and No Wave [sic] music, this notion of the subversive potential of rough technique and bad taste was exemplified in the 'fanzines' *Film Threat* and *That's Exploitation!*" (Thompson and Bordwell 2003: 533).

5. At least this was the case during the period under consideration here, during the 1960s and 1970s. For Wagstaff looking at the spaghetti western, and this current study looking at the *giallo*, the main films under consideration fall within these two decades. I have seen no scholarship on the changes in film exhibition that have occurred over the past twenty years worldwide, which I am sure have had some impact on Italian moviegoing too.

6. Wagstaff's characterization of the *terza visione* audience is echoed by Christopher Frayling: "Your average low-budget Spaghetti played to audiences which went

to the pictures several times a week, talked through the boring bits, enjoyed plenty
of action and noise, liked heroes who dressed in style and smoked a lot of *toscani* ci-
gars, were accustomed to an arbitrary intermission while the projectionist changed
reels, and unless captivated by a surprise ending like to walk out before the end. This
sociology of cinema going helps to explain at least some of the recurring features of
the films themselves. Franco Nero speculated in a 1993 interview that 'Spaghetti
Westerns were for a certain kind of audience—the workers, I think. Mainly workers,
boys . . . yes, all kinds of workers—and the workers that fantasize a lot, and they
would like to go to the boss in the office and be the hero and say "Sir, from today,
something's gonna happen." And then—bam, bam! they want to clean up the whole
world.' He was probably right. In this sense, the Italian Westerns hark back to the era
of silent movies in America, or 'B' movies of the 1930s, when films made direct contact with similar audiences (in the city and the country), and when the horse did as
much thinking as the itinerant cowboy" (Frayling 1998: xi). Although obviously
talking about the spaghetti westerns, I think much of what Frayling identifies here is
applicable to the *giallo* audience.

7. The original Italian title, *Reazione a catena*, literally means "Chain Reaction."

8. Without applying the *terza visione* audience hypothesis, as I did, Troy Howarth
recognized that Bava's formula had some kind of meaning to it: "Even if the me-
chanics of plot are not Bava's primary consideration (this is most evident in challenging *gialli* like *Blood and Black Lace* and *Twitch of the Death Nerve*, which alienate
many viewers by refusing to conform to the standards of conventional mystery plotting), this does not mean that his work is one-dimensional" (2002: 9).

9. Some preliminary discussion of the filtration process was noted in the previous chapter. In addition, I also discuss it in Koven 2004.

10. Now incorporated into *Sight and Sound*.

11. Tom Savini is a renowned special makeup artist known for particularly grisly
effects. Savini has a tremendous cult following, on a par with certain horror movie
directors.

12. Dyer and Vincendeau use these terms unproblematically as synonyms. Space
does not allow me to engage in that particular problem.

13. The world as we live and experience it.

14. While this study is focused on the study of one particular form of a single
country's vernacular cinema, these arguments are applicable well beyond the study of
the *giallo*. Michèle Lagny noted the same prejudices against the *peplum*, although she
seems to agree with the elitist perspective, saying that it "does not appeal to 'sophisticated' filmgoers (with the exception of a few wayward enthusiasts); and film critics
tend either to dismiss the genre with mild sarcasm or to lambaste it for being ideologically unsound" (1992: 163). Agustin Sotto, on the other hand, relates the Filipino action film to the vernacular culture that is the audience for these films, despite
equal derision from the critics: "The film critic has much to complain about in local
mainstream production—logicalities, anachronisms, cross-cultural borrowings, lack

of subtlety in characterization, stock situations, and stereotypes. Many of his complaints are perhaps justified from the point of view of aesthetics. However, looking at the same problems from a sociological standpoint, one begins to see direct relationships between film conventions and cultural values" (1987: 12). And in a series of articles on Bollywood cinema, Sheila Nayar argues likewise for an approach to popular cinema from a more vernacular perspective (1997, 2003, 2004, and 2005). Nayar even argues, quite independently of me, that such an approach needs to use Walter Ong's psychodynamics in order to understand the cinema's vernacular construction (2004). Also see Koven (2003b).

CHAPTER THREE

~

Space and Place in Italian *Giallo* Cinema: The Ambivalence of Modernity

In *La Dolce Vita* (Federico Fellini, 1960), the lead character, Marcello (Marcello Mastroianni), a reporter, cruises contemporary Rome, ostensibly on assignment covering a variety of "human interest" stories, but perhaps it is more accurate to say he is traveling around enjoying "The Sweet Life," as the translation of the title would have it. As Pierre Leprohon noted, "It is significant that the central character of *La Dolce Vita* is merely a *witness* of a world to which at the outset he does not belong" (1972: 168). The Catholic Church saw Fellini's film as highly controversial at the time, blasphemous for its depiction of a spiritually degenerate society (Leprohon 1972: 168). Despite, or maybe because of, the Vatican's condemnation of the film, *La Dolce Vita* became an international success and brought further attention to Rome as an exotic holiday destination, filled with glamour, wealth, and the most beautiful people in Europe. Rome, in many respects, rivaled Paris as exemplifying the glamour of postwar Europe. In a phenomenon typical of bourgeois fads, the satirical commentary in Fellini's film seemed to be lost on most audiences at the time; audiences did not pick up on the film's condemnation of this spiritually bankrupt society and, instead, embraced the film for its glamour.

The degeneration of Italian society, seen through the eyes of the "beautiful people" of Rome, in Fellini's film, was the logical conclusion to a period of massive cultural and economic development and expansion in Italy, known as "the economic miracle." Pierre Sorlin characterized it thus:

From the middle of the 1950s to the middle of the 1970s, structural transformations, namely greater applied scientific knowledge, a market-based industrial

45

economy, and the rise of an urban society, triggered a sustained expansion in the retailing of consumer goods. With modernization, the economic benefits of domestic self-sufficiency and the saving of money vanished, but for people to recognize this and act accordingly required a radical change in attitudes. Family self-sufficiency, which was a necessity, especially on farms, was ideologically justified by traditional values supported by religion, the kinship system and gender roles. For this to evolve, a new cultural environment, dominated by secular, individualistic rationality, had to arise. To what extent did mental attitudes and expectations really alter? This is a question open to discussion. It has been argued, for instance, that the rapid decline in the birth rate, one of the most impressive features of Italian demography since the middle of the twentieth century, must be seen not as cultural "modernization" but rather as the realization of the traditional values of home and family in a world of new opportunities. The fact remains that people believed that a new era had begun. (1996: 115)

But *La Dolce Vita* was a single film in this period that received international recognition and further established Rome (and metonymically, Italy) as the sine qua non of "the sweet life" that Europe had to offer. After Fellini's satirical attempt at critiquing Roman fashion, the *giallo* films went even further, turning *la dolce vita* into *la dolce morte*.

This chapter is concerned with understanding how these *giallo* films use and reflect geographical space, a consideration of the spaces and locations these films situate themselves within diegetically. What I hope to demonstrate is that these films reflect ambivalence toward modernity, a position affected by the filmmaker (ideally) reflecting these films' vernacular audiences. The settings and locations of these films are more than stagnant backdrops however; certain character roles are often fulfilled by foreigners and outsiders, and part of this cinema's ambivalence is in these liminal roles: sometimes they are the killers, sometimes they are the victims, sometimes they are the suspects. Sometimes even the role of the amateur detective is fulfilled by someone not part of the diegetic community.

Location

Pierre Sorlin, although he omits any reference to Italian horror pictures, addresses the Italian practice of dubbing films regardless of their country of origin or original language thus: "Language, in this instance, does a strange trick, it camouflages an object which belongs to the national cinema (people see it like any genuine Italian picture) while being alien to it (nobody thinks that the action takes place in Milan or Rome)" (1996: 11). Applied to the *giallo*, a pan-European Italian-ness begins to emerge through the language of these films: despite their non-Italian locations, at least those set outside of the Italian peninsula, everyone speaks the same middle-class Roman Italian (this procedure works backward too, when watching Italian films dubbed in English—particularly American English). Italian becomes the *lingua franca* of Europe. But the ambivalence that Sorlin noted operates to suture the Italian audience member into the film's locale while constantly drawing attention to its own artificiality. "Dubbing can evoke an immediate sense of otherness, a detachment and sensory dislocation created by the mismatching of an actor's lips and the dubbed voice" (Thrower 1999: 152). This artificiality of the dubbing procedure is partially underlined by the often internationally recognizable casts (no one believes that George Lazenby, John Mills, or Carole Baker are actually speaking Italian in the *gialli* they appear in—and this is verified if one can lip-read), but also invokes a self-conscious myth about an Italian *koine* which unites all of Europe and cuts across class boundaries. So the first site of ambivalence is geographical: that these films recognize the "Jet-Set" aesthetic, the involvement and interest in other parts of Europe, and yet also recognize how artificial these representations are.

Thinking about these films' use of geographical space, as Italian films, it should not be too surprising to find the vast majority of them set in Italy, and more specifically based in and around Rome. Although a few films situate themselves in and around other parts of the country (specifically Venice, Padua, Milan, Florence, Turin, and Parma, as well as regions like Tuscany and Apulia), Rome and its surrounding areas, being in close proximity to the Cinecittà studio, make up the largest single urban setting.

Many *gialli* are set outside of Italy and across Europe, with two films at least partially set in New York City (*Tenebre* and *The New York Ripper*), and two others geographically unspecified but implied to be somewhere in the United States: *Delirium* (*Delirio caldo*) and *Stagefright*. The European settings for a number of these films are extensive, although the most popular location for *gialli* outside of Italy is London, which acts as the setting for several films. Other European locations include such tourist destinations as Dublin, Paris, Barcelona, the Costa del Sol, Hamburg, the Swiss Alps, Vienna, and Prague. At least one *giallo* is even set in Australia (*The Pyjama Girl Case*). Gary Needham referred to these films' reflecting their literary generic origins through their disparate locations as mise en abyme (2003: 136). However, Needham's argument can be pushed even further, for the *giallo* is not just a "literary" genre, it is a "popular" literary genre, and therefore, by extension, there is a suggestion that these films are the cinematic equivalent of "vacation novels," the kind of stories one might consume while on holiday, and the *gialli* locations are a reflection of this. Needham noted "the obsession with travel and tourism not only as a mark of the newly emerging European jet-set (consider how many *gialli* begin or end in airports), but representative of Italian cinema's selling of its own 'Italian-ness' through tourist hotspots (initiated by the murder on the Spanish Steps in Bava's [*The Girl Who Knew Too Much*] as well as countless deaths in or around famous squares, fountains and monuments throughout the *giallo*; and of course fashion and style)" (2003: 136).

The connection between the *giallo* and travel reveals the literary origins of the genre: Laura Marcus argued that the rise in mass-produced popular literature coincided with the rise in railway travel, at least in the United Kingdom.

> "Railway fiction" emerged soon after the growth of the railway system in the early to mid-nineteenth century; cheap books or "yellowbacks" were produced to be sold at the railway bookstalls which W. H. Smith began to take over in 1848. In the same year, Routledge initiated its "Railway Library," and a number of other publishers swiftly entered the competition for the production of cheap editions. The growth of the railways is thus directly linked to the production of literature (popular and "improving") with a mass circulation. (Marcus 2000: 209)

As "popular" literature, crime novels, as Walter Benjamin pointed out, often featured trains or train journeys, for example in the Sherlock Holmes stories, particularly as spaces and times for the detective to meditate on the puzzle and ultimately come up with the solution (Marcus 2000: 215). Hercule Poirot was also partial to train travel (he actively despised travel by boat), although in Christie's hands, trains were just as likely sites for murder as contemplation of the murder. Here we see a clearer example of mise-en-abyme: the parallel and mutually reflective rise in cheap popular literature (including crime literature) and cheap rail travel. Crime literature begins to frequently feature train journeys, and such novels would, as likely as not, be read *on* trains by the emerging commuter class. Jumping forward seventy or so years, the airplane has replaced the train as the main form of mass transit, which is now reflected in these films. This does not mean that the train has been entirely replaced, particularly in Europe: both Sergio Martino's *Night Train Murders* (1975) and Dario Argento's *Sleepless* (*Non ho sonno*) (2001) feature commuter trains quite extensively. For the Golden Age of detective fiction, around the turn of the last century, both the train and cheap paperback novels were signs of modernity. By the 1970s, these had been largely replaced by the plane and movie. Yet, like the Orient Express, these modernist forms of mass travel still had some cachet of sophistication about them; this was before budget airlines, after all. We can see the *giallo* films as shadows of jet-set European sophistication: a simplified, more vernacular commentary on the "economic miracle" than Fellini's *La Dolce Vita*. Once again, *la dolce vita* has been transformed into *la dolce morte*.

That sophistication can be seen elsewhere in *giallo* cinema. Needham noted the proliferation of transatlantic airline icons, usually the corporate logo on the tail section of the aircraft, in the many airport sequences these films feature. Here is a quite literal understanding of the jet-set lifestyle these films are depicting. Needham also mentioned, almost as a throwaway, the prevalence of "the promos for every traveller's favourite drink—a J&B whiskey. This must be the most plugged product in the history of European Cinema" (2003: 143). Alerted to these whiskey "promos," I can concur: they most certainly are ubiquitous across Italian cinema in this period, not only in the *giallo*.

I contacted J&B Whisky in order to ask their marketing department about how the product was being marketed during that period. Sue Cohen, the marketing representative I was in contact with, was unaware of their product's use in these films, so the first real importance of this product's placement is that it was done willingly, and not because J&B's advertising departments paid for it to be there, as more contemporary strategies of "product placement" have done. The use of J&B, then, has some specific connotation that the filmmakers—not just across *giallo* cinema, but also across most European cinema—wanted to convey.

Cohen also pointed out the strong association the whiskey had in the United States, particularly among the "Rat Pack" during their Las Vegas years. Cohen informed me of a photograph the J&B archive had only recently acquired of Frank Sinatra and Dean Martin having a great time in a nightclub booth, with a bottle of the whiskey prominently displayed on the table in front of them—the label (and therefore logo) turned toward the camera. So as a product, J&B was associated with the then fashionable Las Vegas lounge set, epitomized by such *Italian*-Americans as Sinatra and Martin. The iconic status of singers like Dean Martin, in particular, who in the late 1950s began recording Italian-language love songs, would have signified sophistication, wealth, luxury, and masculinity to an Italian cultural audience, and would then have transferred those attributes to any kind of artifactual material in the Rat Pack's presence, including this particular type of whiskey.

At the same time, the brand was gaining popularity in the United States, eventually to dominate the American market. As Cohen tells the story:

> Our distribution company in Italy at that time was called Dateo Import and a chap called Gaetano Bandini wanted to distribute J&B across Europe, but J&B

only gave him North Italy. His first order was for 50 cases of J&B but because the USA took most of our stock at that time we could not fulfill the order and had to supply it in 2 parts. Gaetano had extremely good business sense and really grew the brand in Italy. He knew a lot of influential people so perhaps it was down to him knowing the "right people" that got J&B such prominent face within these films. (personal correspondence)

So Bandini, marketing J&B to all the right people, getting the brand name in the newspapers through careful placement of the product just before the paparazzi could take a picture, much like in the Rat Pack photo mentioned above, and working from the association the whiskey already had in the United States with such fashionable icons as Martin and Sinatra (particularly in Italy) and *their* association with glamour, wealth, success, and masculinity, meant that the Italian *public* imbued J&B with these attributes, at least in marketing theory. Yet, the predominance of the J&B bottle across the *giallo* indicates that, to some degree at least, this marketing was quite successful. There might have been other whiskies readily available when these films were made, but the audience would not necessarily have had the same connotations with these tipples as they did with the ubiquitous J&B brand. The brand of whiskey a *giallo* character drinks, or at least has (prominently) in the house, like with the visual use of brand-name airliners, grounds the *giallo*, not only in an aura of sophistication, or at least *la dolce vita*, but in a consumerist reality that creates some connection with the audience's *liebenswelt*; even if they cannot afford to fly off to London or drink highball cocktails, they at least recognize an assumed value of those signifiers.

Another kind of signifier that grounds the *giallo* in the *liebenswelt* is the use of location footage. As Sorlin noted, "Films shot in actual locations, and intent on respecting the characteristics of the filmed areas, offered highly contrasting interpretation of Italian [and foreign] landscapes" (1996: 139). Sorlin here referred to those high-art, modernist films that set themselves within distinct, often rural or industrial, landscapes, therein making the location one of the film's central characters. But the *giallo* film also used location footage similarly. Most *gialli* tend to feature "traveling shots"; that is, shots, usually taken from a car, that establish the geographical location of the film through a sort of "travelogue" footage, showing key points for tourist interest, as Needham noted above. Most often, these traveling sequences are the background to the opening credit sequence, suturing the audience into the film's location at the very beginning. Even films set in and around Rome feature these sequences, advertising the glamour of the location. Although not necessarily what Sorlin was referring to, *gialli* offer "highly contrasting interpretations" to their diegetic spaces. This is one of the areas in which the genre articulates its ambivalence toward modernity: specifically through juxtaposition of luscious travelogue visual footage with diegetic horror and tragedy.

Take Aldo Lado's *Who Saw Her Die?* for example. Set within the piazzas and courtyards of Venice, the film depicts this northern Italian city in all of its tourist beauty. After an initial prologue depicting the murder of a young girl a few years earlier, and after the opening credit sequence, the film proper opens with an Alitalia airplane landing at the Venice airport, a typical beginning to a *giallo*, as Needham noted above, complete with corporate logo for the airliner. Franco (George Lazenby), a sculptor, is waiting at the airport for his young daughter, Roberta (Nicoletta Elmi), to arrive from London where she lives with her mother.[1] What follows in fairly quick succession (the sequence is less than thirty seconds) are a series of four exquisitely composed shots of Venice, establishing what tourists expect of the city: a piazza filled with thousands of pigeons, Renaissance architecture lining the Grand Canal, a panning shot of more beautiful Renaissance buildings, and finally one of the smaller canals, quiet and romantic, spanned by a small footbridge. On the soundtrack, Ennio Morricone's choral score dominates, effectively suspending the narrative of film in order to establish the beauty of tourist Venice. When we return to the narrative, we observe Franco sitting at a run-down café talking with his friends about how "dead" Venice is, with very little to do, and how much potential the city has for being a cultural capital. This juxtaposition of the historical beauty of the city with how apparently boring it is evokes an ambivalence concerning how Italy advertises itself to tourists versus the reality of *being* there. Venice, here, is all facade. A more significant ambivalence is derived from the main mystery narrative of the film: little Roberta is abducted and later found murdered in one of the quiet and romantic canals depicted earlier. Venice may be lovely to look at, but apparently it is also boring, and your children will disappear only to be found later murdered by a pederast priest. Those romantic canals that grace Venetian tourist advertising are filled with the bodies of murder victims, some children. Tourism may be an important facet of modern Italy's economy, but in *Who Saw Her Die?* that aspect of modernity is depicted as being potentially dangerous, particularly to young tourists like Roberta.

The beginning airport scene in *Eyeball* is largely a red herring: Alma (Marta May) changes her ticket to New York for one to Barcelona, although at this stage of the film, we do not know why. After a few shots of Alma on the plane and being told the plane is about to arrive in Barcelona, the film drops Alma from the narrative to focus on the central characters/victims/suspects, although

Alma is ever present as a structured absence, with other characters wondering where she might be. This shift in character trajectory is not signaled: we leave Alma being told her plane is about to land and pick up on a tour bus leaving the airport, which we assume Alma is aboard, although we cannot see her. This first, reestablishing shot, although initially focusing on the tour bus in the center of the frame, then zooms into a panoramic shot of the city itself. We then cut to the tour guide on the bus, welcoming his passengers to "beautiful Barcelona" and giving them a spiel about the importance of the city. Throughout the subsequent shots (diegetically, the tourists are on their way to their hotel), we are given traveling shots from the interior of the bus of various points of interest, along with the tour guide's commentary. Intercut with this travelogue are shots of the various tourists, and occasional snippets of dialogue are heard (presumably to establish character). One particular snippet of dialogue is particularly relevant here: Robby Alvarado (Daniele Vargas) used to live in Barcelona during the war and is pointing out to his wife, Gail (Silvia Solar), what has changed. Alvarado's own commentary speaks of the changes to the city in the years he has been gone: "That was the location of my old school, right over there on the corner where the bank is." Gail however shows little interest in her husband's past: "Please Robby, no more stories. Your old flat is now a hotel. The area you used to play in is now a parking lot. You're slowly driving me nuts with this nostalgia." This snippet of dialogue pointedly notes that the changes in Barcelona have become increasingly commercial: schools have become banks, homes have now become hotels, and play areas are now parking lots. Gail's mocking reply, however, denotes apathy toward her husband's sense of nostalgia and lost childhood. On the one hand, there has been a remarked increase in prosperity, due partially to tourism (the flat has now become a hotel), but on the other hand, those changes have come at a price.[2] Perhaps even more ambivalent is that no one, including Alvarado's own wife, actually cares.

Setting

Distinct from the geographical locations of these films, the cities and regions in which they take place, many *gialli* confine themselves within clearly bounded spaces. Some restrict their action to apartment blocks or college campuses. By far the most common site for localized *giallo* action is the isolated house or villa; for example, Bava's *Blood and Black Lace* takes place in an isolated fashion house, Umberto Lenzi's *Spasmo* (1974) predominantly in an isolated lighthouse, and Soavi's *Stagefright* largely in a darkened theatre. These locations are on the outskirts of the cities, marginalized and isolated from the modern urban experience, enabling the genre's black-gloved serial killers to move about with greater freedom. Much less common (although *significantly* less common than such a setting will become for the slasher film [see chapter 10]), the action is localized in rural villages (in Italy, Britain, or Germany) or in isolated lake-lands or islands.

Much like in the slasher films of the late 1970s and early 1980s (which the *giallo* certainly influenced and which I discuss in the final chapter), isolating the action, particularly on the outskirts of a major metropolitan city, challenges the complacency of the modern age. The accoutrements of modernity are present or available to the characters but not necessarily *immediately* available to them. It has been suggested by Carol Clover that the killer in the slasher film often uses pretechnology methods—basic weapons and tools such as knives, axes, and the occasional pitchfork (1992: 31). Killers in *gialli* are not so limited and often turn modernity's objects against its consumers, which I demonstrate in chapter 4. And while the police can be expected to show up, due to their workload (and sometimes apathy), they cannot be expected to show up when actually needed.

Another of the fears of modernity that the *giallo* exploits is the breakdown of community. Part of the isolation of living in large apartment blocks is that one is isolated—cut off, as it were—from one's neighbors. *The Case of the Bloody Iris* exemplifies this isolation. Three residents on the same floor discover the first murdered victim in one of the apartment building's elevators. Although for the audience's benefit they need to introduce themselves to one another, throughout the film, much is made of the fact that in this apartment building, no one knows who their neighbors are.

The films that take place in rural contexts are another matter altogether. Here the tension within the film is often regarding the villagers' resistance to modernity. In the small, rural Apulian village of Lucio Fulci's *Don't Torture a Duckling* (*Non si sevizia un paperino*) (1972), the local boys are being systematically murdered. One of the chief suspects is the local witch, Maciara (Florinda Bolkan), whom we have seen scrabbling in the ground next to a modern highway disinterring the skeletal remains of an infant (this is almost the first shot of the movie) and preparing wax figures of the village boys, which she inserts needles in, voodoo-style. Despite being cleared by the local constabulary and the CID officers for the murders,[3] the village men still think she must be the guilty party, as she holds a liminal position within the community as both insider and outsider. As she is leaving the police station, two village men confront her in the church cemetery and beat her to death with chains. She manages to crawl to the side of the highway for help from the passing traffic, but despite being seen by the vacationing motorists, she is left to die there in plain sight.

Sorlin noted, in referring to the opening of 8½ (Federico Fellini, 1963), wherein Guido (Marcello Mastroianni), the film's protagonist, has a dream about being stuck in an enormous traffic jam: "However caustic it was, his opening scene sanctioned a general conviction: ours is the era of individual means of transport, for better or worse we have to use cars" (1996: 119). In the *giallo* films also, the attitude toward cars is ambivalent, as in the case of *Duckling*: they are a symbol of modernity, bringing the modern age to rural areas. We ourselves, in watching *Duckling*, are participating in yet another apparatus of modernity (cinema), but we also are engaged in a kind of tourism. We, like the motorists, drive on by, unable (and unwilling) to help Maciara. Fulci underlines this discourse in the very first shot of the film, in what begins as a pastoral, almost bucolic, landscape of rural Apulia, which pans slightly to the left to reveal an elevated motorway slicing through the idyll. As Stephen Thrower noted:

> *Don't Torture a Duckling* has been criticized in some quarters for painting a big-oted picture of rural life. This is debateable, but Fulci was certainly not alone in depicting the South of Italy as rife with outmoded attitudes and intolerant violence. The perceived dichotomy between educated, sophisticated Northern Italy and the corrupt and threatening South is one which occurs frequently in Italian films. In Fulci's favour is the fact that numerous ironies accumulate around the idea of "sophisticated" city-dwellers, whose detachment from the problems of rural life is pointedly attacked. (1999: 71)

Unlike high-art filmmakers, specifically Pier Paolo Pasolini, Fulci is not glorifying the rural way of life per se; yet neither is he presenting an argument wherein modernity equals progress—either position is much too simplistic. Instead, Fulci presents our perception of the landscape ambivalently—at once bucolic and modern. In Fulci's previous film, *A Lizard in a Woman's Skin*, which takes place in London, the sexual repression of the characters is framed against grand Victorian architecture, reflecting that on the one hand the Victorian age built grand churches and the Royal Albert Hall (which is supposed to be the Old Bailey in this film), but also was responsible for the stereotype of the cold, unemotional "stiff-upper-lip," sexually frustrated modern English. In Fulci's films, as in the rest of *giallo* cinema, the effects of modernity are ambivalent.

Time Period

It is worth noting, at least in passing, that almost all of these films are filmed in the present. That is, they are contemporary with when they were made.

The one exception to this (and I am ambivalent myself as to whether or not to include it as *giallo*), is *Kill, Baby . . . Kill!* which takes place in a nineteenth-century gothic German village.[4] In this film, Dr. Eswai (Giacomo Rossi-Stuart), a man of science, is brought to this rural village to perform an autopsy on a young woman who died in mysterious circumstances. The villagers all believe that she was the latest in a series of strange deaths brought on by the ghost of a young girl who died violently a few years before. Bava first sets up a dichotomy between modernity's rational and scientific mind versus peasant superstition (and in this respect, the film is very much an Italian version of Conan Doyle's *The Hound of the Baskervilles*). But then he subverts the rational explanation: it really *is* the ghost of the little girl who is responsible for the deaths, and rather than bring modern science to the village, Dr. Eswai leaves with a new-found respect for the superstitious.

Foreigner/Outsider

The settings and locations of these films are more than stagnant backdrops; foreigners and outsiders often fulfill certain character roles, and part of this cinema's ambivalence lies in these liminal roles. As Needham noted: "The main protagonist of the *giallo* is often the foreigner in Italy or the Italian on holiday . . . [traveling through] 'exotic locations.' . . . Characters don't seem fixed to a home or location; they are always (in)between different places" (2003: 143). Beyond Needham's schema, there are four kinds of roles that foreigners in these films can fulfill: the killer, the victims, the suspects, and sometimes the role of the amateur detective. By foreign, I am not merely referring to non-Italians, for in many of the films that do not take place on the Italian peninsula, the mystery centers on some kind of an outsider or foreigner who disrupts the narrative equilibrium. Nor am I necessarily referring to national foreignness, as sometimes characters fulfill these outsider roles who may belong nationally but are somehow separated from the cultural hegemonic space.

Many *giallo* victims are either foreign or somehow encoded as being outside a hegemonic norm. Some of the victims in these movies are Italians living abroad or gay or lesbian or Afro-Caribbean. Sometimes they are French or Danish or German, sometimes American or of Asian-Pacific origin. Unlike the domestic victims in these films, the deaths of these foreigners or outsiders are viewed differently—not that these people deserved to be murdered, but that their presence within the diegetic society is problematized by their role *as* victim. As Andrea (Franco Nero), the journalist protagonist of *The Fifth Cord*, notes pointedly: "They're coming and going all the time. From all over the world. It's like a hotel." These victims are more than *just victims*; their presence raises the investigative question as to why they are there in the first place.

Sometimes the "Otherness" of the killer in these films is equally marked as being from outside the hegemonic society: although Italian (or at least holding citizenship in the country where the action occurs), the killer might be Jewish, or a witch, or just marked as someone from "outside" the diegetic community. Their difference may be marked according to sexuality if they are gay, lesbian, or transgender (or in the case of *The Fifth Cord* both foreign [Australian] and gay). Again in Carnimeo's *The Case of the Bloody Iris*, the Jewish Professor Isaacs has been murdering the beautiful young women who live in his apartment complex because he blames them for somehow "corrupting" his daughter into "lesbianism." While Isaacs may be a respected resident in the complex by virtue of his profession and his cultural sophistication (he is always carrying a violin case), and not really a suspect in terms of the mystery narrative (unlike his predatory daughter Sheena), he and his motive are encoded as being *different*, not *really* Italian, despite his citizenship. Space does not permit me to adequately discuss the ambivalent representation of Jews in the *giallo*, but for now, let it suffice to note this film's potential anti-Semitism and homophobia, both of which are evident across the entire genre (Jews and Jewish belief traditions occasionally occur in these films; gays and lesbians occur more frequently, but no less problematically). But certainly this demonstrates some ambivalence toward the increasingly overt ethnic and sexual-orientation presences within modern Italy in the early 1970s—Professor Isaacs's status and profession may be accepted, but his Old Testament punishment of those whom he sees as corrupting his daughter is clearly not. The same goes for Fulci's lesbian killer in *Lizard* and the transgendered killer in Lamberto Bava's *A Blade in the Dark*. Other outsider killers may be German, Hungarian, American, British, or Australian. On at least one occasion, in *The Iguana with the Tongue of Fire*, the killer's foreign status actually helps him by bestowing diplomatic immunity.

Nevertheless, although foreign suspects are usually the case, rarely are they the actual murderer. Sometimes suspects can be Italians living abroad, or not foreign but encoded as being different due to sexual orientation or lifestyle (like the hippies in Fulci's *A Lizard in a Woman's Skin*). Other suspects are German, Polish, Greek, Hungarian, but most frequently either American or British. What these three roles for outsiders and foreigners in the *giallo* indicate is ambivalence toward the kind of jet-set, *La dolce vita* culture that permeated Italian cinema in this period. Similarly to what was discussed in terms of setting and location, whereby Italians are free to travel throughout Europe (and get involved in nasty murder mysteries wherever they go), foreigners and "foreign ideas" can enter Italy, and have a potentially lethal impact upon the hegemony.

This ambivalence is expressed in Lenzi's *Eyeball*, focusing on American tourists in Barcelona. The "foreigners" in this film—both the tourists who are literally foreigners, and the "foreign" setting of the film (Spain)—function for all the roles: killer, victims, suspects, and amateur detective. Here the ambivalence toward modern tourism is more about who one travels with than the dangers of the city itself, as in *Who Saw Her Die?* Barcelona is beautiful but benign, as the killer is one of the tourists. Despite the typical *giallo* plot of the film, the victims are either other innocent tourists or the few locals this tour happens upon. Here the ambivalences are more about paranoia regarding who one's traveling companions are, as well as, from the local residents' perspective, who is coming to your city. Italians are not only traveling more but also foreigners are coming to Italy—both of these perspectives on tourism create distinct ambivalences, which films like *Eyeball* evoke. And in many respects, this paranoia echoes that of Carnimeo's film, where one is no longer sure who one's neighbors are.

The perceived ambivalence toward foreigners is also expressed by those *gialli* that are not about foreigners entering another country (or Italians living abroad) but like *Don't Torture a Duckling* are about outsiders to a community who often disrupt a long-standing, or long-repressed, crime. *Duckling's* murderer, the young parish priest Don Alberto (Marc Porel), is murdering these young boys because he witnesses their increasing loss of innocence as outsiders become more frequent visitors to their Apulian village. In the opening shots of the film, we witness cars coming toward the village and one of the potential victims, watching from an overpass. Echoing *Deliverance* (John Boorman, 1972), where the severely inbred banjo-playing child acts as a gate keeper to the wilderness, this child, firing a slingshot at a lizard sunning itself on a rock, stands at this liminal space between the modern world and the idyll of the village. Because that modern world is encroaching on the Apulian idyll, and with it the community's loss of innocence, Don Alberto sends the village boys to Heaven while they remain in a state of uncorrupted grace. While *Duckling's* themes may be more explicit in this regard than in other *gialli*, modernity's shattering of the idyllic isolation rural villages had experienced is more common, and it can also be seen as underlying the narrative logic in *The Bloodstained Shadow* (*Solamente nero*) (Antonio Bido, 1978) and *The House with Laughing Windows* (*La Casa dale finestre che ridono*) (Pupi Avati, 1976). In both of these films, an outsider enters a rural village and innocently discovers the community secrets the villagers have been hiding for years. The similarities, however, do not end there: both these outsider figures are named Stefano, both are art historians—Stefano in *The Bloodstained Shadow* was originally from the village but left to go to university, whereas Stefano in *Laughing Windows* has been hired by the parish to refurbish the local church's fresco in the hopes of making the village a tourist destination—and both characters are played by the same actor, Lino Capolicchio. Stefano—in both films—represents the encroaching hegemony of modernity on the private and isolated rural village life that had been left to its own devices for many years. Here the ambivalence is more transparent: these villages, like the village in *Duckling*, lose their innocence as a result of outsider interference and are exposed to the outside world, an experience close to home for many of the *giallo*'s audience members. In many respects, the village, if left to its own devices, would have survived these murders and continued on as normal. However, murder and extortion are still crimes, and the state has a self-assumed responsibility to punish those crimes.

This disruption is most obviously evident in the role of the amateur detective. Unlike the more standard *poliziotto* narratives, the *giallo* tends to focus on an amateur detective who witnesses the murder and in asking the right sort of questions often exposes the incompetence of the local constabulary. Specifically in films such as *Don't Torture a Duckling, Kill, Baby . . . Kill!, The Bloodstained Shadow, The House with Laughing Windows,* and *Who Saw Her Die?* the detective is from outside the community. Other examples feature Germans, Hungarians, Americans, British, Canadians, and Italians living abroad who disrupt police procedure. These "foreign" disruptions challenge the normal procedures, and while ultimately they are proved correct, their presence underlines the tension between modernity and tradition that is the overriding logic of these films.

Conclusions

The *giallo* is a cinema of ambivalence, specifically, ambivalence toward modernity. It neither praises nor condemns either traditional hegemonic beliefs or modernity's demands on Italy's role as a member of the European community or an International tourist destination. One of those sites of ambivalence is geographical—both culturally and politically. These films problematize the roles and spaces Italians occupy within the world, and the roles others play within Italy. These ambivalences can be summarized as (1) ambivalence toward language, where modernity is represented within the communicative apparatus itself; (2) ambivalence toward modernity's accoutrements and creature comforts, specifically the availability of cars; (3) ambivalence toward modernity's breaking down of the boundaries that make travel easier, thereby allowing Italians to live and travel in other countries and allowing foreign nationals to live and travel within Italy; and (4) ambivalence toward modernity's pluralism and the changing social and cultural mores. It is too easy to simply say that in appealing to the lowest common denominator, these films are conservative, regressive, and reactionary (although they may be); more significantly they open up a discursive space wherein modernity itself can be discussed.

Notes

1. Before we first see Roberta, we do not know whom Franco is at the airport to meet. We see the plane land in the first two shots, and the third shot is of Franco waiting in the arrivals lounge with a large bouquet of flowers (so we can safely assume he is waiting for a woman). The next shot is of the passengers disembarking, and in the foreground is an attractive, dark-haired woman. The fifth shot of the sequence is back to Franco, seemingly scanning the crowd for the person he is waiting for; he sees her and smiles. We still assume the woman he is looking at is the attractive, dark-haired woman in an eye-line match, and we presume the flowers are for her. The sixth shot is of the same pretty woman entering the arrivals lounge and smiling back (again assuming an eye-line match). Shot seven returns us to Franco, as the pretty dark-haired woman walks by, and Franco stretches out his arms to hug someone small enough to be below the camera line, as we first hear a child's voice say "Daddy." Lado in this sequence is clearly playing with the audience's expectations and assumptions, demonstrating the empathic and participatory nature of vernacular films like the *gialli*. Lado is inviting us to "play" along with the film.

2. One of those prices, not explicitly stated in the film, is that in 1975, when this film was made, this Barcelona is still under Franco's fascist regime.

3. Maciara explains that the body is that of her bastard child who died in infancy and that she got nervous when she saw the local boys playing near the gravesite, so she moved it someplace more private; she says the wax figures are unsuccessful protection spells to prevent the remaining boys from being murdered.

4. This film could be classified as *giallo-fantastico*, as I discussed in the first chapter.

CHAPTER FOUR

~

Murder and Other Sexual Perversions

The *giallo* is a murder mystery genre, so naturally, murders are committed in these films, but what distinguishes the *giallo* from other kinds of murder mystery films is the often graphic depiction of the murders. In part, this gory visual sensibility creates ambivalence toward the generic taxonomy of these films: are they murder mysteries or are they horror films? Ray Guins argued that "the *giallo* places equal (if not more) importance on the actual method of killing as well as solving the crime" (1996: 141). Despite the murder mystery narrative, the *giallo* focuses (perhaps excessively) on the murders themselves.

In this chapter, I consider how and why the characters in these films are killed. Perhaps this chapter is overly descriptive; however, such description is justified, I think, since an overview of the killings these films depict is central to an understanding of them. "The traditional *giallo* demands that one observe the numerous murders, thus placing strict attention on acts of violence" (Guins 1996: 142). The seeming randomness of the murders and the horror-movie visual style of these films raises further ambivalence toward modernity: that the prevalence of murder within contemporary society implies that today, we are *living* in a horror movie—that the excesses and violence we see in *giallo* cinema are an impressionistic rendering of modernity.

In addition to murder, the *giallo* also depicts many other kinds of criminal activity and violence. These depictions are not random, I would argue. Crime fiction writer Sarah Dunant points out, "Many readers agree that as a form of fiction it can sometimes be both frightening and violent, but (and I think this is a very powerful 'but') almost always within a fundamentally safe framework—havoc, mayhem, immorality and cruelty may abound, but you will be returned to sanity at the end, the good guys will win, order will be restored" (2000: 10). I will discuss the quasi-social implications of the murder mystery in chapter 5 in more detail, but for now I want to raise the issue of seeing these cinematic acts of violence and murder sectioned off from the mystery narrative context, as meaningful in themselves. Dunant argued that "crime fiction does bring a taboo topic into the open and that in doing so it allows people to feel things that they might not feel elsewhere" (2000: 11). Both the graphic murders outlined in this chapter as well as the miscellaneous kinds of other criminal (or so *perceived*) activities invoke cultural taboos for discussion and debate within vernacular cinema. Dunant, as a practitioner in the genre, suggested, "a corpse or corpses . . . provokes even deeper questions" (2000: 11). In my interpretation of these films, the questions these bodies provoke have to do with how such discourses would be discussed by their intended audiences.

The Murders

The sheer variety of tools used to commit *giallo* murders is extensive, and it appears that one of the "pleasures of the text" in watching these movies is seeing not just ever increasing levels of graphic violence and gore (although that *may* be one of the pleasures), but seeing the filmmakers' imagination at work in the murderous use of a whole slew of normally benign implements. Most victims in these films are stabbed, slashed, or chopped up, and of course, the single most popular weapon for this purpose is a knife—often a large kitchen knife, or failing that, the more easily concealed switchblade knife.[1] But equally lethal damage can be done with any number of other knifelike utensils: straight razors (also aptly known, just for this purpose, as a "cut-throat razor"), scalpels, artist utility knives, or even letter openers can do the job with appropriate visceral impact.

In a few examples, the murders are committed with more decorative weapons, that is, weapons found at the scene, rather than brought to the murder site premeditatedly, which are intended as part of the diegetic décor. A victim may be impaled on a lance or spear; stabbed with an ornate, ceremonial dagger;[2] or, as in one bizarre example, stabbed with a medieval spiked glove from a suit of armor found on site (in Mario Bava's *Blood and Black Lace*). Bava's use of this glove as a murder weapon could be interpreted as a veiled critique of the bourgeois attitude toward museum collections of suits of armor or other "beautiful" implements of war, which were originally intended to kill. Bava is really returning this *objet d'art* to its original usage. Another example occurs in Argento's *Opera* (1987), when a victim is impaled on a handy decorative wall spike. These murders tend to happen to wealthier characters and could be seen as bourgeois antique collectors quite literally having their decor turned against them.

Decapitations are not nearly as common as one would suspect—perhaps this is due to the cost of prosthetic heads. However some *giallo* victims do lose their heads, cut off with a sword or even with a found piece of sheet metal. In Tonino Valerii's My *Dear Killer* (*Mio caro assassino*) (1971), the victim is decapitated with a dredger.

Common garden tools are perennial favorites as weapons in *gialli*. Filmmakers like to take benign, commonplace items and give them a sense of menace. Axes are an obvious example, but chainsaws, pitchforks, and machetes are also employed. Then there is the occasional power drill or saw, a pair of scissors, a meat cleaver. All can be used to create visually satisfying on-screen deaths.

With ever increasing demand for grisly and varied stabbings, *gialli* filmmakers explore their creative sides with other sharp objects—a broken bottle, a medical syringe. In Argento's *Sleepless*, one victim is stabbed to death with a clarinet, while another is murdered with a fountain pen (which, if not mightier than the sword, at least was more readily available at the time). *Sleepless* is a much later *giallo* and a film noteworthy for Argento's return to the *filone* that helped establish his career (or that his career helped establish). But this film is also noteworthy for the self-conscious variety of murders depicted. The film operates almost like a checklist: in addition to death by musical instrument and fountain pen, people are slashed with a knife, chopped with an axe, hanged, bashed fatally into a wall, drowned, and shot. Even the main murders themselves are "thematic," seemingly taking their inspiration from a children's poem (written by Argento's daughter Asia). While *Sleepless* is a particularly self-conscious film, most *gialli* tend to vary their murders: one or two stabbings, a bludgeoning, a drowning (usually in a bathtub), strangulation, being thrown from a height, and so on.

Next to stabbing, slashing, and chopping, the most popular method for killing someone in a *giallo* film is by strangulation. Strangulation by hand, with the killer's hands (often in black gloves) tightening around the victim's neck, is the most common, and diegetically, this is often due to an absence of any of the above-cited weapons within the mise-en-scene. But *giallo* killers have also been known to strangle their victims with a scarf (often the victim's own), a telephone cord (often when speaking to the amateur detective and about to disclose damning evidence about the killer), or a wire. Some clever variations include being strangled with a length of movie film[3] or with a chain. In a few cases, the killer hangs his victims, often to try and make it look like a suicide.

A few *gialli* victims are smothered, usually with a piece of plastic wrap or sheeting, and once with a pillow. In Dario Argento's *Tenebre*, one unfortunate victim is asphyxiated by having the pages of a book forced down her throat, while in the bizarre Antonio Bido debut, *The Cat's Victims*, another is drowned in a pot of stew.

Giallo characters often are bludgeoned. As with some of the other methods used in this cinema, bludgeoning often occurs without premeditation; that is, the weapons used are often readily available and can be found in situ. Such weapons include wrenches, rocks, shovels, bottles, planks of wood, or small statuary. Some victims are killed by being bashed against walls, or even on coffee tables; and although more frequently the cause of death for the killer, some victims are pushed from high places to smash on the pavement/rocks below. Oftentimes, perhaps due to the less visual nature of bludgeoning deaths (hair tends to obscure the trauma to the body), these deaths happen off camera. However, bludgeoning is rarely the actual cause of death and is used mostly to incapacitate the character before some other implement is used to actually commit the murder.

Occasionally, *giallo* killers drown their victims, for example in a canal or a trough. But the most popular method of *giallo* drowning is in a domestic bathtub. The genre demands of visceral violence and full-frontal female nudity partially explain the prevalence of bathtub drowning: it affords the cinematic opportunity for a naked woman, at her most vulnerable, to be shown being savagely attacked. In an interesting reversal of this generic convention, Bido's *The Cat's Victims* features, instead of a beautiful nude woman, the bathtub drowning of an elderly man. The diegetic musical score, an aria emanating from Giovanni's radio, drowns out his screams as the killer drowns his hapless victim. Although from the waning period of the *filone*, *The Cat's Victims* demonstrates a certain self-awareness of the codes and conventions by denying the more standard beautiful naked woman drowned in the bath.

A more uncommon way for these killers to murder is to burn the victim to death. Variations include being burned on a pot-bellied stove, scalded to death in hot bath water, and having acid thrown in the face. Another less common method is to use a vehicle of some variety, the most popular means being running down the victim with a car, but others are cut apart by boat propellers or by the wheels of a train.

Despite being a popular means of murder in the literary *gialli*, murder by poison or other caustic substances is rare in the *giallo* film. Being poisoned, in a traditional Agatha Christie way of consuming a poison-laced drink, occurs in only one of the films surveyed here (Lenzi's *Paranoia*, which is quite early in the *filone* [1969] and tends toward the suspense end of the *giallo* spectrum). In another single-instance method, a victim is injected with poison (Argento's *Four Flies on Grey Velvet*). Poisons are also employed to paralyze the victims in Cavara's *The Black Belly of the Tarantula*, so the victim is awake when disemboweled. And although not poison, in Aldo Lado's *The Short Night of Glass Dolls*, the victims are hypnotized so that they are likewise awake for their disembowelment. In Sergio Bergonzelli's *In the Folds of the Flesh*, cyanide baths are used both to kill a victim and for the killer to commit suicide in. In this particular film, the bodies of the victims are also dissolved by means of an elaborate acid bath setup.

Finally, there are still other murders that largely defy easy classification. For example, in Mario Bava's *Kill, Baby . . . Kill!* Melissa's ghost compels those who see her to commit suicide—this is a metaphysical gray area insofar as although the revenant is guilty of denying the victims' free will (murder), the deaths *are* suicides.

I noted above, that some *gialli* victims are strangled by hanging so that it *looks* like suicide. While the killer in Armando Crispino's *Autopsy* makes it look like his victims have committed suicide, this is the only film surveyed where *faked* suicides are the primary modus operandi. To be sure, the faked suicide is not a common murder method, but it does occur sporadically. Occasionally the victim dies from a heart attack brought on by a fright caused by the killer. If all else fails, the killers can always shoot their victims. And finally, there are a number of incidents where the actual cause of death is denied to the audience; we are just told the victim has been murdered.

Before leaving this issue, it is worth noting that in some cases the victims are not just murdered, but their corpses are also mutilated in some fashion. Most often, this takes the form of a token being taken from the body—frequently an eye.[4] In the case of Dario Argento's *Tenebre*, although the first killer does not take a token from the body of the victim, he does photograph his handiwork after the crime.

The Victims

The assumption with both the *giallo* films and the later *gialli*-inspired slasher films is that the victims are always beautiful young women, demonstrating the inherent misogyny of the horror genre. To be sure, young women do make up the primary victims in a number of these films. In some cases the victims are (at least thought to be) prostitutes, while in other cases the women are college or high school students or fashion models. The misogyny argument is further strengthened by the fact that in so few films are young men the primary victims. But the films in which women are the primary victims are not as ubiquitous as it is assumed to be. The *giallo* is fairly egalitarian in its choice of victims: the vast majority of the films surveyed feature killings of both men and women in pretty equal measure. It would be fairer to argue that, rather than misogynistic, the *giallo* is a misanthropic genre. Stephen Thrower noted:

> The horror ingredient comes from the *giallo*'s frankly perverse dwelling upon violence, and the voyeur in us is likely to be well served by a similarly blatant dose of sleazy sex. Women are by far the most likely victims on the *giallo* hit-list, but the form's overall misanthropy (and desperation to out-manoeuvre its audience) throws up a significant number of female killers too. (1999: 63)

Usually, but by no means exclusively, the subsequent victims were just in the wrong place at the wrong time, and inadvertently witnesses to the primary murder/crime.

The most disturbing and upsetting of these films, intentionally so, are those wherein the primary murder victims are children. In both Bido's *The Bloodstained Shadow* and Lado's *Who Saw Her Die?* the killers prey on little girls—and in both cases the killer is a priest. In Umberto Lenzi's *Eyeball*, two of the victims are young girls, but they are murdered alongside adult victims, and the motive for these killings is not the pederast ones of Bido and Lado's films. Little boys, conversely, are the primary victims of yet another predatory priest in Lucio Fulci's *Don't Torture a Duckling*; however, although equally predatory as Bido's and Lado's priests, Don Alberto's motive is a misguided desire to protect the boys' innocence, not to take it from them sexually. This by no means exculpates Don Alberto from guilt for his murders, but it does demonstrate a gender distinction within vernacular cinema: little girls are seen as potentially *objects* of desire, while little boys are potentially *victims* of desire.

In many of these films, there is no apparent connection between the victims, and the hunt is for a serial killer.[5] Sometimes, however, the connection between the victims is the link that leads directly to the killer: it may be revealed that all the victims know a specific person, perhaps the amateur detective or the first victim, or it may be that the victims all knew the killer's secret somehow. Sometimes the victims all worked together, studied together, traveled together, or belonged to the same criminal gang. In a few of the films, the victims all shared the same locality or were present at the same party or gathering. However, in at least one case, this connection is a red herring: in Antonio Bido's *The Cat's Victims*, although all the victims sat on the jury that sent Pasquale Ferrante (Franco Citti) to prison for a crime he did not commit, he is neither the killer nor the connection between the victims. The actual connection between the victims is a common crime perpetrated in the past, wherein they all played a part in informing on a young Jewish family in hiding from the Fascist authorities.

Criminal Activity

Behind the *giallo*'s murders are often webs of other kinds of "criminal" activity; while not necessarily criminal in the strictest legal sense, in some cases, the treatment of certain activities, such as homosexuality, are often treated as if they *should* be considered criminal. This aspect of the *giallo* offers up a fascinating barometer of a kind of idealized vernacular legal system.

By far one of the most common kinds of background criminality, after adultery, is blackmail. Set against a backdrop of extortion and protection, everyone in *giallo* cinema has something to hide, and there always seems to be someone else who knows this and has the evidence to prove it. Inevitably, money is extorted in order to keep these secrets hidden. Throughout the genre, everyone seems to be blackmailing everyone else, sometimes with photographic evidence. Occasionally, *gialli* characters are blackmailed in order to hide something along the lines of a character's homosexuality or an adulterous affair. But by far the most common form of blackmail pertains to a previous crime one of the characters has somehow gotten away with, including one dim-witted witness in Argento's *Sleepless* who thinks he can extort money out of the film's killer and receives a fountain pen to the head for his troubles. Even as early as 1970, blackmail is so clichéd with these films that Bergonzelli goes so far as to feature an organized blackmail ring in his *In the Folds of the Flesh*.

Drug use, if not the actual trafficking of narcotics, is often presented within these films. For example, as early as Mario Bava's *The Girl Who Knew Too Much*, in a chance encounter on an airplane, a stranger generously gives the film's amateur detective, Nora Davis, a pack of cigarettes. What she is unaware of is that the cigarettes are laced with marijuana, and the gentleman, a notorious trafficker, is arrested as they get off the plane in Rome. At the end of the film she discovers the unopened pack still in her coat and throws it off the balcony; it is picked up by a grateful priest—a nice example of Bava's sense of humor. But within *The Girl Who Knew Too Much* the drug plot is a red herring, introduced early in the film to throw off the audience's ability to predict the film's plot. Although false openings like this are frequent within *giallo* cin-ema, this false drug plot is highly unconventional.

Other examples include Massimo Dallamano's *A Black Veil for Lisa* or Cavara's *The Black Belly of the Tarantula*. In the former, Inspector Bulov (John Mills) is trying to crack an international drug trafficking ring in Hamburg; in the latter, Inspector Tellini (Giancarlo Giannini) is following up on a co-caine smuggling trail he believes is directly linked with the murder of Maria Zani (Barbara Bouchet), but these too prove to be red herrings.

Linked with drug addiction is the more "socially acceptable" form of ad-diction, alcoholism. In Luigi Bazzoni's *The Fifth Cord*, Andrea Bild (Franco Nero) is an alcoholic newspaper reporter fighting through his booze-addled brain to remember a specific party because the guests who had been present keep turning up dead. Here alcoholism acts as an impediment to Bild's abil-ity to solve the murders. In Luciano Ercoli's *Death Walks at Midnight* fashion model Valentina (Susan Scott) is experimenting with a new kind of drug when she witnesses a murder in the apartment opposite hers, and this like-wise calls into question her role as an eyewitness. Again more typically, as in films such as Ercoli's *The Forbidden Photos of a Lady Above Suspicion* and Um-berto Lenzi's *Paranoia*, the alcoholism of the central characters is the linch-pin for their susceptibility to manipulation by their respective blackmailers. Significantly, neither of these films feature murders but are more focused on the blackmail plots; they are suspense thrillers, rather than murder mysteries.

Beyond the violence of the murders that make up the central focus of most of these films, a general atmosphere of violence, or potential violence, is per-vasive. So, for example, in addition to the murders that make up the main narrative thread, there are frequently other murders and attempted murders throughout the diegesis. Sometimes these murders are in the backstory, as in Argento's *Deep Red*, wherein we see a young Carlo (Jacopo Mariani) wit-nessing the murder of his father before we meet him as an adult (Gabriele Lavia) and as one of the chief suspects of the film proper. This is a narrative device Argento in particular keeps returning to: a murder occurs in the past but appears largely unrelated to the current murders except potentially as a traumatic event one of the characters may have experienced, often the killer.

Other films sometimes depict images of cruelty to animals, distressing even when obviously faked, as in Bergonzelli's *In the Folds of the Flesh* in which a dog, snooping around a freshly dug grave, is killed to prevent the body underneath from being revealed. Another is Lamberto Bava's *A Blade in the Dark*, where the caretaker physically abuses his own dog. More trou-bling are films like Argento's *Deep Red*, in which the young Olga sticks a pin through a small newt, or Pupi Avati's *The House with Laughing Windows*, where the simpleminded curate Lidio (Pietro Brambilla) tortures and murders rats for fun. Both of these examples juxtapose the "natural" cruelty of children (or the childlike) with the more focused cruelty of the murderer. This is slightly different in Argento's Inspector Santini (Urbano Barberini) in *Opera*, who kills the opera house's ravens, indicating how cheaply he holds all life. Other kinds of violent acts in these films include kidnapping, usually by the killer; suicide; "legalized" murder (e.g., as a soldier in Renato Polselli's *Delirium*); rape; spousal abuse; and even professional assassins.

As noted previously, adultery is even more prevalent than blackmail in the *giallo*. While this activity is not necessarily "illegal," it does weaken the socio-familial structure, and as a result of the weakening of those bonds, other more serious crimes often follow—namely murder. Some *gialli* may gloss over extramarital affairs, but not if it concerns teachers sleeping with students. This practice is directly addressed and condemned in both Massimo Dallamano's *Solange* and Sergio Martino's *Torso*.

The *giallo* also has occasionally focused on that male-centric fantasy of the older man with a much younger wife (an Italian fantasy that goes at least as far back as Boccaccio, if not to the Romans), but unlike the teacher-student relationships, here the romances are consecrated through marriage. They also (Boccaccio-like) witness the anxieties and jealousies such May-September romances engender: Inspector Bulov in Dallamano's *A Black Veil for Lisa* is worried less about the international drug traffickers he is trying to hunt down than what his young wife, Lisa (Luciana Paluzzi), is up to. Likewise, Inspector Tellini in Cavana's *The Black Belly of the Tarantula* realizes he is spending too much time on his case and not nearly enough time with his new and young wife Jenny (Barbara Bach). These male fantasies are put into even greater relief in those May-September romances where it is the woman who is older, specifically Lenzi's *Paranoia* and Fillippo Walter Ratti's *Crazy Desires of a Murderer*. In the former, Kathryn West (Carroll Baker) is presented as desperate and pathetic in her desire for the much younger Pete Donovan (Lou Castel). Ratti's film goes even further: Ileana (Karole Annie Edel) turns out to be having an Oedipal affair with her son, Leandro (Roberto Zattini).

Also part of this genre's challenging of sexual taboos and mores is the issue of teen pregnancy, a theme that crops up repeatedly in the films of Massimo Dallamano, such as *Solange* and *What Have They Done to Our Daughters?* Directly linked with the issues of teen pregnancy are also issues surrounding abortion. Dallamano's *Solange* again directly addresses this issue, and in this film abortion is the motive for the killer's murder spree. Linda's (Dalila Di Lazzaro) abortion in Flavio Mogherini's *The Pyjama Girl Case* is what sparks off Antonio's (Michele Placido) violence. Significantly, although suspicion surrounds the local abortionist in Bido's *Bloodstained Shadow* as being the linchpin in solving the crimes, it turns out to be a red herring.

Other sex-related "crimes" that crop up in *giallo* cinema include voyeurism, sado-masochism, and incest. Of the incestuous relationships that occur in this genre, no taboo is left unbroken: Dario Argento's *Cat O' Nine Tails* features Electral desire, somewhat mitigated by the fact that Anna Terzi (Catherine Spark) is an *adopted* daughter of the first murder victim, Professor Terzi. But no such mitigation exists in the brother-sister incest in Bergonzelli's *In the Folds of the Flesh*, for although neither Colin nor Falesse/Ester are aware they are brother and sister at first, this revelation does not detract the debauched Colin once their relationship is revealed. The classical Oedipal dynamic between mother Shirley (Martine Brouchard) and son Michael (Stefano Patrizi) in Riccardo Freda's *The Wailing* is yet a further example.

Although some *gialli* victims are prostitutes, the films rarely give voice and agency to such women. An exception is Janet in Enzo Castellari's *Cold Eyes of Fear*, a woman-for-hire who does demonstrate an ability to hold her own against Welt and Quill. Likewise, we see Linda driven to desperation when she finally turns a trick in Mogherini's *The Pyjama Girl Case*. In both of these films, rather than just nameless victims defined by their role as sex objects, we are expected to see these women as people. A film of true ambivalence, *The New York Ripper*, takes this to an extreme level: Kitty (Daniela Doria), the prostitute slowly ripped open by an artist's utility blade in the film's most notorious sequence, has been in a long-standing relationship with the chief investigating officer, Lieutenant Williams (Jack Hedley). Significantly, although we "care" about what happens to Kitty in this sequence, we care not because of what is being done to *her*, but because of what this will mean for Williams; in other words, unlike Linda or Janet, Kitty exists not as an independent character but only in relationship to her male partner. A teen prostitution ring also features centrally in Dallamano's *Daughters*, for the murders being investigated all focus on this ring.

Sex clubs also feature in quite a few of these films. More than just strip clubs, these are performance spaces where sexual "acts" are performed. These run the gamut from naked wrestling, where men are invited up on stage to attempt to pin down the Amazon-like Mizar (Carla Brait) in Giuliano Carnimeo's *Bloody Iris*, through to live sex acts being performed in the grind-house theatre in Fulci's *The New York Ripper*. Perhaps the most interesting of these clubs is the one where Peter and Janet go at the beginning of *Cold Eyes of Fear*. There they watch a play that at first sutures the film audience into believing it is watching a typical *giallo* opening with an intruder wearing the archetypal disguise of black gloves and black trench coat, attacking a woman in her bed—before she willingly succumbs in a perverse live-action rape fantasy. But by far the most perverse of these sex clubs is the Club 99 in Lado's *The Short Night of Glass Dolls*, which is not only a sex club but also the cover for an elite satanic sex cult.

Pederasty makes its appearance among the illicit sexual relations in the *giallo* as well, albeit to a lesser degree. I have already mentioned that Don Alberto, in Fulci's *Duckling*, is not explicitly motivated by pederast desires, and neither is Bido's Don Paolo (Craig Hill) anymore. When it is present, as in Tonino Valerii's *My Dear Killer*, the film condemns the practice as abhorrent. But disturbingly, despite the clear condemnation of pederasty in the film, the sequence in the artist's loft of the film's pederast suspect, Benjamino, features a clearly underage girl wandering around naked. Equally disturbing, in Lado's *Who Saw Her Die?* again despite the film's condemnation of Father James's (Alessandro Haber) pederastic murders, before young Roberta goes missing, her father's friend touches her inappropriately. Clearly this moment is designed to make the friend a suspect in her disappearance, but it also indicates a different attitude toward the sexualized image of children than Anglo-North Americans can tolerate. As Stephen Thrower points out:

> Pederasty plays an uncomfortable role in thankfully few of these films. In Italy there is a greater degree of tolerance for the sexual adventurism of adolescent boys and this extends to homosexual as well as heterosexual activity. If boys "fool around" with each other, the Italian response is more "so what" than "what's wrong?" It's only when boys engage in sex with older men, or when men live with other men "like man and wife" that Italian morality resembles that of the puritan British and Americans, and the weight of taboo comes crashing down. (Thrower 1999: 98)

Homosexuality is, indeed, an exceptionally problematic facet of modernity for these filmmakers (and by extension, one believes for their audience too). Let me be absolutely clear on this point: while the stereotypes and assumptions made in these films about homosexuality, I argue, reflect a cultural ambivalence relevant to the *terza visione* audiences for these films, I in no way condone such stereotypes. Gay men appear as secondary characters (often as suspects) in quite a few of these films. When gay characters appear in *gialli*, they are often camp and effeminate roles for comic relief—such as the gay private investigator Arrosio (Jean-Pierre Marielle) in *Four Flies on Grey Velvet* or the gay Woody Allen–like photographer Arthur (Oreste Lionello) in *Bloody Iris*. But even more problematic is the much-too-frequent equation made in these films between homosexuality and either child molestation or pornography. In

Bido's *The Bloodstained Shadow*, Count Pedrazzi[6] (Massimo Serato) may give piano lessons to young boys, but he is known more as a gay child molester among the locals of the village and is even referred to as a "moral threat" to the society, although it is unclear whether Pedrazzi is a threat because of his pederasty or his homosexuality. Likewise, the decadent lawyer Bonayuti (José Quaglio) in *Who Saw Her Die?* is both gay and a child molester, but he is further suspicious because of his apparent obsession with a string of child murders in Venice, even to the point of collecting newspaper clippings about these crimes. The connection feels so rife within these films that the term "gay child molester" implies no mutual exclusivity for the filmmakers. Lesbians come off somewhat better, as they are only presented for (heterosexual) male scopophilia, like Katia (Angela Covello) and Ursula (Carla Brait) in *Torso*.

Other Crimes

The ornate mystery plots of these films demand that many of the killers work with accomplices. The husband-and-wife team of the Ranieris in Argento's *The Bird with the Crystal Plumage* is perhaps the most famous example, wherein husband Alberto (Umberto Raho) attempts to take the rap for wife Monica's (Eva Renzi) murder spree. Or there are the lovers Max (Cameron Mitchell) and Contessa Christina (Eva Bartok) in Mario Bava's *Blood and Black Lace*, wherein Max murders the models of Contessa Christina's fashion house, but the Contessa must also shed blood in order to direct police attention away from her *inamorata*. Perhaps the most interesting of the accomplice teams is that of Welt and Quill in *Cold Eyes of Fear*: for while Welt is merely interested in clearing his name, Quill has repressed his love for his former cell mate, despite using the pretense of only being interested in the money Welt promised him.

Thefts and robberies frequently occur in these films too: the break-in to Peter's uncle's house in *Cold Eyes* is but one example. Most of these thefts are petty, pieces of jewelry or other personal items stolen by one of the secondary characters, and function really only to cast further suspicion on the thieves. Of course, the most notorious break-in of *giallo* cinema is the one that sparks off the events surrounding the Terzi Institute in Argento's *Cat O' Nine Tails*, wherein it turns out Dr. Casoni broke into the offices in order to steal the incriminating files that identify him as having the XYY chromosome.

Many of the crimes within *giallo* cinema are centered on greed. Bava's films tend to exploit the greed of his bourgeois characters; thus, for example, in *Five Dolls for an August Moon*, all the characters being picked off on the isolated island are after Professor Farrell's (William Berger) new industrial resin, which will make whomever he sells to extremely wealthy. Similarly, in Bava's *Bay of Blood*, Renata (Claudine Auger) and Albert (Luigi Pistilli) are trying to buy up all the available property surrounding a local lake in order to develop the region into a resort, and they are willing to stop at nothing, including murder, to achieve their goals. *Bay of Blood* also has one of the highest body counts in *giallo* cinema; with (to my count) eleven murders, the relationship between greed and murder is made explicit. Greed is also the motivating factor in the murders of Valerii's *My Dear Killer*. Sometimes, as in *Bay of Blood*, the greed manifests itself in the characters' trying to obtain an inheritance, and sometimes, as in Ercoli's *Forbidden Photos*, it is to access insurance money.

Every so often, the *gialli* like to play with the idea of trying to drive one of the characters insane. Umberto Lenzi has dealt with this theme in at least two films, *Paranoia* and *Spasmo*, but it is the former film, where the elaborate plot mechanisms of Peter (Lou Castel) and Eva (Colette Descombes) to drive Katheryn (Carroll Baker) insane in order to inherit her late husband's fortune, that is perhaps the most extravagant.

Still other crimes in the *giallo* include the more macabre end of the criminal scale: Dario Argento has twice dealt with grave robbing, in *Cat O' Nine Tails* and *Sleepless*. Satanism, witchcraft, and black magic also appear in a few of the films, but I shall be dealing with those issues in more detail in chapter 7.

Finally there are some "crimes" in these films that cast a distinctly ambivalent light on Italian vernacular culture in this period. In Mario Bava's *The Girl Who Knew Too Much*, Nora is obsessed with murder mysteries (*giallo*), and has been sent to Italy in an attempt to cure her of this unhealthy addiction. Likewise, one of the prime suspects in Carnimeo's *Bloody Iris* is addicted to horror comics. In both of these cases, the interest in horror and mystery is derided as abnormal and in need of being corrected. But how much of this is a joking nod to the audience, who are after all, watching a horror mystery movie?

Conclusions

Cynthia Freeland, in discussing the slasher film, noted, "Realism is the key factor that differentiates slashers from their predecessors in horror. Here the monstrous killers are not undead, supernatural vampires of hairy hulking werewolves but living, breathing men" (2000: 162). Freeland calls this phenomenon "realist horror," and it is worth thinking of the *giallo* also as realist horror. I have noted throughout this chapter a variety of ambivalences toward modernity that is observable in these films. As realist horror, the *giallo* confuses the genre borders between murder mystery and horror. John Cawelti noted, particularly for the classic period of detective fiction in the early twentieth century, the similarities between detective fiction and the nineteenth-century Gothic story (1976: 101); implied in this connection is that the Gothic mutated into the detective story. Space does not permit me to fully explore the connections between the Gothic and horror, but if my syllogism is correct, then we can extend this equation to include horror: the Gothic is linked to the horror story; the Gothic developed into the detective story; therefore there is a link between the detective and the horror story. This is by no means an attempt to alleviate the genre ambivalence in the *giallo* between horror and crime cinema, but to the contrary, to highlight this "border crossing" between the two. Freeland's term, "realist horror," succinctly summarizes this ambivalence by effectively rejecting the common equation between horror and fantasy; for Freeland, and for myself, horror can also be grounded in our own world.

Also implicit within Freeland's term "realist horror" is that we are living in a veritable horror film ourselves. The world around us, particularly in the criminal activities that permeate modernity, is full of the stuff of a horror movie. Everyday objects, whose normal uses are benign, can so easily be turned against us with murderous intent. Violence and danger are everywhere in the modern world, and we experience this danger on a daily basis. The *giallo* seems to argue that if any object can be a murder weapon—pens, shovels, and dredgers—then *anyone* can be a killer.

In Sam Peckinpah's *The Wild Bunch* (1969), the film opens with a group of children torturing to death a scorpion with a colony of red ants. This "natural cruelty," Peckinpah's film seems to suggest, is inherent in all of us, not just the so-called criminal classes. We see this natural cruelty of children (and the childlike) in the *giallo* too: Olga in *Deep Red* or Lidio in *The House with Laughing Windows*. These images of cruelty are juxtaposed with the cruelty of the film's murderers. These films' other crimes—adultery, addiction, abuse, abortion, blackmail, perversion, prostitution, and (for this vernacular audience, perhaps even) homosexuality—recognize that in all likelihood, at some level, we are all guilty of certain crimes. The final ambivalence then, at least for this chapter, is that if we are all guilty of *something*, what makes us any different from the *giallo*'s killer?

Notes

1. Cynthia Freeland argued, "As we watch the killer deliver orgiastic thrusting motions, the knife or other weapon obviously functions as phallus. Everyone knows . . .

this is what such violence 'means'" (2000: 181). Although Freeland is discussing the slasher film, her comments can be equally relevant for the *giallo*. I have not engaged the knife-as-phallus argument here, as it would detract from my overview, but it is worth noting, at least in passing. The *giallo* film's preference for beautiful, young female victims, whose often naked (or at least scantily clad) bodies are "penetrated" by these weapons, wielded by "deviant" male killers, surely argues for such an interpretation. When the killer turns out to be a woman, equally strong arguments could be made about the monstrousness of the phallic woman, drawing upon Barbara Creed's work (1993). While I am not developing this argument here, I recognize the centrality within film studies of such an interpretation. I wanted to simply note this interpretation, without actually making it the focus of this chapter.

2. The ornate dagger as murder weapon does seem to be preferred by Dario Argento, as he uses this murder weapon in three films—*Cat O' Nine Tails*, *Deep Red*, and *Opera*, although Sergio Martino also uses this weapon in *All the Colors of the Dark*.

3. This occurs in Lamberto Bava's *A Blade in the Dark*. Being killed with a length of film seems to welcome a self-reflexive reading for Bava's film—that cinema itself can be used as a weapon in the wrong hands. Unfortunately, such readings do not really lead anywhere beyond clever observances.

4. This occurs in both Lenzi's *Eyeball* and Ratti's *Crazy Desires of a Murderer*, just in case anyone wants to keep score.

5. "Serial killer" is a problematic term within an Italian context, as I discuss in chapter 6.

6. While it is understood that *giallo* cinema is an obvious cinema, some filmmakers and screenwriters can have fun with the obviousness demanded, including giving pederastic characters names like "Count Pedrazzi."

CHAPTER FIVE

~

Watching the Detectives:
Amateur Detectives and the
Giallo as Detective Cinema

In the world of the *giallo*, the police are rarely able to solve the crime—these films are not police procedurals after all. Often the only person able to solve the crime and bring the killer to "justice" (whether for trial, hospitalization, or entombment) is an amateur detective. In this chapter, I explore the amateur detective, the *giallo*'s everyman hero, who must seek help from some other kind of agency—a witness, a private (professional) detective, or even someone intimate with the killer. These "helpers" are occasionally "false helpers," who appear to be assisting the hero in solving the crime but in actuality are misdirecting him or her. In almost all cases, the false helper is the killer. As Stephen Thrower noted:

> The *giallo* crossbreeds the murder mystery with horror. It's a form where murder and intrigue, those staple features of popular drama, are taken to baroque extremes, frequently bordering on the ridiculous. Suspicion in the *giallo* is ubiquitous because *everyone* is hiding something. The general tone is one of moral decay and cynicism, with ever more convoluted plots emphasising morbid details in a Janus-faced world of paranoia and betrayal. The killer, often either masked and gloved or replaced by a proxy camera, flits with credulity-straining ease from crime scene to blood-caked crime scene, while reliable plot information is obstinately deferred: the scriptwriter will try just about anything to thwart our attempts at deduction (and the *giallo* is not above cheating either, as devotees of classic detective fiction will find to their teeth-grinding frustration). Armchair psychoanalysts too are baited by the genre's habits; the killer's motivation is usually as tenuous as his methods are elaborate. (1999: 63)

This chapter contextualizes *gialli* as murder mysteries and situates itself within the generic traditions of both literature and film studies.

Giallo as Formula Story

In the first instance, my approach to vernacular cinema in general, and the *giallo* in particular, is influenced by John Cawelti's work on what he calls "formula stories" as "popular literature" (1976: 35), of which he includes the mystery genre as a particular example.

> Because such formulaic types as mystery and adventure stories are used as a means of temporary escape from the frustrations of life, stories in these modes are commonly defined as subliterature (as opposed to literature), entertainment (as opposed to serious literature), or in terms of some other pejorative opposition. The trouble with this sort of approach is that it tends to make us perceive and evaluate formula literature simply as an inferior or perverted form of something better, instead of seeing its "escapist" characteristics as aspects of an artistic type with its own purposes and justification. After all, while most of us would condemn escapism as a total way of life, our capacity to use our imaginations to construct alternative worlds into which we can temporarily retreat is certainly a central human characteristic and seems, on the whole, a valuable one. (Cawelti 1976: 13)

Cawelti's project is to understand the narrative pattern that structures popular literature. Understanding this narrative structure, he argued, maximizes the genre's escapist qualities as a predictable framework readers can operate within while still maintaining some verisimilitude (34). In many respects, Walter Ong's "psychodynamics of orality," as I argued in chapter 2, echoes Cawelti; the predictability of form and narrative structure, the stereotypical characterizations and agonistic situations, the repetition and redundant elements in the prose, and the conservative ideology of popular literature all have strong similarities with the primary orality cultures Ong discussed. Paradoxically, Cawelti's popular literature is (obviously) writing based, whereas Ong's primary orality cultures are (obviously) orally based and may not have any concept of "writing." Yet both Cawelti's formulas and Ong's psychodynamics are strikingly similar. To overcome this apparent paradox, we need to think differently about popular literature (in a way that Cawelti does not), and recognize through vernacular cinema the ephemeral nature of these vernacular forms (literature and film). Martin Priestman noted that the mystery novel is inherently disposable (1998: 6), paralleling what I argued previously in chapter 3 about the rise in mass-produced popular literature alongside the rise in mass transportation, particularly in Britain. Once we know "whodunit" in a mystery novel, the novel's usefulness is expired. Rarely does one reread a mystery novel. Likewise in vernacular cinema, particularly the vernacular culture of the *terza visione* theaters, when the film changes every few days, if not *every* day, and without our contemporary dependence on video and DVD to "rewatch" movies, cinema was more ephemeral, and in this context of vernacular moviegoing, disposable.[1]

Cawelti's four hypotheses about popular literature and the culture that produces and enjoys it are worth enumerating here, as they do reflect the significance of the *giallo* formula for the vernacular audience. First, "Formula stories affirm existing interests and attitudes by presenting an imaginary world that is aligned with these interests and attitudes" (Cawelti 1976: 35). In the *giallo* film, as we have seen, the action takes place in readily identifiable locations and settings and uses recognizable character types and well-known actors. It would be too simplistic to say the ideology of these films, as expressed, is a *direct* reflection of the audience's own beliefs, but the ideas reflected in these films are recognizably "real"; the audience can recognize that people believe this or that, regardless of whether or not they themselves (or anyone they know) actually do. The world of the *giallo* is recognizable, even if it is not the world the audience lives in (the high-style, bourgeois existence of *la dolce vita* these films tend to depict), and reflects those cultural beliefs that are recognized as existing, even if not held by those watching the film.

Second, Cawelti noted, "Formulas resolve tensions and ambiguities resulting from the conflicting interests of different groups within the culture or from ambiguous attitudes towards particular values" (35). The ambivalence toward modernity, as I have argued throughout, is not an outright rejection of the modern world—reflected in changing sexual mores, women's equality, and immigration and emigration in and out of Italy and the European Union. As agonistic dramas, the *giallo* argues a conservative ideological line, but does so, in Cawelti's phrase, to "resolve tensions and ambiguities." As with Cawelti's first point, to suggest that the *giallo* audience would simply accept the ideology of the film is overly simplistic: it puts forward a conservative argument for debate, but suggests ambivalence in response. These films suggest and recognize a variety of social problems, inherent in modernity, but the solutions to those problems, while hardly "sophisticated" or "sensitive," are intended to be debated, not merely accepted. As Stephen Thrower argued,

> It has been noted that exploitation cinema treats its audience to the very sights and sensations the sometimes blatantly moralistic films themselves deplore. The *giallo* film in all its forms tends to a degree of cynicism and decadence,

both in the characterisations and in the manner in which they are observed. The heyday of the *giallo* was the early seventies, and such attitudes can be seen as a somewhat hardened retrenching into conservatism after the liberal idealism of the late sixties. (1999: 73)

"Formulas enable the audience to explore in fantasy the boundary between the permitted and the forbidden and to experience in a carefully controlled way the possibility of stepping across the boundary" (Cawelti 1976: 35). To raise the debates surrounding various ambivalences toward modernity, the *giallo* film creates fantasies where intentionally ideologically conservative and overly simplistic representations of those issues are explored. Would that life was as *la dolce vita* as it appears in the *giallo* films (at least within the male heteronormative culture of these films). While I do not automatically accept psychoanalytical interpretations, particularly in film studies, the *giallo* film does seem to invite interpretation as a form of social wish fulfillment; the ambivalences toward modernity are here expressed as wishful fantasies.

Christopher Frayling, in his study of the spaghetti western, noted that vernacular cinema, despite the temptation to either read these films as ideologically conservative or against the grain and undercutting conservative ideology, was much more complex. Frayling noted that

the concept of the "Ideological State Apparatus" (much loved by these fashionably *marxisant* critics) has recently been misinterpreted to mean that social knowledge is produced by the ruling class, and transmitted through cultural and educational institutions controlled by the bourgeoisie into the otherwise empty minds of the working class; it thus ignores (in John Mepham's words) that "it is not the bourgeois *class* that produces ideas, but bourgeois *society*. And the effective dissemination of ideas is only possible because, or to the extent that, the ideas thus disseminated are ideas which for quite different reasons do have a sufficient degree of effectiveness both in rendering social reality intelligible and in guiding practice within it for them to be apparently acceptable." In other words, the dominant ideology may set the limits of "popular" forms of knowledge (as we have seen), but it rests for the most part on the voluntary and spontaneous "consent" of subordinate classes (rather than *directly* on repressive State Apparatuses), and is, in consequence, most significantly manifest in commonsense, everyday "knowledge." (1998: xx; emphasis in original)

The social result of seeing the *giallo* as vernacular formula cinema appears to move toward a partial integration of these ambivalences toward modernity into the hegemonic life of the audience. Cawelti concluded by noting "literary formulas assist in the process of assimilating changes in values to traditional imaginative constructs" (1976: 36). As a subaltern populace, vernacular cinema audiences are introduced to the contemporary cultural debates through popular literature and cinema. The kind of populist and vernacular morality that was presented by these films is rooted in "common sense." As Pierre Sorlin noted, "Italian films display a moralism common to the various cinemas of the western world, what was nicely called, in the 1960s, 'a mixture of the Ten Commandments and the common law,' that is to say, a mild moralism, neither deferential nor resentful, sometime superficially subversive, which depends on limited competition, limited conflict and limited coercion" (1996: 6). These kind of moral debates are almost an essential aspect of Italian culture, as Mira Liehm noted, "The Italian mentality is strongly imbued with a sense of strict morality. Italians love to pass moral judgements in life as well as in art" (1984: 187). While watching a vernacular film, such as a *giallo*, cultural fantasies are played out in a recognizable world, facing recognizable issues, but through a cultural ambivalence that invites the issues to be debated within the vernacular social networks of the *terza visione* theater, cafes, bars, and homes.

Giallo as Crime/Detective Cinema

Steve Neale noted that film studies have tended to focus on *film noir* and the hard-boiled tradition of detective films while almost ignoring outright any crime film that could not be categorized as *noir* (2000: 72). "Because of the preoccupation in Film Studies with *noir* and the hardboiled tradition, many of the findings and ideas derive from research on detective fiction rather than from research on the detective film as such" (Neale 2000: 72–73). Within the scholarship on detective fiction, Cawelti noted,

> The fundamental principle of the mystery story is the investigation and discovery of hidden secrets, the discovery usually leaning to some benefit for the character(s) with whom the reader identifies. The discovery of secrets with bad consequences for the protagonist, as in the case of Oedipus, is indeed the result of a mystery structure, but a use of this structure outside the realm of moral fantasy. In mystery formulas, the problem always has a desirable and rational solution, for this is the underlying moral fantasy expressed in this formulaic archetype. (1976: 42–43)

Edgar Allan Poe's Dupin stories, "The Murders in the Rue Morgue" (1841) and "The Purloined Letter" (1845), the first "detective" stories, Poe referred to as "tales of ratiocination" (tales of logical and methodical reasoning). Martin Priestman, in preferring the North American term, "mystery," to define this genre, based his preference on identifying "the puzzle element of the form—a puzzle addressed to the reader as well as the protagonists" (2). There is another paradox here: the puzzle or game element of a mystery novel requires an individual reader's attention, focused on solving the puzzle, and this detracts somewhat from my argument of the disinterested (or semi-interested) viewer of vernacular films. But, as I noted in discussing Cawelti's hypotheses with regard to formulaic popular literature, similar cognitive processes are going on, but emphasized and expressed slightly differently. It is further possible that, with a potentially diverse audience, the puzzle aspect of a *giallo* is there for anyone who wants to follow the film, and as I argue in chapters 8 and 9, for those audiences who want the shock and visceral entertainment, the puzzle plot of these films is just the pretense on which to hang these set-pieces.

Xavier Mendik, on the other hand, argued that the *giallo* attempts to disrupt the ratiocination of the classic detective story, particularly at the level of problematizing issues of identity (Mendik is heavily influence by Lacanian psychoanalysis):

> However, if the Classical Detective functions as an "armchair rationalist" marked by stability both in sexual identity and access to the law, then the *giallo* provides a transgressive counterpoint to this position. It details the activities of amateur detectives, whose own identity, sexuality and subjectivity is as compromised as the murderers they seek to expose. . . . Unlike the classic detective, the *giallo* hero's inability to extricate himself from the site of the real is reiterated at the level of the narrative's structure. Specifically it is indicated by the failure to close off the act of crime from that of its investigation. (1996: 43)

I will discuss the role of the amateur detective below, but I introduce Mendik here to point out that the rationalism and positivism seemingly inherent within the mystery genre can be read alternatively, particularly in the *giallo*.[2]

The Police Procedural

As *gialli* are murder mysteries, it is logical to conclude that the police are somehow involved. But this leads to one of the highly problematic issues of *genre*: if the film takes the narrative perspective of the police in investigating and finally revealing the machinations of the plot, then rightly the film is more of a police procedural thriller than a *giallo*, a *poliziotto*. The *poliziotto* genre has its own history and trajectory in contrast to more traditional *gialli*. A number of films in this period and under consideration here clearly fall within the cycle of the police procedural. For example, Paolo Cavara's *The Black Belly of the Tarantula* runs the gamut between *giallo* and *poliziotto*, privileging the investigative perspectives of an amateur detective, Paolo Zani *and* a police officer, Inspector Tellini.

When focused on the police investigation, some of these films demonstrate the tensions between police as insiders, investigating communities they belong to, versus those who are outsiders to the community and come in to investigate. Lucio Fulci's films, most notably *Don't Torture a Duckling* and *The New York Ripper*, foreground this tension between insiders and outsiders; while Lt. Williams, in *The New York Ripper*, is a New York cop investigating a series of murders in New York (an insider investigating his own community), *Duckling* depicts jurisdictional tension between the local *cabineiri's* investigation and incoming federal officers who do not trust the competence of the local force. Other than in those films that fall within the *poliziotto* genre, a good number of *gialli* do feature the police investigation as competent and active in the diegesis, but their role is restricted to the narrative background, thereby allowing the amateur detective to be the focus of the film story. In some cases, the police are given the all-important role of relating the final explanation, putting all the pieces together both for the amateur detective and for us, the film's audience. Echoing Todorov's observation of the two-story structure of the detective story, a "first story" of the crime itself and a "second story" about the investigation into the "first story" (1990: 33), Martin Priestman noted, "the final unmasking of the perpetrator—can happen only once, at the very end, which is also the moment when the hitherto concealed 'first story' comes to be told in its entirety" (1998: 5). Cawelti noted too, "The announcement of the solution is as important as, perhaps in some instances, more important than, the actual apprehension and punishment of the criminal" (1976: 87). As the role of the final explanation is key to the genre, to have this role returned to the official and hegemonic power of the police gives a strong conservative ideological message, but as Cawelti implied above, the ideological position the film appears to take does not mean the audience can or should be expected to accept that hegemonic position.

More typically in the *giallo*, the police are completely ineffectual. Quite often, they are rarely visible, if not completely absent from the narrative. As Morando Morandini noted, "A number of films deal with the dysfunctional state of the police and the magistracy, and with the connivance between the political-economic classes and organized crime" (1996: 592). In many of these films, the police are either useless in trying to solve the crime, or the mystery completely baffles them. Police incompetence is signaled, for example, in Michele Soavi's *Stagefright*, by having a police cruiser on watch outside of the isolated theater waiting for Irving Wallace (Clain Parker) to arrive, unaware that the film's psycho-killer is already inside the theater. The two police officers eat and chat, oblivious to the carnage being wreaked just beyond the padlocked door beside them. More political, but just as problematic, the police in Dallamano's *What Have They Done to Our Daughters?* are functionally useless too, but in this case it is due to high levels of police corruption. This critique of contemporary Italian police work is explicitly echoed in a more direct translation of the Italian title, *La Polizia chiede aiuto* ("The Police Need Help"), at once signifying that the police need assistance in solving this murder but also more help in stopping the flow of corruption within the force itself.

In some cases the police are depicted as being so overworked that they are unable to give the murder case their full and undivided attention. In Tonino Valerii's *My Dear Killer*, although Inspector Peretti (George Hilton) is dedicated to solving the mystery, his assistant Moreau is so bored to distraction that he keeps falling asleep during the investigation. Although this depiction of police apathy is extreme, it does give some indication of how the police were seen by these films' vernacular audiences. Dario Argento's *The Bird with the Crystal Plumage* features police whose hubris leads them to place excessive emphasis upon their (ultimately flawed) forensic evidence at the expense of the old-fashioned technique of believing the eyewitness. In other films, the legal system is too constricting and the police need to work outside of those constraints. Sometimes this may involve the use of a private investigator, such as Arrosio (Jean-Pierre Marielle) in *Four Flies on Grey Velvet*, or the police may intentionally leak information to the amateur detective(s), enabling them to proceed into areas of the investigation that the police cannot, as in *Cat O' Nine Tails*.

Still other films use the "this time it's personal" scenario of a rogue cop who undertakes the investigation alone, literally, in that the cop is by him- or herself, and figuratively, in that he or she acts without legal/departmental support. Argento's detective, Anna Manni (Asia Argento), in *The Stendhal Syndrome* is one such copper. After surviving a rape attack by the film's central killer, she goes after him herself and is ultimately successful in bringing him down. Likewise, in Riccardo Freda's *The Iguana with a Tongue of Fire*, ex-detective John Norton (Luigi Pistilli) takes the mystery personally as he is sexually involved with one of the suspects, the ambassador's daughter, Helene (Dagmar Lassander), and goes after the killer by himself.

Giallo cinema also features a few retired rogue cops who come out of retirement for the sake of the mystery. The central crime in Flavio Mogherini's *The Pyjama Girl Case* comes to light on the day that Inspector Thompson (Ray Milland) retires, and he is allowed to privately investigate this case "for old times sake." Likewise, retired rogue detective Ulisse Moretti (Max Von

Sydow) in Argento's *Sleepless* is brought back to solve a mystery on which he originally worked several years earlier, but now the killer seems to be continuing his activities. The figures of Thompson and Moretti function in these films as representatives of an "old way" of police work—based on interviewing, following leads, and deduction. They are placed in opposition to more "new-fangled" forms of police work, such as psychology, forensic evidence, and profiling, none of which make sense to these seasoned veterans. The ambivalence toward modernity here is in a questioning of the accuracy of these "new" methods in police work; after all, killers were detected and caught before these newer techniques were instituted. If we depend too much on modern technology, these films posit, we lose the human intuitive dimension. And yet at the same time, the technology of modern police work can often limit human fallibility in erroneous conclusions; after all Moretti never did correctly identify the killer in the backstory.

While the mystery is most often solved by the amateur detective, even beyond the police procedural cycle of *gialli*, the police are occasionally given a success or two in bringing the killer to justice, or at least solving the case first.

The Amateur Detective

One of the features that distinguishes the *giallo* from the police procedural is the role of the amateur detective. In the *giallo* someone unconnected to professional detection takes up the central investigative role. Frequently, it is an innocent bystander, but in almost every film, the amateur detective becomes obsessed with the mystery. Perhaps the role of the amateur detective can best be defined by what it is *not*. Above, I discussed that when the person involved in solving the mystery is professional, that is, someone whose paid job it is to solve mysteries, then properly the film is a *poliziotto*. However, in the absence of an amateur detective, the film is, I would argue, something different still. In chapter 10, I consider the similarities and contrasts between the *giallo* and the slasher film, and I note that the role the amateur detective holds in most *gialli* is replaced by the "final girl" in the slasher film. Therefore, one of the defining characteristics of the *giallo* is this role of the amateur detective. Even within the *giallo*, there are premonitions of the later slasher film: specifically in two films by Mario Bava. The more famous of the two, *Bay of Blood*, features no amateur detective role at all, but then there are no real *suspects* either. The murders themselves propel the narrative of *Bay of Blood*, rather than an investigation into them. Similarly, Bava's previous film to *Bay of Blood*, *Five Dolls for the August Moon*, features no amateur detective per se: everyone stranded on the island is a suspect until they show up dead.

Conversely, it could be argued that not only are all the characters in *Five Dolls* potential suspects, but they are all also amateur detectives too.

Returning to the amateur detective, frequently they are drawn into the mystery because they have witnessed the primary murder. Both Argento's Sam Dalmas (Tony Musante) in *The Bird with the Crystal Plumage* and Mark Daly (David Hemmings) in *Deep Red* are archetypal examples: both men witness the first murder in their respective stories as they are walking late at night in Rome. Occasionally the amateur detective recognizes him- or herself as a potential victim of the killer, and so their investigation is motivated as much by self-preservation as by determination to solve the mystery. These hapless heroes are drawn into their mysteries unintentionally, and this initial unwillingness is the basis for *giallo* cinema.

Beyond being a witness, however, *giallo* amateur detectives have other diegetic roles. For example, in Aldo Lado's *Who Saw Her Die?* the amateur detective role is taken by Franco Serpieri, the father of Roberta, one of the missing girls. The opposite, where the child hunts for the killer of the parent, as in Argento's *Sleepless* or Mario Bava's *Hatchet for the Honeymoon*, is sometimes the case. Other times it is a victim's spouse who takes on the role, as in Cavara's *The Black Belly of the Tarantula*, or in Umberto Lenzi's *Seven Blood Stained Orchids* (*Sette orchidee macchiate di rosso*) (1971). Relative strangers can also play amateur detective, as when a neighbor is murdered (in Bido's *The Cat's Victims* and *The Bloodstained Shadow*, or in Carnimeo's *The Case of the Bloody Iris*), or as in Bazzoni's *The Fifth Cord*, where the amateur detective, Andrea Bild (Franco Nero), may have been at the same party as the victims.

Tonino Valerii's *My Dear Killer* complicates the amateur detective's role insofar as he does not appear within the film narrative beyond the first scene, where he is murdered. Although most of the film centers on Inspector Peretti's (George Hilton) investigation into Mr. Paradisi's decapitation, what emerges is that Paradisi, in his role as an insurance adjuster, was investigating the disappearance and deaths of young Stefania Moroni (Lara Wendel) and her father, thereby fulfilling the amateur detective role. Paradisi, although a professional (insurance) investigator, is not a police officer; he represents a civilian authority, which is why I would consider him an amateur detective, as he has no "official" role in investigating crime. However, as a result of Paradisi's investigation, Inspector Paretti is able to follow the clues to solve the case.

When not solving murders, the amateur detective in *giallo* cinema can hold a number of different jobs; although frequently they are newspaper reporters (as in Argento's *Cat O' Nine Tails*, Bazzoni's *The Fifth Cord*, Fulci's

Don't Torture a Duckling, Lado's *The Short Night of Glass Dolls*, and Tessari's *The Bloodstained Butterfly*). This allows them, without too much of a stretch of the imagination, access to resources not available to everyday people. In both Argento's *Sleepless* and Mario Bava's *The Girl Who Knew Too Much* the amateur detectives are unemployed, Giacomo (Stefano Dionisi) and Nora, respectively, are therefore free to investigate the murders at their leisure, and as with the reporter investigators, their inquiries do not take them away from any kind of paid employment. Playboys and socialites who populate some *gialli* could also fit into this category (for example, in Lenzi's *Spasmo* and Martino's *Next!*). One could even extend this further to include Argento's *Phenomena* and Sergio Martino's *Torso*, in which the amateur detectives are students—and these films seem to imply that students have too much free time on their hands as well.

In many of these films, the amateur detective is an artist of some variety: a composer/musician (in Argento's *Four Flies* and *Deep Red*, Lamberto Bava's *A Blade in the Dark*, and Bido's *The Cat's Victims*); an opera singer (in Argento's *Opera*); a writer (in Argento's *The Bird with the Crystal Plumage* and *Tenebre*); a sculptor (in Lado's *Who Saw Her Die?*); a painter (in Avati's *The House with Laughing Windows*); a photographer (in Fulci's *The Black Cat*); a puzzle designer (in Argento's *Cat O' Nine Tails*); a fashion designer (in Mario Bava's *Blood and Black Lace* and *Hatchet for the Honeymoon* and Lenzi's *Seven Blood Stained Orchids*); and even an actor (in Freda's *The Wailing*). With the students and unemployed amateur detectives we could add tourists (as in Bava's *The Girl Who Knew Too Much* and Lenzi's *Eyeball*). The main thing is that all these types of people have sufficient time on their hands to travel about their respective cities investigating mysteries—particularly the tourists and reporters, as traveling about is precisely what they would be doing anyway.

Although less common, some characters in the professional ranks take on the role of amateur detective. In both Bava's *Kill, Baby . . . Kill!* and Armando Crispino's *Autopsy* the amateur detectives are medical pathologists, thereby explaining how they came into contact with the mystery in the first place. Likewise, in Renato Polselli's *Delirium*, the amateur detective is a psychologist, Dr. Lyutak (Mickey Hargitay), again, maintaining the logic of the diegesis by explaining how the amateur detective became involved in the cases. Other professionals playing the amateur detective are a bit more of a stretch to credibility: in Giuliano Carnimeo's *The Case of the Bloody Iris*, Andrea Barto (George Hilton), the film's amateur detective, is an architect; his connection to the murders is that they seem to be focusing around one of the elite high-rise apartment complexes he designed. Oftentimes the amateur detective, particularly when it is a person with a professional occupation, is investigating the mystery in order to clear his or her own name, as is the case with Paolo Zani (Silvano Tranquilli), an insurance broker in Cavara's *The Black Belly of the Tarantula*, or Henry Rossini (Fabio Testi), a school teacher, in Massimo Dellamano's *Solange*.

The amateur detective's function in *giallo* cinema is, obviously, to solve the mystery, which most do. In some cases, the amateur detective is even able to kill the killer. However, in a few of the films, it is the amateur detective who is murdered by the killer, rather than the other way around. The ending of Pupi Avati's *The House with Laughing Windows*, however, is ambiguous: Stefano, the film's amateur detective, is confronted by the killers, two psychotic sisters, who laugh maniacally at his prone position as the police pull up to the isolated titular house. Previously we have seen Stefano running through the village asking the residents for assistance, but all close their shutters to him, including the town's mayor, who then calls the police himself. If the corruption within that village is so pervasive that Stefano cannot get help from anyone, *why* have the police arrived? Avati leaves the film ambiguous as to whether the police have arrived to help Stefano or the sisters.

There is another scenario a few of the *giallo* films follow, which I refer to as the "Roger Ackroyd Scenario" after a novel by Agatha Christie. In *The Murder of Roger Ackroyd* (1926), Christie turns the tables on her readers by revealing that it is the narrator himself, Dr. Sheppard, whom the detective, Hercule Poirot, accuses of the titular murder. Similarly, in a few *giallo* films, the amateur detective turns out to be the killer all along. In the Argento films *Tenebre* and *The Stendhal Syndrome*, as well as in Duccio Tessari's *The Bloodstained Butterfly* (*Una Farfalla con le ali insanguinate*) (1971), there are actually two murderers, one of which is the amateur detective him- or herself. And in Bava's *Hatchet for the Honeymoon*, John Harrington (Stephen Forsyth), who narrates the film as well, admits in his voice-over in the opening seconds of the film that he is a murdering psychopath. But the twist endings in Fulci's *A Lizard in a Woman's Skin* and Polselli's *Delirium* are surprises, appropriate to the "Roger Ackroyd Scenario," because we find that the films' killers are, respectively, Carol Hammond (Florinda Bolkan) and Dr. Lyutak, the films' protagonists.

The Helper

Inevitably, the amateur detective is unable to solve the mystery alone, bringing into play a role function known as "the helper." Usually these helper figures are intentionally assisting the investigation; that is, they are aware that they are supporting the amateur detective in his or her quest. The helper figure typically has specific information the amateur detective requires to solve the mystery. This information may be already known to the helper figure, who is just waiting to be asked the right question, or the helper figure may have access to information sources that the amateur detective does not. Very rarely do helper figures in *gialli* have any narrative purpose beyond splitting the detective role in two so as to potentially be in different locations at the same time. Because of the narrative roles of the helper figures, their function within these mysteries must have a definite and distinct purpose. In fact, in *The Stendhal Syndrome*, it is the helper figure of Dr. Cavanna (Paolo Bonacelli), Anna Manni's psychiatrist, who actually solves the mystery.

The helper figure often has some expertise that is used to assist the amateur detective in solving the crime. Thus, criminal psychology professor Dr. Paul Davis (Paolo Malco) helps Lt. Williams in his investigation into the sex-murders of Fulci's *New York Ripper*, and Professor Dover (Raf Valenti) likewise helps Sam Dalmas in *The Bird with the Crystal Plumage*. Both of these psychologists are called upon as experts in the field of criminal psychology, and their professional expertise, often drawing upon reasonable-sounding psychoanalytic jargon, creates a kind of verisimilitude with the real world and what the film's audience may have heard on television or read in a newspaper. Journalists are also useful to have as helpers in murder investigations, as is Gianna (Daria Nicolodi) in *Deep Red*, Andrea Landini (Dante DiPaolo) in Bava's *The Girl Who Knew Too Much*, or Jacques (Mario Adorf) in Aldo Lado's *The Short Night of Glass Dolls*. These helper figures are often able to access the kinds of information that a "regular person" would not. Criminal friends, like the falsely accused Pasquale Ferrante (Franco Citti) in Antonio Bido's *The Cat's Victims*, can also be useful in accessing areas most people could not.

Just as not all detectives are professional investigators, neither are all helpers professional contacts either. Artists (in *The Bird with the Crystal Plumage*), filmmakers (in *A Blade in the Dark*), theater directors (in *Opera*), musicians (in *The Bloodstained Butterfly*), and even neighborhood children (in *The Pyjama Girl Case*) are just as able to assist their respective amateur detectives as any professional. Although they may not have direct access to significant information, like the professional-class helpers, they may still hold specific clues to the mystery. Sometimes these helper figures are romantically linked with the amateur detective, as in *Tenebre*, *The Bloodstained Shadow*, *The Case of the Bloody Iris*, *Solange*, *Don't Torture a Duckling*, and *Eyeball*. To be sure, the most bizarre of any of these helper figures has to be paraplegic etymologist John McGregor's (Donald Pleasance) chimpanzee in Argento's *Phenomena*, who is also responsible for killing the killer at the end.

While most helper figures intentionally lend a hand in the amateur detective's investigation, some do so inadvertently, as in Lucio Fulci's *Don't Torture a Duckling*, where Don Alberto's developmentally challenged little sister is seen by the amateur detectives Andrea (Tomas Milian) and Patrizia (Barbara Bouchet) strangling her doll, mimicking how the young boys in the film were murdered, and this leads them to the killer priest. Occasionally, the helper figures are murdered before a vital clue can be passed on to the detectives, inevitably preceded by the doomed helper figure saying that they cannot or will not pass on the information over the phone but will see the amateur detective(s) later to pass on this vital clue. Whenever that or similar comments are made, the savvy *giallo* audience member anticipates that this character is about to die. Finally, sometimes a piece of art can hold the vital clue to uncovering the identity of the killer: the disturbing painting of a young girl being attacked in Argento's *The Bird with the Crystal Plumage*, the seemingly missing art in Argento's *Deep Red*,[3] the semiautobiographical film in Lamberto Bava's *A Blade in the Dark*, or the fresco of St. Sebastian in Avati's *The House with Laughing Windows*.

If there is a helper figure, then inevitably there must also be a "false helper," who appears to be assisting in the investigation but is consciously leading the amateur detective astray. Almost always, the false helper is the killer him- or herself. Inevitably, the false helper is someone who the amateur detective would normally trust absolutely, like a priest (in *The House with Laughing Windows*, *The Bloodstained Shadow*, *Don't Torture a Duckling*, *Who Saw Her Die?* or *Seven Blood Stained Orchids*); his or her best friend (in *Sleepless*, *The Girl Who Knew Too Much*, *The Short Night of Glass Dolls*, *Paranoia*, or *Next!*); or even the detective's spouse (in *Four Flies on Grey Velvet* and *The Forbidden Photos of a Lady Above Suspicion*). In terms of understanding the formula of the *giallo*, as I noted above, the helper figure must have a narrative use within the mystery; if a character seems to be fulfilling the helper role, but has no discernable "use" in getting the amateur detective new information, then in most cases this helper is a "false helper" and probably the killer.

Suspects

All good murder mysteries must have an array of suspects, and in part, this is one of those facets of the *giallo* that separates it from the slasher film—in the *giallo*, the killer must interact with the other characters without murdering them, whereas in the slasher film, the killer is *always* killing—like Irving Wallace in *Stagefright*. In many cases, the amateur detective, too, is one of the suspects, if not the prime one, and as I noted above, this would be one factor in the amateur detective's obsession with solving the mystery—clearing his or her name. Other times, the amateur detective's significant other may be a suspect, and the motivation is to clear that person's name. Other frequently used suspects include relatives of the victims (*The Case of the Bloody Iris, Autopsy*, and *My Dear Killer*); relatives of the amateur detective (*The Black Belly of the Tarantula, Autopsy*, and *Eyeball*); and the local handyman (*A Blade in the Dark, Autopsy*, and *Don't Torture a Duckling*), who in *giallo* cinema seems to have replaced the butler from the literary tradition of murder mysteries.

From the literary origins of the *giallo* cinema comes what I have called "the murder mystery plot," which, like most Agatha Christie novels and the like, features an array of suspects, all with their own motives for the murder(s) (*Blood and Black Lace, Five Dolls for an August Moon, The Fifth Cord, The Bloodstained Shadow, The Iguana with a Tongue of Fire, The Pyjama Girl Case*, and *My Dear Killer*). Related to the murder mystery plot is a slightly more cinematic variant, wherein rather than being told what a character's motive might be in committing these murders (a highly literary device), we *see* those motivations demonstrated, as in *Black Belly of the Tarantula, The New York Ripper, Who Saw Her Die?* and *Seven Blood Stained Orchids*. *My Dear Killer* reveals the indebtedness of the *giallo* to the work of Agatha Christie and the classic period of detective fiction quite explicitly: at the denouement of the film, Inspector Peretti gathers the members of the extended Moroni family together in a single room of their mansion and outlines the solution to the crime, much like Hercule Poirot does in the Christie mysteries. He all but says "one of you is a murderer." As Martin Priestman noted in characterizing this kind of murder mystery,

> With the Christie-style whodunit, the emphasis shifts from the brilliant detective's following-up of clues through a range of territories, to the successive investigation of the stories and half-truths of a reasonably large group of suspects, immobilized in place and, effectively, in time. To maintain our interest in them, it is important that each suspect should have, or appear to have "something to hide": usually a less important crime, an unacknowledged sexual or other relationship, a desire to protect another party, or some other private obsession. (1998: 20)

Based on the nature of the killer's disguise, we are often given visual clues as to who among the suspects the killer is. The archetypal *giallo* disguise—black hat, black raincoat, black gloves—intentionally obscures not only the identity of the killer, but also the killer's gender. Usually, when the killer turns out to be a woman, we have been led to assume the killer is a man. Likewise, when we are given clues that the killer is a woman, the killer inevitably turns out to be a man. For example, in Lamberto Bava's *A Blade in the Dark*, we are given very clear (and clearly misleading) clues that the killer is a woman—the slightly high-heeled women's shoes, the bottom hem of a summer dress, and carefully manicured and painted nails.

More problematic, but also highly significant, is when the visual clues as to the killer's identity are again slightly high-heeled shoes, the hem of a black dress, and occasionally a veil—and the killer is revealed to be a priest. Where the killer in *Who Saw Her Die?* is assumed to be a transvestite, it is ultimately revealed to be a priest's cassock we have mistaken for a woman's dress. What does this say about these films' presentation of the priesthood? Priests are cross-dressers? These visual codes became transparent very quickly. Dallamano, in *Solange*, uses icons that earlier that same year (1972) in Lado's *Who Saw Her Die?* indicated ambiguity between woman and priest, but here they only refer to a priest, and in this case, the killer is only *dressed* as a priest. Avati reverses this trend even further in *The House with Laughing Windows* by having the local parish priest reveal *herself* as the second murderous Legnani sister.

The Amateur Detective as *Flâneur*

To conclude this chapter I want to turn my attention back to the figure of the amateur detective in the *giallo*, but recast him in light of Walter Benjamin's notion of the *flâneur*, in particular because the figure of the *flâneur*, and *flânerie* in general, is directly tied to issues of modernity, and, as I shall argue, the amateur detective signifies a strong ambivalence toward the modernity of the *flâneur*.

Ralph Willett, in his *The Naked City* (1996), offers a useful summary of the figure of the *flâneur*, particularly as it has been appropriated to define the modern detective in crime fiction. Willett summarized the *flâneur* thus:

> As masterfully interpreted by Walter Benjamin, the *flâneur* is, on the one hand, an observant classifier of the city's population "who reads people's characters not only from the physiognomy of their faces but via a social physiognomy of the streets"; and on the other, a dandyish connoisseur of metropolitan pleasures and delights, increasingly the offerings of a commercial culture. Celebrated in the work of Balzac and later Baudelaire, he provides a surrogate for the watchful (male) detective of popular fiction, one who listens, searches and above all, like the private "eye," sees and deciphers the signifiers of that labyrinth of populated spaces and buildings which forms the modern metropolis—strange and menacing but also intoxicating. Benjamin claims that whatever track the *flâneur* as hunter follows will lead him to a crime. (1996: 2–3)

Benjamin's equation of the nineteenth-century *flâneur* with the twentieth-century private detective is highly problematic. These problems derive largely from linguistic slippage: while Benjamin seems intent on using the detective in a metaphoric relationship with the *flâneur*, Benjamin and later writers trip under their own rhetoric in seeing the *flâneur* and detective as synonymous. We need to be very careful in not confusing metaphor and actuality.

Keith Tester, in his introduction to an edited collection of philosophical and cross-discipline applications on the idea of the *flâneur*, recognized that different disciplines have appropriated Benjamin's metaphor for their own ends. Tester noted,

> Originally, the figure of the *flâneur* was tied to a specific time and place: Paris, the capital of the nineteenth century as it was conjured by Walter Benjamin in his analysis of Charles Baudelaire. . . . But the *flâneur* has been allowed, or made, to take a number of walks away from the streets and arcades of nineteenth-century Paris. Not least, the figure and the activity appear regularly in the attempts of social and cultural commentators to get some grip on the nature and implications of the conditions of modernity and post-modernity. (1994:1)

In Benjamin's reading of Baudelaire, the *flâneur* was the figure of the dandy who strolled the streets of Paris, with no purpose other than to observe the life around him. So leisurely was the *flâneur*'s pace, there was a brief fad in the mid-nineteenth century of taking pet turtles for walks through the Parisian arcades and letting them set the pace in, what Benjamin argued, was a protest against modernity's fast pace (Tester 1994: 15). The *flâneur* engages in *flânerie*, which can "be understood as the activity of the sovereign spectator going about the city in order to find the things which will occupy his gaze and thus complete his otherwise incomplete identity; satisfy his otherwise dissatisfied existence; replace the sense of bereavement with a sense of life" (Tester 1994: 7).[4] The emptiness of modernity, its meaninglessness and therefore the meaninglessness in the lives of modernity's residents, demanded a search for some kind of meaning. For the *flâneur*, this meaning was sought for on the city streets (the prime locus for modernity's existence). As Rob Shields argued, for Benjamin, the *flâneur* becomes a "detective of street life" in searching for this meaning (Shields 1994: 61). David Frisby noted, "The *flâneur* as observer cannot therefore be reduced to the spectator, to the mere idler or to the gaper. . . . Rather, the activity of watchful observation in the modern metropolis is a multifaceted method for apprehending and reading the complex and myriad signifiers in the labyrinth of modernity" (1994: 92–93).

Like the detective, the *flâneur* wanders the city streets looking for meaning within an inchoate modernity. But the detective is paid to do a job, whether as a private detective or public employee, and is not looking for personal meaning in the modern world, although in some cases this may be found. The same problem applies to the figure of the newspaper reporter or journalist, despite some critics likewise linking the journalist to the *flâneur* (see Frisby 1994: 92–93 and Willett 1996: 3); they too are *paid* to wander the streets looking for meaning. Central to the *flâneur* is that this is a *leisure* activity, and without taking too much of an essentialist position, paid *flânerie* is highly paradoxical. Returning to the *giallo*, those amateur detectives who either do not (need to) work or whose *flânerie* is outside of their paid employment can more accurately be considered a *flâneur*. Perhaps this explains why the *poliziotto* is a separate genre/*filone*; the police investigating a series of murders as part of their job is a different phenomenon to an amateur investigating on their own. The amateur detectives in these films have an alternative vested interest in solving these cases and are not motivated by the base capitalist desire to get paid. The *giallo*'s amateur detective is most often of the bourgeoisie. Consider Chris Barber's characterization of Mark (David Hemmings) in Dario Argento's *Deep Red*:

> In *Deep Red*, Hemmings is a wealthy, affluent bourgeois, with an ingenious, apparently innocuous nature. Though attempting to transcend his condition towards a wider social homogeneity, he succeeds only in showing his naiveté and ineptitude. (Although there is also a suggestion that group/serial unity is an illusion, and social reality is an inescapable heterogeneity). His first conversation is with another, very drunk pianist (Gabriele Lavia). His unruly behaviour embarrasses Hemmings, as does his insistence that he is a proletarian pianist, while Hemmings plays the piano for pleasure. Later, Hemmings repeats his naivety when he visits this colleague and is confronted by his homosexual partner. (2003: 85–86)

The distinction between Mark's leisure piano playing and Carlo's playing for money is almost metaphoric of the *giallo*'s relationship to the *poliziotto*. Mark is searching for meaning, in his music and in his life, and this search for personal meaning within modernity becomes displaced onto the search for meaning in the case of who murdered Helga Ulmann. The search for meaning within modernity was also noted by John Cawelti as an integral aspect of popular literature, specifically the murder mystery:

> The particular combination of cultural factors, which generated this combination of needs—such factors as the decline in traditional religion, the growth of uncertainty about the social order, together with a general acceptance of the ideas of individual achievement and the family circle—were most evident at precisely the

time the classical detective formula reached its widest general popularity, the early twentieth century. Furthermore, I would guess that these factors were strongest among that group who were apparently the most enthusiastic devotees and even addicts of the formula—successful, highly educated professional people whose backgrounds were mostly firmly in the middle-class tradition. It would follow from this line of reasoning that the classical formula would be less popular among working-class readers and those members of the middle class who had risen from a lower class, as in the case of self-made businessmen, since in these cases the combination of cultural and psychological factors would be quite different. Random observation tends to bear out this hypothesis, since those who have most enthusiastically testified to their love of classical detective stories have been middle-class professionals and, in particular, academics. (1976: 105)

Cawelti, despite his myopic view on middle-class readers of popular (detective) literature,[5] assumes there would be little interest among the working-classes for discussion of these issues. But the social and cultural changes inherent within modernity affect other classes too. Vernacular cinema audiences are also aware of the decline in traditional religion, the importance of traditional family values, the changing social and sexual mores, and the contemporary challenges to the social order. The formulas of vernacular cinema address these concerns, albeit differently.

Notes

1. Ironically, while Cawelti extols the virtues of the mystery and suspense novel, he condemns the horror genre outright: "Horror seems especially fascinating to the young and relatively unsophisticated parts of the public" (1976: 48). The prejudices noted previously in chapter 2, about Italian horror films and their absence from the history of Italian cinema studies, reflect Cawelti's quasi-Leavisite bias against the genre, compounded further by Cawelti framing his dismissal in class-based apathy ("unsophisticated parts of the public"). Cawelti continued: "Older, educated people probably learn more sophisticated modes of self-transcendence and become too detached and critical to be terrified by the more primitive modes of monsterdom" (48).

2. Mendik further develops his Lacanian reading of the *giallo*, particularly Dario Argento's *Tenebre*, in a short monograph (2000).

3. Once one has seen *Deep Red* and has become familiar with the solution to the mystery, it is fun to go back to the sequence of Mark running in to try and save Helga to look for the "missing artwork" in the film. Argento is nothing if not meticulous in this film's construction.

4. Tester noted the inherent tautology here: "the *flâneur* is the man who indulges in *flânerie*; *flânerie* is the activity of the *flâneur*" (Tester 1994: 7).

5. Implicit within Cawelti's entire book is the question, "Why would people consume *popular* literature (like murder mysteries) when they should know better?" Mystery writer Sarah Dunant offers an obvious, even if banal, answer: "although literary fiction may be more profound or better written, it is often not as much fun to read" (Dunant 2000: 10).

CHAPTER SIX

~

The Killer's Identity

"Serial murder," as Ellen Nerenberg noted, "is an American Phenomena; it is not European, and it is decidedly not Italian" (2001: 65). Nerenberg goes even further, noting that the concept of serial murder is so foreign to Italians that the language does not have a word for it (65).[1] This is not to say that multiple murders, or several murders by the same killer, do not happen in Italy; quite the contrary, but the phenomenon is rare enough that there is no Italian equivalent for "serial killer." When such killers do strike in the country, the press refers to them as *il mostro*, monsters.

> Designating serial murderers as "monsters" accomplishes an important linguistic (not to mention psychical) operation. It transposes the unthinkable onto the irrational, Gothic, and fantastic terrain where monsters dwell, thus, setting it at a safer distance for an eventual contemplation that will diminish the "monsters" as the stuff of folklore . . . , dreams and nightmares, and artistic artifacts. (Nerenberg 2001: 65)

What makes the concept of the "serial killer" so frightening, at least for me, is its commonness. The frequently cited statistic is that currently in the United States, between fifty and five hundred serial killers are currently on the loose. These killers are so familiar to Americans that the term "serial killer" is common parlance. This everyday association Americans have with the concept of serial murder does not occur in Italy. The Italian, *il mostro*, maintains that mysterious and bogeyman quality to the killer. It is not part of everyday life.[2]

Within the context of classic detective fiction, serial killers are also rare. This rarity is not linguistic in origin, as in the *il mostro* issue, as much as it is due to the incompatibility of serial murder with the project of the classic detective story.[3] David Schmid noted,

> The serial killer, who typically murders for non-rational motives and who usually murders strangers, challenges some of the most cherished assumptions of traditional detective fiction, namely the belief that murderers always have "rational" motives for murder, such as greed or jealousy, and the belief that murderers always have some kind of personal relation with their victims. (2000: 75)

Using a single literary example, Agatha Christie's novel *The A.B.C. Murders* (1936) appears to have Poirot and Hastings following the trail of a serial killer, using a railway timetable as the only tangible link between the murders. But Poirot's "little grey cells" reveal that the killer has actually planned this entire spree in order to carry out a single, "traditional" murder based on the killer's desire to inherit a fortune. Five murders are executed in order to cover up the fact that only one was motivated. What appears to be a serial killer narrative Christie reverses into a much more traditional classic detective story.

Quite a few of the *giallo* films surveyed here use this *A.B.C. Murders* device: it appears that the killer is unknown to the victims, but in reality the primary motive is behind only one of the murders. Frequently it is the police themselves who assume the murders are the work of *il mostro*, not making the connection between the deaths that the amateur detective is called upon to piece together. But there are a few true homicidal maniacs in the *giallo* canon, killers who enjoy random murder. Examples include Dario Argento's *Tenebre* or *Sleepless*, films where the killer uses a template for his murders—Peter Neal's novel in the former and a children's poem in the latter. But what fuels the *giallo* is less the random killer than the game of trying to find the connection between the murders, both for the amateur detective and for the audience.

In the majority of films, the victims know their killer, at least in some capacity. Mario Bava puts forward a satirical commentary on capitalism's tendency toward "consuming" its workers in two of his *gialli*. In both *Blood and Black Lace* and *Hatchet for the Honeymoon*, the killer is the victims' employer. This power relationship between employer and employee and killer and victim is extended to the teacher-student relationship in Dario Argento's *Phenomena*, albeit without Bava's sense of humor, where the killer is one of the teachers at the Richard Wagner School for Girls. Although the killer of Massimo Dallamano's *Solange* is *thought* to be one of the teachers at its diegetic school, this turns out to be a red herring. Occasionally, this employer-employee relationship is reversed; where the killer is the employee, rather than the employer. In Umberto Lenzi's *Paranoia*, for example, Brion (Tino Carraro), the one who orchestrates the plot against Kathryn, is her attorney. In Fillippo Walter Ratti's *Crazy Desires of a Murderer*, it is Berta the maid (Isabelle Marchal) who is responsible for the grisly crimes—and while not quite "the butler did it" solution of the old cliché, it is similar. These films foreground the power dynamics in the worlds of work and education, and extend them to the correlative roles of killer and victim. Some *giallo* killers are even known to murder their friends (in Mario Bava's *Five Dolls for the August Moon* and in Flavio Mogherini's *The Pyjama Girl Case*) and spouse (in Lucio Ercoli's *Forbidden Photos*).

The Killer's Relationship to the Amateur Detective

The amateur detective often does not know the killer when his or her identity is finally revealed. However, in some cases, the two *do* know each other. In Riccardo Freda's *The Wailing*, for example, the killer is Shirley (Martine Brochard), amateur detective Michael's (Stefano Patrizi) mother. In both Antonio Bido's *The Bloodstained Shadow* and Umberto Lenzi's *Spasmo*, the killer is the amateur detective's brother. And in Dario Argento's *Sleepless*, the killer, Lorenzo (Roberto Zibetti), has been amateur detective Giacomo's (Stefano Dionisi) best friend since childhood.

In a few *gialli* the killer and amateur detective are sexual partners, as in Dario Argento's *Four Flies on Grey Velvet* where the killer is finally revealed to be Roberto's (Michael Brandon) wife, Nina (Mimsy Farmer), or Luciano Ercoli's *The Forbidden Photos of a Lady Above Suspicion*, wherein Minou (Dagmar Lassander) is being driven insane by her husband Peter (Pier Paolo Capponi). The killer can be the amateur detective's lover, as in Armando Crispino's *Autopsy*, Lucio Fulci's *The New York Ripper*, or either of Umberto Lenzi's *Paranoia* or *Eyeball*.

In chapter 5, I noted that Agatha Christie's *The Murder of Roger Ackroyd*, wherein the killer and the protagonist are the same person (a closer personal relationship would be hard to find), indirectly inspired a few *giallo* films. However, it is also worth noting that in none of these "Roger Ackroyd"–like *gialli* is the killer/amateur detective any kind of "split personality"; there is no evidence given in these films that the amateur detective is *unaware* that he or she is the killer. Actually, with the exception of Bava's *Hatchet for the Honeymoon* and Renato Polselli's *Delirium*, there are in fact *two* killers, and the amateur detective assumes the role of killer only once the first killer has been disposed of. Argento plays this particular game twice: once in *Tenebre* and again in *The Stendhal Syndrome*.

In most *giallo* films, the killer is male. Significantly however, this is not always the case (often in Dario Argento's films). A few of these films feature multiple killers, mostly male-female teams working together, although in *The Stendhal Syndrome*, once Detective Anna Manni (Asia Argento) has killed the film's rapist-murderer, Alfredo Grossi (Thomas Kretschmann), she takes over his murder spree; here is an odd example of a victim becoming the victimizer in *giallo* cinema. Conspiracy *gialli*, wherein there are several killers, are rarer. Again, these are perhaps indirectly inspired by another Agatha Christie novel, *Murder on the Orient Express* (1934), in which Hercule Poirot concludes that everyone on board the titular train had a hand in Mr. Ratchett's murder. Aldo Lado's debut film, *The Short Night of Glass Dolls*, features a conspiracy among Prague's political and judicial elite, under the guise of a Satanic sex cult, to murder women whom they believe are useless to society and fit only to satisfy their libidinal and violent desires. Thus everyone connected with Club 99 whom investigating journalist Gregory Moore (Jean Sorel) interviews is actually guilty of the murders.

There are even a few examples of killers being revealed as not human, although the consideration of these films as *gialli* may be debated. In Mario Bava's *Kill, Baby . . . Kill!* the killer is the ghost of a young girl who died while the local villagers did nothing to help her. More bizarrely, in Lucio Fulci's *The Black Cat*, the killer is a psychotic kitty who at first may or may not be being controlled by Professor Robert Miles (Patrick Magee) but by the end is certainly *controlling* the parapsychologist.

Disguise

The *giallo* killer is almost always disguised in some way. From a strictly narratological perspective, this obviously obscures the identity of the killer from the audience's deduction until such time as the filmmaker wishes to reveal it. In the slasher film, which I have already noted is indebted to the *giallo*, certain disguises have become iconic—Freddy's glove from Wes Craven's *A Nightmare on Elm Street* (1984) or the hockey mask (goalie mask, to be more precise) that Jason Voorhees wears in most of the *Friday the 13th* series[4] to name but two. In Mario Bava's early *giallo*, *Blood and Black Lace*, the archetypal disguise for the *giallo* was established: black gloves (often leather driving gloves), black raincoat, and black wide-brimmed hat. It is worth pointing out that Bava's film was not the first to use this disguise for the killer (although the first to be used in Italian *giallo* cinema): in George Pollock's *Murder, She Said* (1961), Miss Marple (Margaret Rutherford), while on the 4:50 from Paddington (the title of the Christie novel the film is based on), witnesses a murder in a passing train—a man (we assume) wearing black gloves, dark hat, and overcoat, is strangling a woman to death. In the Christie novel (1957), no such description of what the killer is wearing appears (Christie 1997: 533), but the advantages of this disguise for films are obvious: it not only cloaks the identity of the killer, but also the killer's gender. In the wake of the 1964 Bava film, this disguise became de rigueur for *gialli* murderers.

The black gloves the *giallo* killer wears are fairly ubiquitous. Although some filmmakers tend to vary this: Carnimeo, in *The Case of the Bloody Iris*, has his killer wear yellow kitchen gloves (mise en abyme for *giallo*?), Umberto Lenzi, in *Eyeball*, has his wear red rubber gloves, and in three films, the killer wears white surgical gloves—Bazzoni's *The Fifth Cord*, Bido's *The Cat's Victims* and Ratti's *Crazy Desires of a Murderer*. Significantly, the iconic function of the black gloves became solidified in the *giallo* audiences' lexicon fairly quickly. As early as 1971, Mario Bava begins playing with audience expectations, opening *Bay of Blood* with the elderly Contessa Donati (Isa Miranda) being murdered (by hanging) by an assailant wearing black gloves. The assailant takes off his gloves and reveals himself to be her husband, the count (Giovanni Nuvoletti), but someone else then murders him. Bava upsets the audience's expectations by having the black-gloved "maniac" murdered by the film's real killer. "By 1975 [the black leather gloves] was a *giallo* cliché: the ritualistic adornment of leather, with its connotations of fetishism and sex, suggesting that [in *Deep Red*] the killer isn't just a psychopathic murderer but kinky with it" (Grainger 2000: 123). Even more playful, Argento also made it a habit in his films to don the black gloves himself in these sequences, partially as an homage to Alfred Hitchcock's cameos, but also, as Peter Bondanella noted, as "a humorous act of identification with his killers" (2001: 420).

Sometimes, although statistically rarer than the black gloves, the killer wears a wide-brimmed dark hat,[5] a facet of the killer's disguise that has little variation across the *giallo*. Often the killer wears a dark overcoat—in some films varying in style and color: beige trench coats (in Argento's *Opera* and Valerii's *My Dear Killer*), a red raincoat (in Lenzi's *Eyeball*), or even a white laboratory coat (in Ratti's *Crazy Desires of a Murderer*).

Giallo killers also sometimes disguise their face with a mask of some sort, often a balaclava or a stocking over their head. Massimo Dallamano varies this somewhat by having his killer blacken his face with makeup, in *A Black Veil for Lisa*, or wear a false beard, in *Solange*.

A few *gialli* also try to disguise their killer's voice: the killer has her accomplice make the threatening phone calls in Argento's *The Bird with the Crystal Plumage,* and she alters his voice electronically in Argento's *The Stendhal Syndrome.* By far the strangest example of this is in Lucio Fulci's *The New York Ripper,* wherein the killer disguises his voice to sound like Donald Duck. One of the reasons Fulci's film remains controversial is that this absurdity of the disguised voice is juxtaposed with extremely misogynist and horrific violence. How are we supposed to respond to this film when we are first cued to laugh at it for the ridiculousness of the disguised voice but then are confronted by graphic and horrific murders? Are we to read the film as having our laughter and derision turned against us (or subverted, depending on how much artistic merit one wants to give Fulci) by the disturbing violence? Are we supposed to continue laughing as Kitty's eye and breast are sliced open with a razor blade? It is moments like these in Fulci's film catalogue that make his films the most ambivalent of the *gialli.*

In a very few *giallo* films, the killers use a faked ailment of some kind to mask their violence and raise them above suspicion. In Paolo Cavara's *The Black Belly of the Tarantula,* the killer turns out to be the blind masseur (Ezio Marano), who had only been faking his blindness in order to get a job. Or in Pupi Avati's *The House with Laughing Windows,* the seemingly bedridden and invalid Laura Legnani (Vanna Busoni) is revealed to be one half of a pair of bloodthirsty sisters. But these disguises are rare.

In quite a few of these films, the killer wears no disguise at all. This is all the more surprising, considering how iconic the black gloves are, almost metonymic of the genre as a whole.

Sexual Ambiguity as Disguise

Having a woman killer dress like a man is an obvious way to play upon the audience's assumption that the killer must be a man based on the visual evidence. And while, discursively, such an aspect of *giallo* cinema may seem central, statistically, cross-gendered disguise is relatively rare. Argento uses this device twice—in *The Bird with the Crystal Plumage* and *Deep Red*—and Riccardo Freda uses it in *The Wailing.* I have only come across a single example of the reverse, where a male killer dresses as a woman, and that is the transvestite killer in Lamberto Bava's *A Blade in the Dark.* In this film, we are intentionally misled as to the gender of the killer by means of insert shots of the killer's feet in women's low-heeled shoes, the hem of a summer dress, and carefully manicured fingernails painted a "tasteful" red. We are further misled, when we are shown Sandra (Anny Papa) wearing very similar shoes and having identical fingernails. And yet, according to Jacqueline Reich, *giallo* films are almost *defined* by the killer's sexual ambiguity and cross-gendered identification. She refers to the *giallo* as "a genre dominated by sexually ambiguous villains and monsters offering diverse points of cross-gender identification" (Reich 2001: 89). To be sure, many *giallo* killers are "sexually ambiguous," but not all of them are; the "sexually ambiguous" killer has become so associated with the *giallo*, much like the disguise of the black gloves and hat, that its iconicity is more potent than its actuality within these films.

The most significant cross-dressing disguise in the *giallo*, however, is where a priest's cassock is mistaken for a woman's dress (by a diegetic witness or presented to the audience as misleading information). In particular, in Aldo Lado's *Who Saw Her Die?* we are given privileged visual information about the killer in the form of point-of-view (POV) shots and other insert shots wherein, although denied full visual identification, parts of (ultimately) the killer's body, namely his shoes, appear. The POV shots from the perspective of the killer are particularly informative, as they are slightly obscured by a semitransparent veil that presumably covers the face of the killer. Also the insert shots of the killer's shoes look "feminine"—slightly raised heel, slender and tapered at the toe. We also see what looks, to us, like the bottom hem of the killer's "dress" (which turns out to be a cassock).

Giallo cinema features a number of such killer priests. But what could this signify? The ambiguity of gender with regard to the priest's cassock also points to an ambiguity of gender with regard to priests themselves—they are born men, but cannot live "like men," from the heteronormative context of Italian masculinity and machismo. This is further confirmed in Umberto Lenzi's *Seven Blood Stained Orchids*, where that film's killer priest, Father Saunders (Renato Romano), is punched in the groin and then drowned in a swimming pool by Marco (Antonio Sabato)—effectively, Marco emasculates him before he is able to kill him. By wearing the cassock, a visual equation is made between the priest and "women" insofar as their garment looks like a dress. Priests hold liminal and ambivalent positions within *giallo* cinema, as they occupy those spaces that lie between the genders—neither man nor woman. Furthermore, that most *gialli* priests are revealed to be the killers themselves raises yet another ambivalence about the priesthood in that, perhaps because of their liminal gendered roles, they become monstrous. This idea is demonstrated in Avanti's *The House with Laughing Windows* in the final revelation that the second murderous sister has been living as the parish priest since the end of the war, and, it is assumed by the film, the village was fully aware of this. In addition to Avanti's and Lenzi's films, killer priests who are mistaken as women (or implied to be women by the shots we are presented of their bodies and clothes) occur in Bido's *The Bloodstained Shadow*, Dallamano's *Solange* and Lado's *Who Saw Her Die?*

The Killer's Motive and Past Traumas

The reasons behind the *giallo* killers' activities need enumeration, and this section outlines the variety of motives for murder in these films. Some of these films give no motive and are content with explaining away the killer's actions as merely due to his or her insanity. These tend to be later *gialli*—such as Argento's *Sleepless* or Soavi's *Stagefright*. But, relatively speaking, such avoidances of proper exposition are rare.

Most *gialli* killers have experienced some kind of trauma in their diegetic pasts, which erupts murderously in the diegetic present. Take, for example, the films of Dario Argento, whose films often rely on the revelation of some kind of past trauma to explain their murders. In *Bird*, for example, we are told a psycho killer attacked Monica Ranieri (Eva Renzi) as a young girl, and she was lucky to be left alive. It was this trauma that sparked off her own murder spree, which the film is about. Argento uses a similar narrative structure for Detective Manni in *The Stendhal Syndrome*: she was a victim of the previous rapist, Alfred, and as a result of being traumatized by this attack, she began killing others. Other *giallo* killers were traumatized by witnessing a parent's murder (in Bava's *Hatchet for the Honeymoon*) or a brother's death (in Martino's *Torso*). In the case of Bava's *Kill, Baby . . . Kill!* the killer was traumatized by witnessing her *own* death. In Umberto Lenzi's *Eyeball*, the film's killer, Paulette (Martine Brochard), missing an eye since a childhood accident, resents other young women's beautiful eyes, and so kills them, stealing the requisite token in covetous retribution. Such retribution also motivates the killer in Argento's *Phenomena*: Frau Brückner (Daria Nicolodi) resents the youth and innocence of the girls at the Richard Wagner school, since hers was taken from her when an inmate at the local asylum raped her (through the bars, no less!), and she has been saddled with a monstrous child ever since.

Other retributive murders are perpetrated in revenge for the killer's child's illness. For example, the killer in Dallamano's *Solange* (the film's Italian title, *Cosa avente fatto a Solange?* translates more transparently as "What have they done to Solange?") is dealing out retribution to those girls whom he believes are responsible for his daughter, Solange's (Camille Keaton), abortion, which directly resulted in her madness. Similarly, Peter (Andrea Occhipinti), the killer in Fulci's *The New York Ripper*, is punishing women who have grown up and are sexually active because his own young daughter has a terminal illness and will never reach that stage. Father Saunders, in Lenzi's *Seven Blood Stained Orchids*, murders women whom he blames for his brother's death, and one whom his brother had an affair with. But surely the most disturbing form of parental retribution is that of Professor Isaacs (Georges Rigaud), as he murders the beautiful young women in his apartment block because he blames them for his daughter Sheila's (Annabella Incontrera) lesbianism in Giuliano Carnimeo's *The Case of the Bloody Iris*.

While Carnimeo's film depicts a killer's retribution for his daughter's homosexuality, other *giallo* killers strike because of their *own* homosexuality or other sexual identity issues. Some, like the aforementioned transvestite killer in Bava's *A Blade in the Dark* or Nina Tobias in *Four Flies on Grey Velvet*, strike because of their confused gender roles. In the latter case, it emerges that Nina's father would have preferred her to be a boy, and she spent most of her childhood (presumably until puberty) living as such. Others, like John Lubbock (Maurizio Bonuglia) in Luigi Bazzoni's *The Fifth Cord* are embarrassed by their own homosexuality.

Popular awareness of Freudian psychology permeates the psyches of these *giallo* killers. A quasi-Oedipal dilemma gets played out in Argento's *Four Flies* in Nina's desire to kill her father, whom she blames for her own gender confusion, and in Freda's *The Wailing*, in which Mama Shirley sexually desires her son, Michael. Argento's *Opera* takes these a step further by making the central murders a logical next step from the sado-masochistic relationship Inspector Santini (Urbano Barberini) had with Betty's (Christina Marsillach) mother in the diegetic past.

Outright and explicit misogyny is relatively rare, or rather it is rare for it to be expressed as such. The killer of Martino's *Torso* thinks all women are dolls; this view emanates from a childhood game he was playing when his brother fell to his death, in the diegetic past, and so now he dismembers women like he did with his childhood toys. Whereas the blind masseuse in Cavara's *The Black Belly of the Tarantula* murdered his own wife in a jealous rage, and now he murders any woman who reminds him of her.

While the child murders in Lucio Fulci's *Don't Torture a Duckling* may appear to the audience to be pederasty, given the number of newspaper stories about priests abusing young boys in their care, diegetically at least, Don Alberto's (Marc Porel) motive is to protect his young charges from the corrupting influences of an ever encroaching sexual maturity. Aldo Lado's *Who Saw Her Die?* is not so coy, and the killer priest in this film is a sexual predator of young girls. Likewise, in Dallamano's *What Have They Done to Our Daughters?* the killer is operating a teenage prostitution ring, and most of the murders are contained within his maintenance of it.

A number of *giallo* killers are motivated less by psychosexual issues than simple greed. There is a strong *filone* in the *giallo* tradition where the motives for the murders are financial. In these films, the victims are killed because they stand in the way of the killer's inheritance (in Bava's *Bay of Blood*, Bergonzelli's *In the Folds of the Flesh*, Crispino's *Autopsy*, Lenzi's *Spasmo*, Ratti's *Crazy Desires of a Murderer*, and Valerii's *My Dear Killer*); to control specific business interests (in Bava's *Blood and Black Lace* and *Five Dolls for an August Moon*, Lenzi's *Paranoia* and *Spasmo*); or even to get insurance money (in Ercoli's *The Forbidden Photos of a Lady Above Suspicion*).

Some unfortunate victims are simply in the wrong place at the wrong time, such as witnesses who might be able to identify the killer. These killings seem to indicate that not only does knowledge equal power, but knowledge can be deadly. Those who uncover the killer's secret, either intentionally or accidentally, are fit for the proverbial chop. These secrets might pertain to gender/sexual identity issues (Bava's *A Blade in the Dark*), lesbianism (Fulci's *A Lizard in a Woman's Skin*), homosexuality (Freda's *The Iguana with a Tongue of Fire*), inheritance (Crispino's *Autopsy*), genetic information (Argento's *Cat O' Nine Tails*), or even a previous murder in the diegetic past (Bava's *Blood and Black Lace* and Argento's *Deep Red*). Sometimes, the initial murder in these films is a "crime of passion," unmotivated and accidental. The following murders are then the killer's attempt to keep his or her guilt from being revealed, as in Bido's *The Bloodstained Shadow*, Dallamano's *A Black Veil for Lisa*, Mogherini's *The Pyjama Girl Case*, or Tessari's *The Bloodstained Butterfly*.

The traumatic past event that sparks *giallo* films' murders are fully in keeping with the tradition of detective fiction. Tzvetan Todorov, in perhaps the single most influential theoretical musing on the detective genre, recognized the double-narrative structure of the mystery.

> We know such narratives are constituted by the problematic relation of two stories: the story of the crime, which is missing, and the story of the investigation, which is present, and whose only justification is to acquaint us with the other story. Some element of that first story is indeed made available from the beginning: a crime is committed almost before our eyes; but we have been unable to determine its real agents or motives. The investigation consists in returning over and over to the events, verifying and correcting the smallest details, until the truth about the initial story finally comes out; this is a story of learning. . . . What characterizes knowledge in detective fiction is that it has only two possible values, true or false. In a detective story, either we know who committed the murder or we do not. (1990: 33)

Of course, Todorov is not talking about the *giallo* film, but the classic detective story: in these fictions, the crime is the past event, and the narrative present is concerned with this past crime's investigation. Rarely in the classic detective story are there more crimes trying to cover up the first crime,[6] but the model itself is sound. Martin Priestman noted that "the final unmasking of the perpetrator—can happen only once, at the very end, which is also the moment when the hitherto concealed 'first story' comes to be told in its entirety" (1990: 5). The motive for the killer's murders constitute Todorov's "first story": something has happened in the narrative past that is investigated (often by the film's amateur detective) in the "second story." Ultimately, as Todorov noted, all mystery narratives are "gnoseological," that is, they are about the quest for knowledge (1990: 46). And the *giallo* stays within this generic boundary by its double-narrative structure of past event and present investigation. But as vernacular cinema, these events and investigations need to be presented graphically (visually) and simplistically to be consumed by the vernacular audience. The complexity of the *giallo* narrative, while always present in these films, is irrelevant. It becomes a flimsy framework on which to hang the various set pieces of graphic sex and violence. While these *gialli* can be rationalized as murder mysteries and subjected to Todorovian (or other) theoretical analysis, such analyses become almost an intellectual game the filmmaker plays with "slumming" bourgeois critics, almost daring them to try and figure out these puzzles, while the intended audiences, like the one Pauline Kael discussed, quoted in chapter 2, are rooting for further carnage.

The Killer's Death

The killer's death, by narrative necessity, needs to be spectacular. It is the diegetic moment when any cultural transgressions are reverted back to normalcy. When, as in quite a few *gialli*, it is the police who finally shoot the killer, the power reverts to hegemonic forces of societal restraint, which in many respects the killer's actions were challenging.

However, often it is the amateur detective in these films who not only solves the crime but gives the final *coup de gras* to the killer too. This death can take a number of forms, but one of the most popular is throwing the killer off of a cliff or other high place. This method of death seems to be a metaphoric "fall," whether echoing Satan's fall from Heaven, or our fall from Eden. The fall is almost always spectacular, filmed in slow motion and in such a way as to maximize the visual power of the image. In particular, in Lucio Fulci's *Don't Torture a Duckling*, Don Alberto's fall is not only in slow motion, but Fulci includes insert shots of the physical trauma the killer's face receives by smashing into the cliff's rocks on his way down. At times, Don Alberto's face seems to positively explode as his head grazes the cliff face.

These falls are given tremendous amounts of on-screen time, so they must have some meaning beyond just narrative closure. Perhaps reading a lapsarian metaphor into them is excessive, but the films seem to welcome such analysis.

Killers might also die by being stabbed, shot, immolated, drowned, or even slashed to ribbons by an angry chimpanzee armed with a straight razor, as in the finale to Argento's *Phenomena*. Significantly, as a slasher film, Michele Soavi's *Stagefright* features the film's killer, Irving Wallace (Clain Parker), killed three times—falling from a theatrical scaffold, being immolated, and then finally shot. But unlike slasher films, where the killer keeps getting up and advancing on the final girl, most *giallo* killers are given a single death. I will discuss the differences between the slasher film and the *giallo* in chapter 10, with particular attention to *Stagefright* as an Italian *slasher* film, rather than *giallo*.

Some *giallo* killers would rather commit suicide than permit the amateur detective, or worse, the police, either to take them in or have the satisfaction of a clean kill. *Giallo* killers have been known to deliberately drive their cars into trucks (in Argento's *Four Flies on Grey Velvet*); throw themselves off of high buildings or cliffs (but still echoing the lapsarian imagery noted previously—as in Bido's *The Bloodstained Shadow*, Freda's *The Iguana with a Tongue of Fire*, or in Martino's *Next!*); shoot themselves in the head (in Dallamano's *Solange*); or even asphyxiate themselves with cyanide gas (in Bergonzelli's *In the Folds of the Flesh*). Many Italian filmmakers also tend to play with irony in killing off their *gialli* villains by having them killed accidentally, such as in a car accident (Lenzi's *Paranoia*), accidentally shot (Bava's *Bay of Blood*), hit by a bus (Mogherini's *The Pyjama Girl Case*), garroted with their own necklace (Argento's *Deep Red*), or even impaled on a piece of modern art (Argento's *Tenebre*).

And some killers, rather than shuffling off this mortal coil, simply shuffle off to prison, or get packed into an insane asylum. In the more cynical films of this genre, a few killers even manage to get away with their crimes (Avati's *The House with Laughing Windows*, Lado's *The Short Night of Glass Dolls*, and Lenzi's *Spasmo*). But these last examples are very rare.

Conclusions

As Jacqueline Reich was quoted earlier, some *giallo* killers suffer from gender confusion or are uncomfortable with their sexuality because of it being considered deviant within Italian modernity. But although sexually ambiguous killers appear in *giallo* cinema, their overall percentage is relatively small. These killers may appear in the genre's more famous examples, or are examples that are more useful in certain types of critical analysis, but the sexually confused *giallo* killer is a frequent, but by no means *typical*, character.

What is typical is some past trauma or event that warps the killer's mind. While much psychoanalytic hay might be made from how these films recognize the popular Freudian perspective on the significance of one's early childhood shaping adult behavior, and while such theories are popular enough to be potentially recognized by the films' vernacular audiences, I remain unconvinced the audiences would actually care about such motivations.

The recognition of past trauma on the contemporary Italian psyche is perhaps more fruitful to consider. Let us remind ourselves that these movies are thirty to forty years old now, made (predominantly) in the early 1970s. The characters are approximately in their thirties and forties, which means the characters would have been born between 1930 and 1950.[7] If the past trauma these films' killers experienced was in childhood, or experienced by their parents, doing the math, we find they are traumas occurring during World War II under Mussolini's Fascist rule. The films' audiences are likely to be approximately the same age as the characters, so they either would have had early childhood memories of the war or been more than familiar with their parents' experiences. Are these films reflecting the more cultural explanation of 1970s Italian disassociation resulting from fascism, military defeat (consider how many of the audience members or their parents would have been soldiers during the war), and postwar reconstruction? The war receives explicit mention in only one *giallo*, Bido's *The Cat's Victims*, and that film's killer, the son of a Jewish man seeking revenge on those who denounced his father, is hard to condemn.[8] While the film clearly states a "murder is wrong" moral message (the denounced Jew got his own revenge by becoming a judge and selecting these neighbors for jury duty on the case of Pasquale Ferrante, where he was satisfied that those who had handed him over to the Nazis had lived pathetic and sad lives ever since), the reason for the murders is almost noble. Bido's film makes explicit what the other *gialli* imply: that the real past trauma is not about fathers raising daughters to be boys or watching your brother fall to his death trying to rescue a little girl's doll or even witnessing your crazy mother kill your father. The real past trauma is a historical one: the defeat and emasculation of Italy in the war and under fascism. And this trauma has been haunting Italians ever since.

Notes

1. This argument is based on the Whorf-Sapir thesis, which argues that language and culturally based ideas are inherently linked. Should a concept be significant

enough to be important to a culture, the language will have a word for it. In reverse, since there is no word in Italian for "serial killer" or "serial murder," then, based on the Whorf-Sapir thesis, the concept is of little relevance to the culture.

2. It is worth noting here that in the early 1990s, an Italian black comedy was produced about the Italian response to serial murder. *Il Mostro* (Roberto Benigni, 1994) is essentially about a wrong man accused of being a notorious serial rapist and murderer, played, of course, by Benigni himself.

3. Of course there are *crime* novels about serial killers, but these tend to be more police procedurals than classic detective stories, which focus on the private investigation of a crime, as I discussed in chapter 5.

4. First donned in *Friday the 13th Part 3* (Steve Miner, 1982) and worn ever since.

5. Bava's *Blood and Black Lace* was the first *giallo* to do this, but Argento also availed himself of the wide-brimmed hat in *The Bird with the Crystal Plumage*. So too did Cavara (*The Black Belly of the Tarantula*), Dallamano (*A Black Veil for Lisa*), Lado (*Who Saw Her Die?*) and Lenzi (*Seven Blood Stained Orchids*).

6. Although in many of Agatha Christie's novels the action is perpetuated with further murders in order to cover up the initial crime, much like these *gialli* do. Her novel *Death on the Nile* (1937) immediately springs to mind as an example.

7. If one consults the Internet Movie Database (www.imdb.com) for information on the various actors in these films, we find they were also born in this twenty-year period.

8. Marcia Landy noted another significant Jewish representation in *giallo* cinema, in Argento's *Deep Red*: "Parallel to the 'primal' scene of murder (a reversal of the child as victim), but contributing to the problematic of understanding what is seen, are the discovery that Helga was Jewish (as we learn from her funeral, where the mourners recite Kaddish). . . . In the case of Helga's death and the discovery of her Jewishness, the spectator is invited to make comparisons between these murders and the destruction of the Jews in the Holocaust" (2000: 358). While Helga's Jewishness is indeed odd insofar as it does not seem to serve any narrative or thematic purpose, I am not as convinced of the Holocaust echoes in this film as Landy is; I think the explicit Holocaust reference in *The Cat's Victims* is a much stronger argument.

CHAPTER SEVEN

~

"Weird Science of the Most Egregious Kind": The Ambivalence of Belief in the *Giallo* Film

In this chapter I wish to consider how the *giallo* manipulates folk superstitions and demonstrates modernity's ambivalence toward more traditional belief traditions. The directors discussed here evoke echoes of traditional folk beliefs in order to create some vague and inchoate verisimilitude with the traditions of their audiences. The films resonate with folklore the audience may have heard before, rooting the horror/mystery narrative within some reality for them. Other *gialli* feature urban legend material regarding certain contemporary scientific beliefs. These treatments of legend also demonstrate a certain amount of ambivalence toward modernity.

Superstitions

The word "superstition" should raise a red flag for scholars because the term can have pejorative associations: one's own belief is often regarded as the "truth," while someone else's belief is thought to be less well founded, less rational—and therefore "superstitious." That said, I am consciously using the term here to be provocative, in part because the way in which these films present traditional belief systems counter to a hegemonic Italian Catholicism implies their being perceived as "superstitions" by the filmmakers. These "non-canonical" belief systems, it is presumed, reflect the sensibilities of the films' vernacular audiences (Pratt 1996). But more specifically, I am using the term "superstition" to denote an ambivalence toward some kind of foreign belief tradition, be it foreign in spatial terms (from a cultural and geographical

111

Other) or temporal terms (from a perceived "older" tradition, but still adhered to). This is the sort of superstition portrayed in these films.

Consider Lucio Fulci's *Don't Torture a Duckling* from a slightly alternate perspective. Recall that in this film the young boys of an Apulian village are being systematically murdered by the local parish priest, who is trying to prevent them from being corrupted by encroaching modernity, symbolized by the elevated motorway that literally cuts through the pastoral and bucolic landscape, as well as graphically across the cinema screen, exemplified by the very first shot of the film. It begins as an establishing shot on a rural mountainside, panning left while zooming into the motorway that slices through both the terrain and the image. Throughout the opening sequence, Fulci juxtaposes the motorway, symbolic of modernity's presence, with traditional folkways. First we see the local witch, Maciara, disinterring the skeletal remains of an infant, and then one of the local boys, disenfranchised and bored, firing a slingshot at a sunning lizard. Both of these actions are set contextually *beside* the new motorway, the modern and the traditional, existing uncomfortably side by side. Later on, and throughout the first half of the film, we see Maciara fashioning dark figurines of young boys out of (what we later learn to be) black wax and inserting pins into them. The audience is given no explanation for either the disinterred remains or the black voodoo-like figures until Maciara is completely exonerated for the crimes.

Until Maciara is arrested and charged with the murders, the film literally denies her a voice; we have only these enigmatic outward behaviors, keying us to interpret her actions as suspicious. It is when the "Law of the Father," the police, demand an explanation of what she was doing that we first hear her speak and give her own account. We are presented with Maciara's actions, specifically the creation of her little voodoo dolls, as directly linked to the boys' deaths. We know she is suspicious because we saw her disinter the remains of a baby—again with no explanation offered. Fulci's film suggests that *we*, the presumably technologically adept modern audience, immediately view with suspicion that of which we are denied an explanation. We are positioned by the film to view, again with suspicion, religious practices that seem "foreign" to us or different; it is not what the audience might recognize as religion, an increasingly myopic category within predominantly Roman Catholic southern rural Italy. But up until the time of these murders, Maciara has lived unperturbed within the village setting, or at least on its outskirts as a liminal figure. Pierre Sorlin also noted a similar dynamic: "In many parts of the peninsula, especially in the countryside, the old ways survived well into the twentieth century, but cinema contributed to estranging people from habits they themselves still observed" (1996: 4). Modernity,

Fulci's film suggests, has the ability to take us to remote regions of the country to experience the folkways of rural Apulia, but while doing so, it presents those traditions suspiciously. Nevertheless, as suspicious as Maciara may be, it is the local representative of the Catholic Church who is the real killer: an ambivalent perspective to be sure.

Sergio Martino's *All the Colors of the Dark* is similarly ambivalent. Jane Harrison (Edwige Fenech) and her common-law husband, Richard (George Hilton), are drawn into a world of cult activity after they have survived a car accident in which Jane lost their unborn baby. The film depicts paganism as something inherently evil and dangerous. In one sequence, which we are not sure is an "actual" ritual or a hallucination of Jane's, we see the coven leader (Julian Ugarte) sacrifice a puppy before forcing Jane to drink its still-warm blood; the cruelty here becomes an icon of evil. The cult's lieutenant, Mark (Ivan Rassimov), a man with piercing, wolflike eyes, murders three people who attempt to take Jane from the coven, stabbing them with a ceremonial dagger. This depiction of witchcraft is typical of the horror film. But it is the actions of Jane's partner, Richard, that begin to complicate the presumed polarity between "good, normal people" and "evil, wicked Satanists": in protecting Jane and himself from the coven's evil clutches, he murders just as many people as Mark. Richard kills Mark with a pitchfork, shoots Jane's sister Barbara (Susan Scott) dead for also being a member of the coven, and ends up pushing the coven leader off the roof. If Richard kills just as many people as the coven does, what is the difference between the two? It is true that Richard does not torture puppies, but he is having an affair with Barbara while her sister is recovering from losing *their* baby, and then he ends that relationship by shooting her. The film vilifies witchcraft as an evil practice, but the actions of the supposedly heroic characters undercut that moral certainty.

There is less ambiguity in Aldo Lado's *The Short Night of Glass Dolls*, which features a clearly evil Satanic sex cult that abducts and then murders beautiful young women in Communist Prague. Here the ambivalence between two equally repressive political systems, the capitalist West and the Soviet occupation after 1968, is exemplified by Club 99, a secret society that boasts members from all corners of the Prague elite—legislative, judiciary, and executive. What is particularly significant here, however, is the address to a supernatural agency in Club 99's organization; the film notes that "99" in numerological traditions has a particular power, and that within the coded registers of "black magic" denotes "Amen." While much of this is contrived nonsense, Lado has picked up on certain traditional threads within numerological belief, namely the idea that formulaic numbers have some kind of power.[1] Lado's appeal to the supernatural dimension can be regarded as one part generic convention (in a horror movie) and one part further vilification of the Soviet expansion into Eastern Europe, by claiming for the "Evil Empire" a sort of demonic inspiration. This is further supported by the villains of the film; all the members of Club 99 are the elite of Prague, and neither the people living under Soviet rule nor those idealist Western Communists and socialists who came east to work (like the film's hero, Gregory Moore (Jean Sorel), a left-wing American journalist) are to blame for the corruption. What is significant about *The Short Night of Glass Dolls* is the ambivalence of the ending: the members of Club 99 are neither caught nor punished, for all the agencies that could punish them are controlled by Club 99 members and executives.

Other kinds of supernatural and superstitious belief traditions exist within the margins of *gialli* cinema. Spiritualism, for example, occurs in both Dario Argento's *Deep Red* and Mario Bava's *Hatchet for the Honeymoon*. Linked with these examples is a later film, *Phenomena*, in which Argento explores issues of telepathy (in this case between humans and insects) as well as somnambulism. What these examples demonstrate is that despite the murder mystery's rational, Cartesian approach to detection, at the periphery the *giallo* recognizes the existence of nonrational traditions of belief as well.

Other superstitions appearing in *giallo* films include those that the murderer himself adheres to. So, for example, in Luigi Bazzoni's *The Fifth Cord*, the murders are determined by astrology; in Armando Crispino's *Autopsy*, the murders are linked to sunspot activity; and in Mario Bava's *Kill, Baby . . . Kill!* the deaths are a result of a ghostly apparition. Still other superstitions lurk incidentally in these films, such as the belief that *Macbeth* (whether Shakespeare's play or Verdi's opera) is cursed, featured in Dario Argento's *Opera*, or the belief that photography steals one's soul, which appears in Riccardo Freda's *The Wailing*.

Lucio Fulci's *The Black Cat* and Mario Bava's *Kill, Baby . . . Kill!* directly foreground the *giallo*'s tension between science and superstition, although they are *giallo-fantastico*. The Mario Bava film appears to fit into the supernatural/Gothic tradition (as a ghost story), while its narrative structure and ambivalent themes seem to put it into the *giallo filone*. Again, although I have discussed this film earlier, it is worth considering it in light of this current discussion about belief. Dr. Eswai demands a more rational explanation for these mysterious deaths and sets out to discover what is "really" going on. On the surface, this appears to be almost a reversal of Conan Doyle's *The Hound of the Baskervilles*, because the events in the village deny a scientifically rational explanation: it *is* a ghost that *does* compel those who see her to commit suicide. Instead of the villagers putting aside their superstitious beliefs in favor of rationalism, the voices of modernity—Dr. Eswai and his medical assistant/lover Monica (Erika Blanc)—come away from the village profoundly touched by the supernatural. Certainly Bava's film demonstrates a different kind of ambivalence than the other films, and (at least according to Bava fans) indicates the director's sense of humor in reversing expectations like this, and yet this film is the most rooted within an actual folk tradition.[2]

Fulci's film, on the other hand, attempts to fuse the scientific with the superstitious: Professor Robert Miles (Patrick McGee) attempts to tape record voices "scientifically" from beyond the grave in order to prove the existence of life after death. Despite the film's depiction of rational explanation of paranormal events, it also presents the folk belief that cats can control (or at least influence) human thought. These films, and to some extent Fulci's *Don't Torture a Duckling*, foreground the debate between the rational, modern science, and the superstitions of "folk belief," but none of these films takes a predetermined position on either side. Instead, they pose an ambivalence regarding these "superstitions," indicating that, while fewer and fewer people may believe in them, they continue to persist, and sometimes they may even be right.

Talismans and Lucky Charms

In a different way, Aldo Lado's *Who Saw Her Die?* offers another perspective on the ambivalence toward belief. Franco's search for the person who abducted and murdered his daughter Roberta reveals, like a number of *gialli*, that the killer is a psychotic priest. Notably, despite Franco's modernist and secular lifestyle, the daughter wears a zodiac pendant that acts as a good luck charm. The killer's first attempt at abducting either Roberta or her playmate is averted by the sudden appearance of the other girl's mother, who also takes Roberta home. During this sequence, the zodiac pendant hangs conspicuously around Roberta's neck. Only after the other neighborhood children steal Roberta's good luck pendent is the killer able to abduct her.

While there is no indication that Lado actually believes in the agency of good luck charms and pendants, it is a significant motif to include. In the rational Cartesian worldview these films espouse, luck or talismans may seem to have no place; and yet it is more than coincidental that Roberta is abducted moments after her pendant is lost. Just as Fulci is equally suspicious toward both traditional folk beliefs and the Catholic Church, Lado is not entirely willing to discount more traditional belief systems in favor of modernity. The *giallo* cinema in general tends to reject a simplistic Manichean distinction between traditional belief and modernism; it invokes, instead, a more ambivalent position.

Other lucky charms make an occasional guest appearance in *gialli* cinema. In Riccardo Freda's *The Wailing*, the heroine is protected against murder by wearing the "Seal of Solomon," the only talisman, the film tells us, powerful enough to ward off black magic. Interestingly, this talisman is the six-pointed Star of David, indicating perhaps a conflation of magic with Judaism and thereby exoticizing "the Jewish Other." Helga Ulmann (Macha Méril), in Argento's *Deep Red*, is less lucky; although she owns a table decorated with this symbol, she is still murdered by the killer. (Perhaps she should have been wearing the talisman rather than using it as a coffee table.) Max Lindt (Robert Hoffmann) in Massimo Dallamano's *A Black Veil for Lisa* has his own personal lucky charm—a silver dollar that stopped a bullet fired at him—and like little Roberta in *Who Saw Her Die?* Max is untouchable until he loses the talisman, after which things go awry for him.

As with the numerological suggestions in *The Short Night of Glass Dolls*, many of the talismans are used by the filmmakers as signifiers of guilt or evil. In Martino's *All the Colors of the Dark*, Barbara is discovered as belonging to a coven by her tattoo of the cult's cabalistic symbol, which initiates use as a form of protection. The tattoo does not protect her, however, as Robert, the film's protagonist, shoots her dead upon the discovery. Umberto Lenzi also employs the talisman as a signifier of guilt in *Seven Blood Stained Orchids*. In this film, the killer leaves a crescent-shaped medallion in the hand of all of his victims as a calling card. But Elena (Rossella Falk) recognizes the medallion, and thereby is able to identify the killer to the film's amateur detective Mario.

Pseudoscience and Urban Legends

As some *giallo* films evoke echoes of traditional folk belief, so others feature material from urban legends. Though employed differently, the legends also demonstrate a certain amount of ambivalence toward modernity. Consider again Armando Crispino's *Autopsy*. A period of intense sunspot activity (the literal translation of the Italian title, *Macchie solari*, is "sunspots") is the reason given for a rash of suicides around Rome, but it is actually a natural cover for Edgar (Ray Lovelock) to kill anyone who stands in the way of his inheriting a small fortune, including his sometime girlfriend, Simona (Mimsy Farmer), a pathology student. It is her research into faked suicides (murders made to look like suicides)—and their accompanying forensic evidence—that gives Edgar the idea of using the atmospheric phenomenon as cover. The legend pattern that the narrative takes, using the core belief as the backdrop, if not creative impetus, is typical in *giallo* cinema.

In 1971 Dario Argento produced two films, both built with components of legend. The legend material emerges at the denouement of the films, rather than at the beginning, in keeping with the murder mystery tradition.[3] The final clues are embedded in the legend itself, which enables the amateur detective to solve the mystery.

Released first, *Cat O' Nine Tails* tells a convoluted tale of murder and blackmail around a science institute that is currently working on genetic research into the relationship between the double Y chromosome and criminality. The killer in the film, Dr. Casoni (Aldo Reggiani), has this double Y chromosome and, in order to protect his reputation, murders anyone who discovers his secret. Within the popular discourse of the late 1960s and early 1970s, an extra Y chromosome was thought to be linked to criminality, and this is the cultural environment in which *Cat O' Nine Tails* was produced. As this is the final key to the solution of the mystery (the motive for the murders themselves), the belief is unquestioned in the film. The link between double Y and criminality has long been discredited, although it occurs in film again as late as the 1990s in the science fiction sequel *Alien*[3] (David Fincher, 1992), in which Ripley crash-lands on a penal colony designed specifically for "double Y" chromosome inmates.

Argento's second film appearing in 1971 is the provocatively titled *Four Flies on Grey Velvet*. In this picture, a rock musician, Roberto Tobias (Michael Brandon), is attacked by an old man, and in defending himself, he inadvertently stabs the elderly fellow. Believing himself to be a murderer, Roberto runs home, but over the next couple of days photographs keep appearing in his house documenting the event. As Roberto attempts to decipher the circumstances, more murders occur. The only clue is lifted off the retina of one of the victims: as folklore tells us, the last thing a person sees before he dies (particularly if murdered) is forever imprinted on the retina. In *Four Flies*, forensic science has progressed to the point that science can now lift those images photographically. And off of this victim the police are able to lift an image that looks like the titular four flies on a gray background. As the police are trying to interpret the image, Roberto meets up with his wife, Nina (Mimsy Farmer), who is wearing an odd piece of jewelry—a medallion made of a fly encased in clear plastic—which would have been swinging from side to side when she was stabbing the victim.

These two Argento films integrate fragments of urban legends into their plots, but the question remains as to *how* Argento uses them. Insight into this creative process comes from Argento's close collaborator on the two screenplays and fellow exploitation filmmaker, Luigi Cozzi. In Maitland McDonagh's *Broken Mirrors/Broken Minds*, Cozzi is quoted as noting that the double

Y chromosome storyline was influenced by a British film called *Twisted Nerve* (Roy Boulting, 1968), which explores the link between Down syndrome and criminality (1994: 66). Although Cozzi remembers the double Y plot deriving from *Twisted Nerve*, the link is a vague connection between genetics and criminality. More likely, the plot was inspired by popular scientific discourse at the time. Since then, McDonagh recognizes, the connections have been deemed tenuous at best, a fact reflected in the comments of Rose, Kamin, and Lewontin in *Not in Our Genes: Biology, Ideology and Human Nature*:

> Males who carry an extra Y (XYY) have sometimes been described as "supermales," and efforts have been made to prove that they have higher levels of "male" hormones or are unusually aggressive or criminally inclined. Despite a flurry of enthusiasm for such claims in the late sixties and early seventies, they are now generally discounted. (1984: 50)

However, Cozzi remembers much more clearly the plot genesis for *Four Flies*, a direct link to popular scientific beliefs of the time:

> Cozzi also claims that the idea for the camera that photographs the last image on the dead woman's eye came from a newspaper account. Though the superstitious notion that dead man's eyes can convict a murderer was popular in the 19th century and survived into the early 20th (leading some Depression-era gangsters to shoot out their victims' eyes), it's weird science of the most egregious kind. (McDonagh 1994: 77)

Popular scientific theories circulated by news media (of all descriptions) often unintentionally propagate components of contemporary legends (see Oring 1990 and Smith 1990). Crispino's *Autopsy* is another case in point. The news media published stories regarding the connection between sunspot activity and, if not suicides, at least bizarre human behavior. Crispino himself confirms this:

> The sunspot idea came from a newspaper article that I noticed together with the scriptwriter, Lucio Battistrada. It was about an increase in apparently inexplicable suicides which all happened together during the summer, but which in reality were caused by a strange solar phenomenon that produced paratoxic reactions in psychologically vulnerable individuals. We researched this strange phenomenon in the press and decided to write a story about it, partly because it meant that we could use the unusual background of Rome in summer, which is fascinating in a thriller. It was that phenomenon that decided the setting and around this setting we built the story around the character of a young nurse working in a mortuary. (quoted in Palmerini and Mistretta 1996: 39)

Cozzi's comments about the two Argento films, and Crispino's regarding *Autopsy*, reveal the popular newspaper as a source for film stories, or at least the ideas behind those stories. Crispino, significantly I think, notes that the "research" he did for this film was "in the press," unproblematically accepting newspapers as an infallible source of information. And, as I noted above, newspapers often (unintentionally) circulate urban legends; that is, urban legends often appear in newspapers as news, the reporters seemingly unaware that these stories are legends. Horror cinema, however, has long had a tradition of drawing its inspirations from newspaper reports. Cynthia Freeland noted in reference to the slasher film that

> the ties between fact and fiction have become increasingly intricate and ramified. The fictions of *The Silence of the Lambs*, a story about a cannibalistic killer . . . based partly on Ed Gein,[4] permeated media coverage of the arrest of cannibalistic serial killer Jeffrey Dahmer; publicity over Dahmer's arrest in its turn threatened the box-office take and opening date of the horror film *Body Parts*. Like these movies, other horror-film stories may begin in the newspapers and then move swiftly on to Hollywood and contracts and major motion pictures. (2000: 162)

Italian horror cinema, particularly when the genre was in such high demand to supply the *terza visione* theaters, likewise looked to the newspapers for its inspiration.

Although released in Britain and North America with the title *Torso*, throughout Continental Europe the film was either known by the Italian title *I Corpi presentano tracce di violenza carnale* or abbreviated outside of Italy and anglicized as *Carnal Violence*. The 1973 trailer for the film throughout the Continent reflects this use of newspaper-circulated urban legendry as plot devices for the films. The extent to which *Torso/Carnal Violence* explicitly employs legend texts is slim, and it really only picks up on popular psychological terms such as "psychosexual killer." But the graphics of this exclusively European trailer imply a "ripped from today's headlines" story. The fonts and graphic design used for the cast members' names, as well as the title of the film itself, mimic typical newspaper-style fonts, in photographic negative, suggesting that these graphics were taken from microfilmed newspaper archives. Much like the other *gialli* that use echoes of traditional folk beliefs, these "newspaper legend" films are intended to resonate with the audience's sense of verisimilitude—suggesting that they too may have read, or otherwise heard about, actual events similar to those in the films. The graphic images of the European trailer for *Carnal Violence* merely reflect this conceit.

Aldo Lado's *Glass Dolls*, again, concludes with an urban legend motif: the film begins with Moore's presumably dead body being found. The journalist is not dead, but totally paralyzed through hypnosis, although his brain is very much awake. *Glass Dolls* charts Moore's attempts to reconstruct the events that brought him to this position and his attempts to prove to the attending doctors and pathologists that he really is alive. The film concludes with Moore on the autopsy table of an anatomy class, about to be surgically cut into, when he finally regains movement of his right hand and signals to the pathologist (Fabijan Sovagovic), whom he remembers from Club 99. The pathologist recognizes Moore, and in noticing that he is alive, proceeds quickly with the dissection. The "buried alive" legend here mutates into a more contemporary form, about a cadaver coming alive in the dissecting room tale.[5]

The final identifiable urban legend text in *giallo* cinema is a variation on those stories circulating about "snuff" movies, which purportedly document actual murder on camera. Unlike some of the *mondo*-like shockumentary movies, such as the infamous *Faces of Death* (John Alan Schwartz, 1978), wherein actual documentary sequences of people being killed are presented for audience enjoyment, snuff movies are murders orchestrated specifically *for* the camera. While there are a number of films *about* snuff movies, and one fallaciously purported film, this is not an area that *giallo* cinema has tended to explore. Perhaps the reason is purely chronological: Snuff movies entered the popular culture arena late in the 1970s, with the release of *Snuff* (Michael Findlay, Roberta Findlay, and Horacio Fredriksson, 1976). The film is an attempt to cash in on these legends by amending a faux-snuff coda to a cheaply acquired South American exploitation film, and then trying to pass it off as authentic. The point is that the controversy surrounding snuff movies, particularly in the wake of the limited release of *Snuff*, was too late in the *giallo* cycle to get picked up, because most Italian exploitation film-makers had moved into other realms of horror by then. One potential variant does emerge, however, with Pupi Avati's *The House with Laughing Windows*. In the film, Stefano is brought to a tiny island village to restore and complete a fresco depicting the death of Saint Sebastian begun in the fascist period. Stefano comes to discover that what he is working on is in fact a "snuff painting"; the artist's two deranged sisters would acquire victims to be murdered and then the artist himself would paint them in their death throes. The timing of Avati's film coincides with the appearance of *Snuff* in 1976, so the echoes may be intentional. By changing the artistic medium from film-making to painting (specifically fresco painting), Avati seems to be suggesting that regardless of the presumed contemporary nature of these snuff stories, they are—anachronistically—as old as Italy's artistic traditions.

Conclusions

In the same way that *giallo* films present an ambivalent perspective toward traditional folk beliefs, other *gialli* present ambivalent perspectives toward the beliefs embedded in modern legends—specifically those found in contemporary scientific legends. But, for scholars of urban legends, this should not come as any surprise, because the legend is an inherently ambivalent genre. As Robert Georges's oft-cited definition of legend posits:

> A legend is a story or narrative that may not be a story or narrative at all; it is set in the recent or historical past that may be conceived to be remote or antihistorical or not really past at all; it is believed to be true by some, false by others, and both or neither by most. (1971: 18)

Inherent here is the recognition of the genre's ambivalence. The meaning of a legend lies less in the actual text itself than in the metatextual discussion that any legend text immediately provokes (Oring 1986: 125). The *giallo* films work similarly, particularly with regard to issues of belief: both modern science and traditional belief traditions are held up with ambivalence, begging for discussion among audience members, after the film has ended.

Notes

1. Stith Thompson noted that this motif occurred frequently and significantly enough to warrant it a unique entry in his *Motif-Index* (motif Z71.6). The number nine, he observes, is particularly powerful in numerological belief traditions (Thompson 1955–1958).

2. Thompson includes this motif, "Ghost leads people to commit suicide" (E266.2). However, he notes its origin as American rather than Italian or German (Thompson 1955–1958).

3. I would refer to such a narrative structure as a "resultant narrative," wherein the film leads up to the revelation of the legend being told (see Koven 2002).

4. On this point, Freeland herself falls victim to the confusion between fact and fiction as reported in the newspapers and general knowledge within popular culture: the connection between *Silence of the Lambs* and the true-crime story of Ed Gein has nothing to do with Hannibal Lector's taste for human flesh, but Buffalo Bill's creation of a "woman-suit" made from the skin of dead women. It has never been proven that Gein was a cannibal, but that idea and belief circulates in rumor, legend, joke, and other forms of oral folklore.

5. Barbara Mikkelson (1999) gives a lengthy description of various cases of someone being buried alive, including a few reviving on the dissection table.

CHAPTER EIGHT

~

"A Perverse Sublime": Excess and the Set Piece in the *Giallo*

So far, this book has explored the *giallo* predominantly within the context of popular (vernacular) crime cinema—looking at these films as murder mysteries and detective stories. But the vast majority of fans of Italian *gialli* are not aficionados of Agatha Christie and Edgar Wallace (although some may be), but fans of gory horror cinema. The dominant feature that separates the *giallo* film from more traditional murder mysteries and detective cinema is the focus, within these movies, on the murders themselves, which I have already discussed. These murder sequences are often protracted, longer than they need be to further the plot alone, and act as spectacles in themselves. Considering that the *terza visione* audience for these films is less likely to be interested in following a complex and literary-modeled mystery plot than the graphic sequences of gore and sex, this chapter will consider those sequences themselves within the context of horror cinema. This requires a slight change in analytical tack, moving away from the discourses of mystery or thriller cinema to horror. This chapter will attempt to theorize what these (predominantly) gory "set pieces" mean beyond an overly simplistic sense of "thrill seeking" for the working-class audiences that tend to consume these pictures.[1]

In a highly influential article, Linda Williams considered the cognitive category commonly referenced as "gross." Williams noted that the term "gross" cuts across genres: it can refer to gory horror films, emotional melodramas, or romantic/sexual moments in films (1999: 701). It is malleable insofar as, while it exists as a cognitive, that is understood, category of meaning (we know what is meant when something is referred to as "gross"), that understanding is heavily informed by the generic context we initially know the film to be situated within. While there is no reason why an actor like Bette Midler could not be in a horror film that features extensive sequences of gory carnage, should we be told that the new Midler movie is "gross," we would tend to assume the grossness comes from its melodramatic and emotionally overwrought content, rather than the promise of any exploding head sequence. Likewise, one would not tend to assume that a new George A. Romero movie identified as "gross" would feature extensive emotional sequences.

Williams goes on to explore what the notion of "gross" has in common across these three uses—horror, melodrama, and sexuality.

> Alone or in combination, heavy doses of sex, violence, and emotion are dismissed by one faction or another as having no logic or reason for existence beyond their power to excite. Gratuitous sex, gratuitous violence and terror, gratuitous emotion are frequent epithets hurled at the phenomenon of the "sensational" in pornography, horror, and melodrama. (1999: 702)

This "excitation" of the spectator—to sexual arousal, nausea, or tears—is partially to account for other, related, negative epithets hurled at such films and film genres (in Williams's argument, she is referring to the melodrama, horror, and pornography simultaneously), such as being "manipulative" or as "lowest in cultural esteem" (1999: 703). Within Williams's argument, the emotional "excitation" of the spectators is (implied to be) a direct reflection of their identified surrogate on-screen (cf. Mulvey 1999). Williams continued:

> I suggest, however, that the film genres that have had especially low cultural status—which have seemed to exist as excesses to the system of even the popular genres—are not simply those which sensationally display bodies on the screen and register effects in the bodies of spectators. Rather what may especially mark these body genres as low is the *perception* that the body of the spectator is caught up in an almost involuntary mimicry of the emotion or sensation of the body on the screen. (Williams 1999: 704; emphasis added)

While Williams is less direct in her assumptions about audience mimesis than Mulvey, there is still a sense that direct connections between on-screen action and audience response exist, despite this conclusion being slightly ameliorated by her use of the word "perception," that such a connection *could be perceived*. This connection between the screen action and the audience is further underscored in Williams's discussion of those moments when audience "mimicry" is denied, specifically in comedy films. Williams noted "[gross-out comedies have] not been deemed gratuitously excessive, probably because the reaction of the audience does not mimic the sensations experienced by the central clown" (Williams 1999: 704). In other words, in comedies those "gross" filmic moments when the affect is parodied—bodily harm, arousal, or emotion—are distanced by the comedic frame, whereby the spectator is invited to laugh *at*, rather than identify *with*, the on-screen action.[2] But how do we know when the frame is intended to distance the audience (i.e., to be laughed at) or for mimesis (i.e., to be moved by the on-screen action)? Williams does not address this question. Stephen Thrower noted, in what could be considered a retort to Williams:

> There are all sorts of ways in which fans are prevailed upon, but the surrounding discourses hostile to the genre, to assert that the very scenes they so like in these films don't really work, don't really disturb, or shock, or don't require us to take them seriously. Thus, fans might start to mutter about the unconvincing special effects, the bad dubbing, the cheesy music, the less than serious acting, or whatever. (1999: 154)

Within her analysis, the context of *all* horror films is to "frighten," just as all pornography is to arouse, and all melodrama is to evoke emotion. Such essentialism breaks down in the face of the *giallo* film; how do we know if the murders, particularly the outlandish and over-the-top murders in some of these films, are meant to evoke terror or distance us?

Williams's argument, provocative though it is, fails to consider the "gross out" on its own terms. The gruesome murders in *giallo* films, as I have argued in a previous chapter, are those moments that are intended to capture the attention of a half-attentive audience. As such, they need to be considered as meaningful on their own. To approach these sequences within an integrated and holistic approach to a specific *giallo* film, as Mendik does with *Tenebre* (2000), is to look for, in Kael's criteria, the logic behind the gore. But such an approach violates the basic demands of vernacular cinema. How can we approach these sequences on their own terms, without contextualizing them within the film as a whole?

The Set Piece

To return to Jonathan Rosenbaum's review of *Torso*, which I discussed in chapter 2, he recognized that attempting to impose classical models of narrative on this film was redundant, since it consciously eschewed such logic and was designed to give the audience what the filmmakers thought was wanted from vernacular horror cinema—beautiful women in various stages of undress, graphic violence and dismemberment, gratuitous lesbian sex scenes, and a basic plot on which to hang these grotesque show-stoppers. L. A. Morse, as a token example of fan-writing on vernacular cinema, echoed Rosenbaum's view, seeing these films as centered on a movement from one sequence of graphic violence or sex to another. What both of these critical approaches have in common is recognizing that vernacular cinema audiences do not necessarily watch (or want to watch) movies as a classically integrated whole, but are sufficiently entertained by a series of graphic "set pieces."

Within the context of Italian horror cinema, Donato Totaro defined what a set piece is:

> A set-piece is a choreographed scene that usually, though not exclusively, takes place in one location. By an "elaborate" set-piece, I mean a situation or set of actions where narrative function . . . gives way to "spectacle." In other words, the scene plays on far longer than what is strictly necessary for the narrative purpose. (2003: 162)

Italian horror films, not just *giallo*, are notorious for their graphic and "elaborate" set pieces, to appropriate Totaro's term. In part, this is what separates them from other kinds of horror cinema, a seemingly irreverent attitude toward "the logic behind the gore," to pick up again on Kael's phrase. Totaro continued:

> This manner of set-piece typifies an aspect of the transformation that perhaps best differentiates the Italian horror film from its American counterpart, which is more character-based, plot-driven and attentive to verisimilitude. The focus on spectacle as a mode of entertainment often comes at the expense of narrative coherency and characterization, but is a conscious decision based on many varied factors (economic, aesthetic and stylistic). Therefore, when mainstream critics complain about the "weak" narratives in Italian horror films, they are missing the point. (2003: 163)

Cynthia Freeland goes so far as to argue that by stopping the plot these set pieces demand that the audiences of graphic horror pause and consider the sublime beauty and power of cinema itself (echoing Pasolini's cinema of poetry, which I discuss in chapter 9) (2000: 256).

Here I want to consider the set piece as an integral aspect to the rhetorical discourse of vernacular cinema. Vernacular cinema, as has been noted, needs to periodically grab its audience's attention, and one of the main ways this is done is through these set pieces. The problem is, as evidenced by the bourgeois reviews that criticize these films for being too dependent on spectacle at the expense of plot, we lack a critical vocabulary for dealing with these sequences *apart* from their integrated narrative whole—and as Totaro noted above, such a separation needs to be made.

One way of approaching an understanding of the set piece, and by extension, better understanding vernacular cinema, comes from a (presumably) flippant comment by Kim Newman who refers to the set pieces in the films of Dario Argento as being akin to musical numbers (1988: 107). Newman goes so far as to refer to Argento as the Vincente Minnelli of horror, rather than Alfred Hitchcock or Fritz Lang, to whom he is more frequently compared (Newman 1988: 107; Hunt 2000: 330–31).[3] Newman's comments underline a vernacular understanding of the set pieces in vernacular cinema, that they are like unique minimovies within a larger filmic context that break from the diegetic "reality" the plot of the film has so far established.[4] These set-pieces, however, despite their similarity to "numbers" in either pornographic or musical films, also need to conform to Totaro's description above; that is, they are extended pieces of action, usually in one location, and last for longer than is necessary for strictly narrative purposes. These set pieces, like the musical number, are designed to be appreciated in their own right. As Freeland argued,

> Numbers in graphic spectacular horror function in at least three ways: (1) they further the narrative, so part of a film's form or structure; (2) they produce its central emotional and cognitive effects: dread, fear, empathy, awareness of the monster or of evil; and (3) they provide certain aesthetic pleasure that have to do with the audience's knowledge and appreciation of the genre. (2000: 257)

We can divide the various kinds of set pieces into different categories, each of which has its own rhetoric and affect: the suspense sequence, the sex sequence, the violence sequence, and the murder sequence. As noted above, each of these sequences, as set pieces, is held longer than is typically necessary for narrative purposes. Basically, the narrative information they convey is subordinate to the visual pleasure they impart.

First, let us consider the "suspense sequence"; as the description implies, these are sequences constructed around the delayed gratification—sexual or violent—of the promised spectacle. Of course, suspense may be incorporated into other kinds of set pieces as well, particularly in murder sequences before the final gratification of the grisly spectacle. When the sequence promises a gory kill, but delays it for an "extended" period of time, it is what I would call a "suspense set piece." Consider for example the murder of Professor Giordani (Glauco Mauri) in Argento's *Deep Red* (perhaps my personal favorite sequence in all *giallo* cinema): in terms of narrative, Giordani has just discovered the identity of the killer, and is trying to contact Mark to warn him. Giordani is alone at home, putting his evidence together, when the killer strikes. But the sequence is a relatively long one, running for almost five minutes. Argento extends the suspense before Giordani's murder to put the audience on the edge of their seats. We know that Giordani is about to be murdered, not only by understanding the genre's conventions but by how the sequence is keyed.[5] In this sequence, the audience is keyed primarily through Argento's use of sound. The film, in leading up to this set piece, has shifted between Mark's discovery of the child's painting under the villa's crumbling plaster and Giordani attempting to contact the amateur detective with the results of his own investigation. The music for much of this lead-in sequence has been Goblin's *Tubular Bells*–derivative score, but when we enter the suspense set piece that immediately precedes Giordani's death, the nondiegetic soundtrack cuts sharply off and our attention is grabbed by its absence. The sequence is almost silent, apart from the sound of Giordani's quiet footsteps echoing distantly down the corridors as he makes himself a cup of tea and goes back to his desk. On his return, disrupting the eerie quietness of the sequence, a whispering voice calls out, "Giordani." At this moment the nondiegetic soundtrack kicks back in with a driving riff, effectively informing the audience that something is about to happen. Giordani is clearly unnerved by hearing his name called by an unseen person, and he arms himself with a large letter opener, trying to ascertain where the voice was coming from. In a shot-reverse shot, we see Giordani looking anxiously around him, followed by a long shot, from his perspective, of the room out in front of him. With this shot, the music once again cuts off. While up to this point the editing of the sequence has been appropriately rapid, Argento holds this single shot as we wait for the killer to jump out from either edge. Instead, a cupboard opens in the rear of the mise-en-scene and a clockwork doll walks out, laughing maniacally; in fact, it is only the doll's creepy laughter that can be heard on the soundtrack. Giordani strikes out at the doll with his knife, splitting open its head, which continues to move and laugh dementedly. As Giordani strikes at the doll, the music cuts back in, as the killer jumps out from the right, first bashing the professor's mouth on the mantelpiece, then the desk edge, before picking up the letter opener and stabbing him through the neck. The sequence ends as the camera "cranes" up from blood pooling under the desk to the dead face of Giordani. The nondiegetic score does not return until the film finally cuts back to Mark.

As far back as *The Bird with the Crystal Plumage*, Argento has been playing with sound in his set pieces. The attempted murder of Monica Ranieri (Eva Renzi) in the gallery is a case in point. The sequence begins with Sam Dalmas (Tony Musante) happily returning from a meeting with his publisher holding a check large enough to get him home to the States. He is whistling to himself, and except for his footsteps on the empty Roman streets, no other noise is audible. As he passes the Ranieri Gallery, he witnesses what he believes is a murder in progress, and rushes to help. As he is caught between the sliding doors at the front of the gallery, he is effectively cut off—auditorily too: he cannot hear what is going on either in the gallery or on the street, and no one can hear him. Argento plays with the soundtrack reflecting that auditory alienation; characters speaking on the street cannot be heard when the camera is where Sam is diegetically standing.

Another technique of drawing attention to a forthcoming set piece is a visual trope typical in Italian vernacular cinema and often disparaged in non-Italian criticism—the sudden zoom, either in or out on the subject of the shot. In Umberto Lenzi's *Eyeball*, as young Jenny (Verónica Miriel) leaves the flamenco demonstration in the hotel's nightclub, the camera pauses on her and punctuates this shot with a zoom-in to her face. As Jenny has been a minor character until this point, the zoom calls attention to the film's own rhetoric, and when we continue to follow Jenny out of the nightclub and by the swimming pool, we are anticipating an attack. This is further confirmed when, through an insert shot, we see the killer's distinctive red raincoat in the bushes and the glimmer of her switchblade. Here the zoom keys the audience to anticipate a forthcoming set piece, although in this example Jenny escapes by jumping into the swimming pool. What distinguishes the suspense sequence from other kinds of set pieces is, as in this sequence from *Eyeball*, that the spectacle is withheld; we are denied the spectacle of watching Jenny slaughtered. But the denial of spectacle is often just as compelling for vernacular cinema as the spectacle itself: in the same sequence, just before Jenny is attacked, she stops by the swimming pool, kicks off her sandals, and from behind her in a medium close-up, we see her pull down her dress, promising the audience the spectacle of seeing her naked. This is further promised by an insert shot of her tossing her dress down beside the pool. But as we return to the previous from-behind medium close-up, she lifts her long black hair to tie it atop her head, revealing a bikini strap around her neck. Lenzi promises us two spectacles in this sequence, either seeing Jenny naked or murdered, if not both, and both are denied. Here we see the common connection made in these films, as well as in the literature on the horror film (Italian and non), between eroticism and murder.

The *giallo* often promises sex, as well as violence and gore, although admittedly in smaller amounts. And these sexual set pieces are equally keyed to draw the audience's attention back to the screen. For example, in Sergio

Martino's *Torso*, in one sexual set piece, Ursula (Carla Brait) and Katia (Angela Covello) make love in what Rosenbaum recognized as one of the film's highlights, its "gratuitous lesbian sequence" (1975: 132). This sequence is clearly marked by a shift in Guido and Maurizio de Angelis' score: from mysterious incidental music, as we occupy the viewing position of the killer watching Dani (Tina Aumont) through a partially opened window, to a soft, jazzy piece as Ursula does a seductive dance for Katia in the privacy of their room, keying the audience that we are about to witness some soft-core porn. As the two women make love, this soft jazz continues, even when our viewing position shifts back outside, looking in through another partially opened window. The music can still be heard as the killer, stalking outside, comes across a peeping Tom enjoying watching the girls make love, and chases him from the premises. The music does not fade out altogether until the killer has chased the man well off the property and through the village. Then his gasping breath and the sound of his shoes on the cobblestones dominate the soundtrack. This sex sequence then segues into a suspense/murder sequence (much like the Giordani sequence) and is similarly keyed. The mysterious music part of the score does not reappear until the peeping Tom has found himself cornered in an abandoned shed and the killer finally slashes his throat with a scalpel.

The sexual spectacle dimension of the *giallo* appears in several films, but perhaps none so self-reflexively as in Giuliano Carnimeo's *The Case of the Bloody Iris*. In this film, we are treated to a sequence in a "gentleman's club" where model Mizar (Carla Brait, again), wearing nothing but a bikini, challenges the men in the club to a wrestling match; if they can pin her within three minutes, they win a prize, but no one has ever been able to claim it. The sequence opens in an establishing shot of the interior of the club in almost total blackout; just a few patrons are visible in the dim lighting. Within the same shot, a pink light illuminates the figure of Mizar standing on a center platform with the customers surrounding her, seated at their tables. Still within the same shot, the light turns to yellow and then to white, becoming brighter and illuminating more of Mizar's presence with each change. When the light goes to white, the camera fast zooms in on Mizar's face as she delivers the first challenge directly to the camera, "Are there any volunteers here tonight who'd like to try it?" Clearly, within the diegesis, she is addressing this to the audience at the club, but this self-reflexivity is further stressed when the manager of the club throws her a flashlight, which she uses to illuminate any potential volunteers for her wrestling challenge. But as with her challenge, Mizar first points the flashlight directly at the camera/cinema audience, and assuming a cinematic audience for this film, rather than a video audience (which would have been unthinkable in 1971), the film takes on something of an erotic challenge to the men in the cinema, challenging their safety and masculinity within the darkened cinema space. But again, as we saw with *Eyeball*, the fast zoom-in is usually a precursor to some kind of extended set piece, marking this sequence as something noteworthy.

The set pieces, including the sexual sequences, are the moments within *giallo* cinema that the filmmakers demonstrate their true technical abilities. Most of Carnimeo's *Bloody Iris* is visually quite flat and prosaic; characters tend to move either left to right or front to back of the frame—a criticism of most *gialli*, if not most vernacular films. But if most of *giallo* cinema is occupied by prosaic moments of narrative, it is the set pieces wherein the poetry of cinema, namely image and sound, come together. For example, Carnimeo films the central love scene between Andrea (George Hilton) and Jennifer (Edwige Fenech) differently. Here, architectural features within Andrea's house often frame the lovers, reflecting thematically how Andrea himself is being framed by the architecture he designs; that is, he is the prime suspect in the murder mystery because he is the architect of the building. Carnimeo fast zooms in and out on the sexual action, disrupting the sense of space and time within the sequence, reflective of the character's own suspension of space and time in their bliss. Granted, this sequence from *Bloody Iris* is clichéd, but the intention is clearly to offer visually something more "poetic" than prosaic in this sequence, even if the result is not necessarily "good" poetry. I shall discuss these "poetic" moments with regard to Pasolini's theories about a "cinema of poetry" in the next chapter.

Lucio Fulci's films truly come into their own during the set pieces. At best, he is a mediocre filmmaker during the more prosaic moments of his films, but during his set pieces, he is technically on par with revered *auteurs* like Argento and Mario Bava. The brutal whipping to death of Maciara in *Don't Torture a Duckling* is a case in point. In this violent set piece, the director eschews his almost signature fast zooms for a handheld camera, which gets exceptionally close to the violence perpetuated on Maciara, alternating between subjective points of view alongside her tormenters. But most significant is his use of music in this sequence. As the sequence begins, Maciara has just confessed (not to the murders of the young boys, of which she is innocent, despite community accusations) to having a baby as a teenager, and to trying to use witchcraft to protect the young boys from being murdered. Maciara slowly walks alone out of the village as the local women whom she passes spit on the ground; at this stage Riz Ortolani's score is soft and sad, echoing, along with the whitewashed adobe village, the spaghetti westerns. Ortolani's score disappears from the soundtrack once she has left the village; here it is mostly the sound of insects and a distant woman's voice in the hills singing an Apulian folk melody. But the sequence really comes into its own when Maciara reaches an abandoned churchyard. There she is met by several village men, who impose a kind of vigilante justice on her by whipping her almost to death with chains. Here the music is diegetic, from the radio in one of the men's cars, playing a high-energy rhythm and blues track that gives the sequence a sense of excitement and energy. But then Fulci does something curious: he has the radio announcer interrupt the song and say, "A change of mood now. Let's listen to the lovely voice of Ornella Vanoni," and the soundtrack goes into the Italian diva's "*Quei giorni insieme a te*."[6] This shift in music, from a high-energy, rocking track to a soft and sad love song about loss, changes the mood of the sequence. No longer are we energized by the violence inflicted on Maciara's body, but are suddenly struck by how sad and meaningless it is. The stress on Vanoni's song is not accidental, for Fulci keeps this on the soundtrack well after her attackers have left, as Maciara crawls to the roadside begging for help and dies.

Unlike Dario Argento, Lucio Fulci, while certainly not one to shy away from depicting carnage, tends to keep his murders off screen. He leaves his set pieces to focus on the violence around us. Consider, for example, the bat attack sequence in *A Lizard in a Woman's Skin*. Carol Hammond (Florinda Bolkan) is running from a mysterious man in a motorcycle helmet. For much of this sequence, the music is Ennio Morricone's jazz-rock score, heavy on the electric bass. But as the chase enters an abandoned church, the music disappears, replaced by ambient diegetic sounds—footsteps, breathing noises, and creaking doors. Carol, in attempting to evade her attacker, climbs into the church towers and locks herself in a dark room. As she explores her new surroundings, she accidentally puts her hand on a dead bat. Her scream awakens a swarm of bats, which attacks her in an extended sequence of violence. The scene is obviously intended as homage to the sequence in Alfred Hitchcock's *The Birds* (1963) wherein Tippi Hedren is attacked in the attic of the Bodega Bay house: similar lone heroine, attic room, escape route closed off, and hundreds of winged creatures. Certain shots, particularly from her perspective of the bats coming for her face, seem lifted directly from the Hitchcock film. Fulci uses some intriguing camera work throughout this sequence, much of it filmed using a handheld camera, heightening the intensity of the suspense and getting quite close to the action. But during the bat attack itself, Fulci uses repeated zooms in and out to convey a sense of the unrelenting attack. Fulci returns to this sequence in a later film, *The Black Cat*, almost frame for frame, reproducing the bat attack on Jill when she attempts to escape from the mad Professor Robert Miles and finds herself in a similar bat-infested room. In this later film, Fulci seems to be almost parodying himself. In *Lizard*, the sequence ends with the helmet-wearing attacker finally breaking into the room as Carol manages to break through a boarded-up window. The attacker can only manage a single stab in Carol's arm with his switchblade knife. In *The Black Cat*, Jill likewise manages to get out of the bat room, but in a rather anticlimactic and almost comical conclusion to the sequence, is met by Professor Miles, who knocks her unconscious with a two-by-four.[7]

Fulci's sense of parodying the set piece can be seen in the conclusion of *Don't Torture a Duckling*. Don Alberto (Marc Porel) is thrown from a cliff by reporter Andrea Martelli (Tomas Milan). In most *gialli*, this sequence would be shown in a long shot, of the body hurling down to earth, perhaps with, as Fulci includes here, flashbacks of how Don Alberto committed the murders. But what the director includes, in addition to these stereotypical shots, are close-ups of Don Alberto's face as he descends, hitting the rocks, which rip huge and gory chunks out of him. What is added to this film by this truly excessive display of violence? As I discussed in chapter 6, falls such as these seem to indicate a metaphoric fall from grace. But Fulci goes even further than that by focusing on the priest's destroyed visage, having his face torn off by the rocks. The perverse poetry of this and other set pieces becomes almost mocking. If Fulci challenges his audience to see the pathos in Maciara's death, he takes an equal measure of delight in Don Alberto's fall.

By far set pieces occur most commonly during the key murders. Dario Argento is perhaps the *giallo*'s greatest murder director, and his reputation as an auteur is primarily built around these murder set pieces. But even in more run-of-the-mill *gialli*, the murder sequences are set apart and keyed as something worth paying attention to. Typically, the shift is to a handheld "killer-cam" perspective, as the killer stalks the next victim, oftentimes silently entering the person's apartment and finding the victim either taking a bath or getting undressed for a bath. Carnimeo's *The Case of the Bloody Iris* varies this slightly by having one of the murder set pieces on a busy Rome street. In this sequence, the stalking does not at first seem to key a set piece, as many street scenes use handheld cameras for budgetary reasons and do not necessarily indicate killer-cam. Carnimeo, in order to demonstrate that this is indeed from the killer's perspective, includes an insert shot of the killer looking down at his own hands, revealing his deadly scalpel, which he has hidden in a rolled-up newspaper. But such visual rhetoric is the exception that proves the rule that shifting perspective into killer-cam, usually accompanied by a shift in the soundtrack to diegetic ambient noise, keys the audience to expect a murder set piece.

Argento, who quickly became the master of the murder set piece, added to the tools used for such key sequences. I have already discussed at length the sequence in Argento's *The Bird with the Crystal Plumage*, where Sam Dalmas witnesses what he thinks is the murder of Monica Ranieri. Here, I want to discuss two other key Argento murder sequences: the murder of Helga Ulmann (Macha Méril) in *Deep Red* and Betty's boyfriend in *Opera*, as both of these sequences highlight what is remarkable about murder set pieces.

Helga's murder sequence in *Deep Red* is of relatively normal duration, and perhaps slightly too short to be considered a set piece, remembering that, according to Totaro, such sequences must be longer than is necessary for narrative purposes alone. However, the sequence is actually given two "movements"; that is, we see the murder in two different segments separated by a dialogue interlude of about four and a half minutes. In the first segment, Helga is struck four times with a meat cleaver at her front door.[8] Although only running for approximately two and a half minutes of screen time (including the suspenseful lead-in to the murder where the child's song can be heard diegetically on the soundtrack before the killer strikes), Argento inserts shots, in extreme close-up, of the cleaver striking Helga. While graphic and intense, this sequence does not appear entirely out of the ordinary in terms of what would normally be expected from a horror film murder sequence. As Helga lies dying on the floor, the killer moves over to the notes Helga was making before she was attacked and grabs them.[9] The film then picks up on Mark and Carlo discussing the politics of piano playing, as I noted in chapter 5. During this discussion, a woman's scream is heard. Mark continues his walk home through the darkened streets of Rome. He stops to light a cigarette, looks up, and sees Helga framed in her window, screaming. While this first image of Helga in her window is shot from a long way off, Argento immediately cuts to a medium close-up shot, still from outside, of Helga in her window screaming. Argento cuts back to Mark, in an eye-line match from Helga, and then cuts closer to Mark realizing what he is actually looking at. The shot-reverse-shot pattern continues, returning to Helga framed in the window in the previous medium shot. But then Argento cuts back to the same image of Helga in her window, but from a distance, creating greater visual verisimilitude with Mark's perspective. It is from this long-shot perspective that we can see the figure of the killer raise the cleaver behind Helga and bring it down on the back of her head. Argento cuts closer to this action, but still from Mark's perspective, as the force of the killer's blow pushes Helga forward through the window. As Helga is pushed through the window, Argento presents us with an inserted extreme close-up of Helga's neck falling onto shards of the broken window. This second movement, where Helga's head smashes the window, is barely a minute long. But in dividing the murder sequence into two movements separated by a seemingly irrelevant discussion, Argento creates a variety of perspectives of the murder (omnisciently in the first instance, and from Mark's perspective in the second) that bracket this sequence off as different.

Again, Argento's use of editing, sound, and music is significant in establishing his set pieces: in this sequence, despite the on-screen running time of only two and a half minutes, the first movement of Helga's murder features at least thirty-seven separate shots. In the four and a half minutes of Mark's discussion with Carlo, Argento includes only twenty-two shots, most of which are made up by shot-reverse-shots of the two men talking, there are only about half a dozen different shots in that longer sequence. Most of this sequence features lengthy tracking shots of the actors talking. The second movement of Helga's murder, despite being only a few seconds long, features ten different shots in its composition. Argento alternates the editing of this extended sequence, showing Helga's murder not once, but twice, in two sets of rapid editing, which frame the leisurely paced and static conversation between two of the lead characters.

As I noted above, Argento also plays with sound in this sequence; for much of the first sequence, there is a notable absence of nondiegetic music, much like in the Giordani sequence. At first, we are given only diegetic surface noise, as Helga is on the telephone. The editing is leisurely in this sequence too, but it becomes much more rapid when the killer begins to play the child's song, which acts as her leitmotif throughout the film. As Helga approaches the door, the sound again returns to the diegetic surface noise, and the nondiegetic music does not kick in until the killer has struck the first blow. Again, in the second of the murder movements, Argento only uses diegetic sounds as Mark witnesses Helga's murder and impaling upon the broken window, but the musical score kicks in as Mark races upstairs to try and save her.

Jumping forward a decade, *Opera*'s first major set piece sees Betty (Christina Marsillach) and her new boyfriend, Stefano (William McNamara) celebrating her debut in Verdi's *Macbeth*. The two have just made love and Stefano goes off into the kitchen to make them both a cup of tea. The killer grabs Betty from behind, binding and gagging her. He ties her to a pillar and then inflicts perhaps the most visual and visceral punishment of any of the director's victims—the killer places two sets of sewing needles, secured by pieces of tape, underneath Betty's eyes.[10] Forced to keep her eyes open or else impale her eyelids on the needles, Betty is thereby forced to watch her lover murdered. Stefano emerges from the kitchen and, confused by the sight of Betty tied up, approaches her. As Stefano nears Betty, the killer strikes from behind a curtain, plunging his dagger under Stefano's jawbone and up through his mouth. Stefano falls back as the killer pounces, finishing the young man off. The killer takes the opportunity to fondle Betty's breast, calling her "a bitch in heat" before cutting the rope that binds her hands and leaving. With her arms now freed, Betty removes the remainder of her bindings and runs out to the street.

The entire sequence only runs for approximately three and a half minutes. And unlike Helga's murder in *Deep Red*, the editing, while tightly constructed, features less rapid cutting. *What* Argento chooses to focus on here is less Stefano's murder, than the torture of Betty being forced to watch it. The violation to Betty's eyes, the placing of the tape with the needles in it, runs as a continuous sequence for forty-one seconds and consists of twelve separate shots, focusing on Betty's terrified look, with a drop or two of blood on the needles themselves. Stefano's murder, on the other hand, features eight shots across thirty-four seconds, although added to this are insert reaction shots of Betty's eyes. Three of the shots of Stefano's murder are the same actual composition—likely a continuous sequence that has been intercut with images of the killer stabbing Stefano (from the victim's perspective) and horrified reaction shots of Betty watching. In this sequence, Argento includes several extreme close-ups, mostly of Betty's eyes with the needles in front. But one shot in particular, as it is so unique within horror cinema special effects, is worth noting: as Stefano is stabbed under his jaw and into his mouth, Argento includes an extreme close-up of the young man's screaming mouth where we can see the tip of the dagger blade inside, beside his tongue. One shot that Argento keeps returning to, of Stefano on his back being repeatedly stabbed from the perspective of the killer himself, seems to be highlighting Sergio Stivaletti's special effects work. *Deep Red* had needed extreme close-ups of the penetrating cleaver to convey the savagery of the murder, but it was abstracted as an image due to the limits of special effects technology and budget. By 1986, however, special effects had progressed to the point where Stefano's body could be shown repeatedly penetrated in a continuous medium shot.

And yet, despite the development in special effects makeup since the 1980s,[11] Argento is not against using some of his older tricks in *Opera*. The sound in this sequence is mostly diegetic surface noise, dominated on the soundtrack by the killer's heartbeat rhythmically pounding. It is unclear as to whether the sound of the killer's heart is audible to Betty or if it is intended to suture the audience further into the perspective of the killer. Either way, the point is that, as in *Deep Red*, the suspense section of this set piece features no nondiegetic sound. And again, as in *Deep Red*, when the killer first plunges his dagger into Stefano, the nondiegetic music kicks in, this time with a driving heavy metal track, and it dominates the soundtrack during Stefano's murder.

Conclusions

Shock cinema, to which, for all its artistic pretensions, the *giallo* films ultimately belong, is predicated upon transgressive images of sex and violence. These films are largely structured around various kinds of set pieces. In between these sequences, the mundane and almost prosaic stories are rarely worth paying any kind of close attention to. The audiences within the *terza visione* houses would view the film's narrative as almost an irrelevancy, their attention grabbed only when the set pieces were keyed. Sound, music, and killer-cam shots create a temporary subjective position in the psychotic minds of these films' killers. The stylistic fusion of a character's subjectivity with the mechanical documentation of cinema itself seem to point toward a kind of "free indirect subjective" voice in the cinema, which Pier Paolo Pasolini noted as a major aspect in his "cinema of poetry" and which I will elaborate on in chapter 9. But the set pieces themselves structure the *giallo* as a cinematic poem, keying the spectator to interpret this free indirect subjective with particular intensity. Within these set pieces we are continually distracted by their material construction—through montage, continuous shots, and prosthetic special effects. But perhaps that is the point of them in the first place. Set pieces in vernacular cinema attempt to grab the audience's attention through the use of sex, violence, and graphic gore and focus it on the screen for five or so minutes before it lags again. Because these are the moments in vernacular cinema when the audience is pretty much guaranteed to be watching, they are also the moments when the filmmakers demonstrate their technical skills (an observation also noted by Hunt 2000: 330).

Grabbing a half-attentive audience's attention through a combination of aural and visual signs, the *giallo* filmmakers create with the set piece a kind of minimovie, around which the plot of the film is constructed. These sequences are spectacles in themselves, much like the song and dance numbers in a Hollywood musical or the various sex acts in a pornographic feature. Michele Soavi's *Dario Argento's World of Horror* (*Il Mondo dell'orrore di Dario Argento*) (1985), which collects together several of Argento's set pieces in a decontextualized anthology of "greatest hits" (greatest kills?) video, is in itself evidence of the market for pure spectacle without narrative structure. Of course, such compilations imply audience awareness of the original films or that they might seek out those films to see these sequences' original narrative context, but obviously the spectacle can entertain on its own.[12]

And yet, as Cynthia Freeland argued, this focus on spectacle within the horror set piece creates a kind of sublime beauty.

> In graphic horror films, the spectacle becomes so vast and overwhelming that it makes sense to consider again how such visual spectacles can be related to the concept of the sublime. That is, perhaps the non-stop visions of blood and gore in these films work like a sublime artwork or natural force, something so huge and vast that it overwhelms the rational self . . . [a] *perverse* sublime. (2000: 243)

However, if Linda Williams is correct, and I do not think she is in this instance, then a video such as *Dario Argento's World of Horror* is pure masochism for the viewer; there would be no relief from the mimetic identification between the spectator and the on-screen victims. Watching this video would be an endurance test of mimetic evisceration. But that is not the effect of watching these compilations; often viewers run a gamut of emotions between mimetic empathy and derisive laughter. At its most successful, this kind of horror, whether contextualized within a *giallo* or excerpted into a "documentary" like Soavi's, highlights the sublime nature of these sequences. Carol Clover (1992) noted the shifting of on-screen identification across gender lines in the "slasher" film; so too, I think, contra Williams, there is a shifting of affect across the genre.

Notes

1. This is an observation Cynthia Freeland also made with regard to the slasher film: "The slasher horror film, by its very hyperbolic excess, may actively encourage the audience in its critical awareness of its own interest in spectacle" (2000: 189).

2. I am not sure I agree entirely with this analysis as the controversy over the wave of "gross out" comedies in the late 1970s and early 1980s, with films like *Porky's* (Bob Clark, 1982), indicates. This is a separate argument however, which requires more attention than can be afforded here.

3. This connection is also made by Freeland (2000: 255).

4. Like the Italian horror film, other forms of "low-cultural" cinema or more vernacular forms of cinema can also be seen as using this musical-number analogy to describe their set pieces. Stephen Ziplow, for example, an American pornographic film producer, breaks down the manufacturing of a typical porn film into a variety of "numbers," akin to the songs in a musical, only instead of dance numbers, love duets, and big finales, the porn film offers lesbian numbers, straight-sex numbers, and orgy numbers (quoted in Williams 1989: 127).

5. Anyone, other than the amateur detective, who receives vital information about the identity of the killer, is due to be killed before that information can be passed on. This is one of the "rules" of the *giallo*.

6. Roughly translated, the song title is "Those Days with You."

7. Fulci also repeats his own set pieces in the opening of *The Beyond* with a chain-whipping sequence that echoes Maciara's from *Duckling*, but with better makeup effects. It could be argued that in Fulci's most productive period as a film-maker, 1979–1982, when he made some of his best-known films, he consciously set out to parody the set piece in its sheer hyperbole.

8. For the record, Helga does not actually answer the door. She is about to open the door to her apartment when she receives a strong psychic impression of what is about to happen to her, causing her to jump back from the door. The killer pushes the door open herself and attacks Helga.

9. Earlier in the film it is established that Helga is psychic and identified the killer in the audience of a public demonstration of her gifts.

10. This image, of Betty's terrified eyes, forced open by the needles, has become a signature image for Argento. Maitland McDonagh uses this image as the cover for her book on Argento, *Broken Mirrors/Broken Minds*.

11. Stivaletti has been Argento's special effects makeup artist of choice since their first collaboration, *Phenomena* (1985).

12. Modern pornographic videos tend to eschew the narrative lines of the "classic" porno film of the 1970s and instead link together several seemingly unrelated sex "numbers" in eight- to eleven-minute segments.

CHAPTER NINE

~

The *Giallo* as Cinema of Poetry

In chapter 8 I discussed the set piece in *giallo* cinema and referred to the sex, violence, and gore as being "poetic." In this chapter I want to consider a variety of other formal cinematic aspects of the *giallo* in light of Pier Paolo Pasolini's theory of a "cinema of poetry." I do not believe in using theory for theory's sake; there are enough film academics who do that already. Revisiting Pasolini's essay, although it is more than forty years old at the time of this writing and never achieved a central place within the pantheon of film theory, is not mere sophistry, reviving some hoary old theory to give an alternative analysis of these films. Central to Pasolini's thesis is the idea that those moments when cinematic naturalism (if one agrees with Bazin 1999) or classical continuity (if one agrees with Bordwell, Staiger, and Thompson 1985) is broken are those moments when the "real film" that the filmmaker wanted to produce shines through. In many respects, the points I was making in the previous chapter about set pieces fall within this rubric: the filmmaker's art is most evident in the set pieces, and not in the integration of those moments within a larger narrative context. Within the imagined *terza visione* context in which many of these *gialli* were first screened, the set piece functioned to hold the audiences' attention for a few minutes before they returned to the social space of the theater. In this half-attentive state, the formal filmic properties discussed in this chapter not only function as a kind of vernacular poetry, opening the text up to associational ideas beyond the text, but also demonstrate audio-visual versions of the psychodynamics of orality that Walter Ong discussed and I noted in chapter 2.

The Cinema of Poetry

During a roundtable discussion at the 1965 Pesaro Film Festival, Pier Paolo Pasolini, along with Christian Metz, Umberto Eco, and G. D. Volpe, began formulating what is commonly referred to as the discourse of film semiology (Greene 1990: 92). Pasolini's presentation, titled "*Il cinema di poesia*" ("The Cinema of Poetry"), liberally peppered as it was with generalized and simplistic slogans about the nature of cinema and reality, was heavily criticized as naive in its approach to film semiotics. Today, Pasolini's essay is still largely dismissed due to what are seen as flaws in his perception and meaning of cinematic sign systems. Scholars such as Teresa de Lauretis and Gilles Deleuze have independently tried to return to the central components of Pasolini's thesis, but still "poetic cinema" as discourse remains marginalized within film studies. This consideration of the set piece in *giallo* cinema, in part, attempts to redress this disregard of Pasolini's ideas. Space prevents me from engaging too much in Pasolini's thoughts on film semiology, although escaping entirely from those debates is impossible, as they are directly entangled with his thoughts on "the cinema of poetry," but my focus will be more on what potentially makes cinema "poetic."

To begin with, Pasolini conceives of "the cinema of poetry" as being dreamlike, that is, antirational, antinarrational, and therefore antiprosaic. He noted that the world *as conceived* is made up of image-signs (im-signs), but that the order and meaning given to these im-signs is linguistic (Pasolini 1976: 544). Prelinguistic meaning transcends ideology, but therefore becomes much more impressionistic and irrational (Pasolini 1976: 545). As Pasolini himself noted, "the word (linguistic sign) used by the writer is rich with a whole cultural, popular and grammatical history, whereas the filmmaker who is using an im-sign has just isolated it, at that very moment, from the mute chaos of things—by referring to the hypothetical dictionary of a community which communicates by means of images" (546). Cinema, therefore, in its most linguistically basic form, is a combination of these im-signs:

> Cinema, or the language of im-signs . . . is at the same time extremely subjective and extremely objective (an objectivity which, ultimately, is an insurmountable vocation of naturalism). These two essential aspects are closely bound together, to the point of being inseparable, even for the needs of analysis. The literary function also is double by nature: but its two faces are discernible: there is a "language of poetry" and a "language of prose" so differentiated that they are diachronical and have two divergent histories. (Pasolini 1976: 548)

Pasolini's grand-project was to try to move cinema away from the rational and narratological world of the prose text toward a more "oniric nature of dreams . . . of unconscious memory" (1976: 549). And to do this, the film poet needed to move away from an ideologically defined sense of "naturalism" toward an increasingly subjective cinema.

It is this combination of im-signs and language that was heavily contested in 1965 (and in many respects still is). Critics such as Antonio Costa saw little value in studying Pasolini's theoretical writings, as they "are of little or no use for the development of a scientific semiology of the cinema, nor for film theory and/or film criticism" (quoted in de Lauretis 1980: 159). But as de Lauretis noted, Pasolini was uninterested in a *scientific* study of film semiology, thereby making Costa's criticism largely moot; on the other hand, neither was there any value in exploring Pasolini's insights into "the relation of cinema to reality and to what he called human action" (de Lauretis 1980: 159). And yet, for de Lauretis, there was still tremendous value in reexamining Pasolini's idea of the "cinema of poetry," despite any problems in his semiotic theory.

Pasolini proposed this combination of reality and human action with the cinema through a cinematic equivalent of "free indirect subjective" discourse within the film. Naturalism and realism are conveyed through the standard (and for Pasolini, prosaic) filmic system of continuity, and these can be considered similar to omniscient narration within written prose. But when moving toward a cinema of poetry, Pasolini equated the subjective shot (the shot-reverse-shot, or an eye-line match) with the cinematic equivalent of direct discourse within literature (550). For Pasolini, the true cinema of poetry would be cinema that would abandon altogether the distinction between character and camera or other cinematic apparatus, a cinema that only existed theoretically. As he stated, "I do not believe any film exists which is an entire 'free indirect subjective,' in which the entire story is told through the character, and in an absolute interiorization of the system of allusions belonging to the author" (551). One example Pasolini cites as coming close to a true cinema of poetry is Michelangelo Antonioni's *The Red Desert* (*Il Deserto rosso*) (1964), on which he comments:

> The "cinema of poetry" . . . characteristically produces films of a double nature. The film which one sees and receives normally is a "free indirect subjective" which is sometimes irregular and approximate—in short, very free. This comes from the fact that the author uses the "dominant state of mind in the film," which is that of a sick character, to make a continual *mimesis* of it, which

allows him a great stylistic liberty, unusual and provocative. Behind such a film
unwinds the other film—the one the author would have made even without
the pretext of *visual mimesis* with the protagonist; a totally and freely expressive, even expressionistic, film. (555; emphasis in original)

For Naomi Greene, Pasolini's "free indirect subjectivity" was his search for a
cinematic equivalent of the literary "free indirect discourse" that "denotes
the technique whereby an author conveys a character's thoughts or speech
without either the quotation marks that accompany direct discourse or the
'he/she said' of indirect discourse" (113). For Deleuze, as Greene argues, the
idea of "free indirect subjectivity" began to get to the value of Pasolini's essay: "Deleuze now suggests that free indirect subjectivity refers to a kind of
mimesis between a character's subjective vision and the camera, which sees
both the character and his vision in a transformed manner" (117).

But how does "free indirect subjectivity" manifest itself on the screen? In
both Pasolini's theoretical construct and his own filmmaking, one needs to
recognize a contrast between cinemas of poetry with cinemas of prose: to wit,
Hollywood's continuity system. If the objective of Hollywood continuity
filmmaking was never to let the camera's presence be felt, then the cinema
of poetry must demand the opposite (Pasolini 1976: 556). Pasolini does note
that there were moments of poetry within classical Hollywood cinema, but
they were often due to cinematic *technique*, and not a specific poetic cinematic *language*. For "the cinema of poetry," Pasolini argued for a rupture in
the continuity system of filmmaking.

Thus one feels the camera, and for good reason. The alternation of different
lenses, a 25 or a 300 on the same face, the abuse of the zoom with its long focuses which stick to things and dilate them like quick-rising loaves, the con-
tinual counterpoints fallaciously left to chance, the kicks in the lens, the trem-
bling of the hand-held camera, the exasperated tracking-shots, the breaking of
continuity for expressive reasons, the irritating linkages, the shots that remain
interminably on the same image, this whole technical code was born almost of
an intolerance of the rules, of the need of unusual and provocative liberty, a di-
versely authentic and pleasant taste for anarchy, but it immediately became a
law, a prosodic and linguistic heritage which concerns all the cinemas in the
world at the same time. (556–57)

The excesses of style and drawing attention to the film's formal construction
create cinema's "double nature," as Pasolini refers to it above. When our attention is focused not on the narrative but on the formal construction of the
image, we are invited to contemplate the materiality of that image, only par-

tially with regard to its mimesis. "Since this 'other' film is created totally through formal means, its true protagonist—and, by extension, the true protagonist of the cinema of poetry—is style itself understood, essentially, as a stylistic liberty that calls attention to itself by breaking the rules" (Greene 1990: 120).

So, for Pasolini, when stylistic liberties rupture the narrative prose and we are asked instead to contemplate the formal means of the image's construction, and when that rupture derives from a character's subjectivity thereby fusing the character's subjectivity with the mechanical reproduction of the camera itself, we are invited, if not *required*, to question the very poetics that are presented to us. Greene goes so far as to attack Pasolini's detractors, who in accusing the writer of naivete merely reveal their own (108). Greene cites Deleuze's observation that what Pasolini was wrestling with was the establishment of "the ontological ground for cinema" (108). For de Lauretis, Pasolini

> is concerned with film as expression, with the practice of cinema as the occasion of a direct encounter with reality, not merely personal and yet subjective; he is not specifically taking on, as [his critics were], cinema as institution, as a social technology which produces or reproduces meanings, values and images *for* the spectators. . . . [For Pasolini] cinema, like poetry, is *translinguistic*: it exceeds the moment of the inscription, the technical apparatus, to become "a dynamics of feelings, affects, passions, ideas" in the moment of reception. (164; emphasis in original)

What Pasolini was offering was a means of, in de Lauretis's words, "reclaim[ing] iconicity . . . not so much *from* the domain of the natural or *from* an immediacy of referential reality, but *for* the ideological" (164, emphasis in original). De Lauretis's example is Pasolini's own film *Salo* (1975), wherein the atrocities depicted on-screen are so dispassionate and extreme "one simply *can not* see: one must decide, choose, will oneself to see it, to look at it, to listen to it, to stay in one's chair, not to get up and leave" (164, emphasis in original). Choosing to watch and subjecting oneself to another's images— whether *Salo* for de Lauretis or the *giallo* films—becomes both ideological and ontological; a distanced engagement with the social act of watching a film and the questions such acts reveal about *our pleasure*.

The *Giallo* as Cinema of Poetry

Although Pasolini was alive and making his own films during the main period of the *gialli* (Pasolini died in 1975), we do not know what he thought of them or if he had seen any of them. Pasolini's area of concern, cinematically, was with modernist high-art forms of cinema (his own included) rather than vernacular cinemas like the *giallo*. Pasolini wrote about friends and respected filmmaker colleagues such as Antonioni or Bernardo Bertolucci, but not about Bertolucci's contribution to Sergio Leone's *Once Upon a Time in the West* (*C'era una volta il West*) (1968), or Bertolucci's co-screenwriter on that film, Dario Argento. What Pasolini identified in Antonioni and Bertolucci was an excess of style used to convey larger and more impressionistic ideas about human action. In many respects, the bourgeois critics, for whom Pasolini had little affection (despite being one himself), who accuse the *giallo* filmmakers of incompetence and being overly derivative (despite the accuracy such claims may have), are only seeing the "front-film" in Pasolini's "double nature"; the prosaic narrative that compares poorly to Hollywood models. With the exception of critics like Morse and Rosenbaum, most critics did not interrogate the "back-film," the film that lay behind the prosaic narrative facade. Throughout this book, I have been trying to get to the ideas that bubble up within this "back-film" and that occasionally bleed through to the "front-film." I now want to look at some of the formal properties of the filmic form the *gialli* utilize, those moments of excess style that underscore the "cinema of poetry," and put forward some tentative ideas about what such styles might mean. Most of the examples in this chapter come from the films of Dario Argento, as he is—debatably—the most technically accomplished of the *giallo* filmmakers.

Point-of-View Shots

The first and most notable visual cinematic device in the *giallo* is the point-of-view (POV) shot, wherein the camera takes the perspective of one of the characters, most often the killer stalking the victim. This highly artificial device, which immediately ruptures the classical text, and calls attention to its own constructedness, has become highly clichéd in the wake of the "slasher" films that followed the *giallo*.

> Even before it became the horror genre's favourite and most mockable cliché (in the wake of the success of John Carpenter's 1979 *Halloween*, which opens with an extended Steadicam shot of the stalking and killing of a teenage girl by a heavy-breathing maniac), the killer's point-of-view shot was a similar device. From a purely functional standpoint, it made it easy to conceal the killer's face without limiting the range of his actions; stylistically it became genre shorthand for the temporary identification with the murderer that's widely considered a major horror movie attraction. But *Deep Red*'s manipulation of

the killer's eye POV provides no easy vicarious thrills—just as one becomes accustomed to seeing through the killer's eyes, the viewpoint shifts; the viewer is kept aware at a distance, always on the outside looking in. *Deep Red* is no roller-coaster ride like *Friday the 13th*; it's an altogether more discomfiting experience. (McDonagh 1994: 114)

Such sequences go beyond cliché, however, and become metonymic with the genre itself, with Dario Argento particularly being a keen user of the killer-cam, although by no means the only one. In many respects, this repeated use of the POV camera to denote the stalking killer is more significant than merely a cliché, it underlines the "tradition" aspect of the *filone* itself. When filmmakers use this visual signifier, particularly within the Italian *giallo* tradition, they are consciously following in the wake of previous successful *gialli* films, probably using Argento as their model. Rather than a "copy cat" visual style, within vernacular cinema, particularly Italian vernacular cinema, this imitation really is the sincerest form of flattery. In Italian, *seguire il filone*, literally meaning "to follow the tradition of" a filmmaker or particular film, features a strong conscious implication that both the filmmakers and the *terza visione* audience are going to be aware of the visual tradition being followed.

When a filmmaker works within a set visual tradition but adapts it, even slightly, the results can be varied. For example, Luigi Bazzoni, in *The Fifth Cord*, goes so far as to restrict the visual field into a "pin-hole" image, thereby increasing the subjectivity of the shot. Other directors have also attempted to put an original twist on this formal aspect: Lucio Fulci, in *The Black Cat*, uses "cat-cam," wherein the camera is at the height of a cat and moves across the set "catlike." Dario Argento uses "bug-cam" in *Phenomena* to give a subjective perspective to the insects helping Jennifer (Jennifer Connelly) in her investigation.

Both Argento and Fulci sometimes avail themselves of other kinds of subjective, or impressionistic, visual styles in order to reflect the psychological states of their characters. For example, Argento in *Phenomena* uses a kind of faux-negative visual style in order to reflect Jennifer's sleepwalking state. More traditional forms of subjective camera work occur in Mario Bava's *The Girl Who Knew Too Much*, such as a slightly out-of-focus lens in order to reflect Nora's concussed state after a mugger has knocked her unconscious.

These POV shots, whether killer-cam or any of the other subjective camera devices, are self-conscious violations of the norms of continuity filmmaking. Pasolini identified this self-consciousness as a hallmark of the "cinema of poetry." These kinds of subjective shots fuse together a character's subjective mental state (here most often the killer's) with the camera itself into what Deleuze saw as a "free indirect discourse." Argento, in particular, tends to film sequences set entirely within the killer's mind, as, for example, we see in *Deep Red*, where we are presented with abstract images from the killer's childhood—toys mostly—completely decontextualized on a black background, that the camera almost fetishistically explores. *Giallo* cinema also has tendencies toward "free indirect discourse" in scenes when the killer fondles his or her weapons before going out to kill. The camera often takes a subjective position of the killer and we view the beauty of the cold, shiny steel, again frequently filmed on a black background to offset the shine. And like the set piece, these sequences go on for longer than is strictly necessary for the narrative to progress. With Argento's almost surreal dream/fantasy sequences, like the one previously noted in *Deep Red*, no narrative information is conveyed, but only a poetic exploration of the killer's mania.

While just using a handheld camera to suggest the killer stalking his or her next victim is not sufficient for the "cinema of poetry" writ large, this often is enough to break the continuity of bourgeois prosaic cinema. While the *giallo* may not be "*cinema* of poetry," subjective visual devices, such as killer-cam, can be seen as poetic *moments* within the film, an introduction of the subjective mind of the psychotic killer. Pasolini recognized that Hollywood, too, would avail itself of techniques like this, and for the same function noted here, but that such usages were more for *technique* itself than the development of a poetic cinema *language*. Maybe this point is where Pasolini and I begin to disagree: the technique itself is often enough to break the continuity system of prosaic cinema, enabling the filmmaker (film *poet*, in this case) to explore more complex and poetic ideas, connecting the camera with the city itself. If, as I argued previously, the amateur detective engages in *flânerie*, then perhaps the killer likewise becomes a *flâneur* when stalking a victim. The main difference here is the filmic device of "free indirect discourse," of using the subjective camera to convey this stalking. When we watch the amateur detective engage in *flânerie*, we watch objectively, prosaically; but when the killer stalks his or her prey and we find ourselves within the killer's mind, wandering the streets or apartment corridors, approaching the victim, we become culpable in the stalking itself. It is *we* who approach the victim, through the camera as surrogate. As both Deleuze and de Lauretis noted above, this visual culpability underlines the ontological nature of the "cinema of poetry," challenging our very notions of why we watch films of this kind.

Extreme Close-Ups and Fast Zooms

Slightly more typical within the *giallo*'s formal palette is the use of extreme close-ups. Argento, for example, tends to use extreme close-ups of the killer's eyes in *Cat O' Nine Tails* and *Tenebre*. In the former, immediately before the killer attacks someone, we see his pupils dilate in one of these extreme close-ups. In many respects, because we are only given these close-ups for the killer himself, these insert shots act metonymically for the killer's presence, much like the *giallo* disguise noted in chapter 6. Argento goes this one further in *Opera* by inserting extreme close-ups of the killer's pulsating brain just prior to an attack. In *Deep Red*, Argento includes extreme close-ups of musical notations as they are written (by Mark) on a sheet of staff paper and also of Mark's piano keys and the hammers attached to those keys hitting their respective strings. These close-ups, and by extension the others used, express a character's intense concentration. This is continued in *Tenebre*, wherein we see extreme close-ups of the killer's pills and a glass of water. These items, as I argue below, act almost fetishistically, and certainly metonymically, to give insight into the killer's frame of mind, his requiring medication to alleviate splitting headaches.

Other *giallo* directors will use extreme close-ups of the witnessing of the murders. The act of being an *eyewitness* to the crime is here literally visualized by the insert shot of the witnesses' eyes in the act of seeing. As Gary Needham pointed out, the Italian term "*testimone oculare*," which means "eyewitness," has a greater resonance within the *giallo* film: literally, testimony of the eye, or even the epistemology of the eye—what the eye *knows* (2003: 140). Certainly at the banal and prosaic level of murder mysteries, the witness of the crime (most often murder) is going to be a useful resource for the police in apprehending the criminal. When the amateur detective is the only eyewitness to the murder, the investigation is sparked by an attempt to understand what he or she *saw*. That internal thought process, which in a literary murder mystery could be rendered prosaically as "What did I just see?" or "John could not believe what he saw," is in the *giallo* film represented visually by the trope of the fast zoom into an extreme close-up of the eyes. We know with the construction of the eye-line match within the continuity system that a minicycle of enigma and resolution is set up: What is he looking at? He is looking at a woman being murdered.

The extreme close-up is, perhaps, one of the most criticized formal aspects of Italian vernacular cinema, after the violence. For example, "Much complaint has been made about *The Black Cat*'s frequent close-ups of eyes. Fulci often uses them, and they proliferate in this film more than any other: it has to be said that as a shorthand for elaborate psychological power-struggles they are indeed inadequate" (Thrower 1999: 190). But I think Thrower misses the point of these close-ups. The fast zoom into an extreme close-up of the eyes is a hyperbolic extension of the eye-line match, intending to grab

the audience's attention and to underscore that what the character is looking at is *very important*. Even if distracted audience members only catch a fast
zoom out of the corner of their eye, *giallo* filmmakers give enough of a pause
following the zoom for them to turn to the screen for the resolution of the
enigma (what is he looking at?) to be conveyed. The emphasis on that close-
up, however, is what makes the zoom-in cinematically poetic. The lens dis-
tortion is abrupt and jarring, certainly not the smooth transition favored by
the continuity system. The zoom calls attention to itself as artifice, and warns
the audience that the following shot will be significant. While this is hardly
a subtle or sophisticated technique, as a poetic trope of vernacular cinema, it
denies the chance for the audience to be sutured into the diegesis.

Of course, extreme close-ups are also used as insert shots during the murder sequences themselves, often of the blade penetrating the victim's flesh.
Here is the *giallo*'s version of the "money shot" in pornography: instead of
presenting sexual penetration, as in hard-core porn, in *giallo* cinema we are
presented with full *bloody* murderous penetration. I have already noted how
in *Deep Red* Argento inserts shots of the cleaver penetrating Helga's body
when she is murdered. These are filmed in extreme close-up, creating almost
abstract images. Their inclusion and the way they are photographed disrupts
the continuity of the sequence. I noted in chapter 8, in a comparison with
Opera, that due to the special makeup effects available at the time or budgetary restraints, Argento needed to insert extreme close-ups of the cleaver
striking Helga in order to convey the savagery of the attack. With *Opera*, due
to a higher budget, improved special effects, or a combination of both, Stefano could be stabbed almost in a continuous take. The insert shots in *Deep
Red* appear to be constructed by means of a stage blood package underneath
a skin of some kind, which is then underneath the same dress Helga is wearing in the scene. With the medium shots of Macha Méril, her body is in motion, fleeing from the attack, but the inserted extreme close-ups of the body
are inert, even for the few seconds of the shots. Not only do these insert shots
disrupt the continuity of Méril's body (we cannot know for certain where she
is being hit with the cleaver), they also temporarily disrupt the rhythm and
flow of the murder sequence by alternating between the fluid movement (of
the actor) and the nonmovement (of the special effect). By way of disrupting the continuity we are asked to think about the image on its own, divorced from the other images in the sequence. Here again, we see Pasolini's
"cinema of poetry": the image of the cleaver penetrating Helga's body becomes an im-sign, separated by the discontinuity of the sequence. While on
the one hand we can see these insert shots as part of a more prosaic whole
(Helga's murder), their artificiality brings to the fore the film's own constructedness, breaking the continuity of narrative cinema.

But is this breaking of continuity intentional or accidental due to sloppy, incompetent, or "best we could do at the time" filmmaking? If sloppy editing and cheap special effects are indicative of a "cinema of poetry," then any "bad movie" could be seen as poetic. This is exactly the point I am trying to make here: for *whatever reason*, when the film breaks the spell the continuity system has spun over us, we allow the ideas sparked by the images to flow freely, often outside of the narrative frame that is supposed to contain them. It is in these moments that we can experience a much freer flow of im-signs than in a more prosaic cinema.

False Opening

Mario Bava's *Blood and Black Lace* opens with a credit sequence unique in *giallo* cinema: each of the actors featured in the film are given their own tableau, bathed in a combination of red and green chiaroscuro lighting, with appropriate black spots. The actors pose in costume as the characters they play in the film, but also within each mise-en-scene is posed a mannequin doppelganger. Sometimes the mannequin is meant to echo the pose of the actor or to act as the actor's shadow, holding the same pose but in the opposite direction. In one playful example, Francesca Ungaro's mannequin appears to be trying to strangle the actress. These tableaux reflect the playful nature of Bava's film, and as noted previously, it was one of the first "proper" *giallo* films. I cannot recall any other film, let alone *giallo*, that features the actors posing so self-referentially in the opening credit sequence.

Duccio Tessari's *The Bloodstained Butterfly* opens much more typically for these films: through a butterfly-shaped iris, the opening credits are projected on the black outside of the cut-out image, while inside the butterfly shape are scenes of Marta Clerci driving around Milan, where the film takes place. After the credits, the butterfly shape disappears and Marta's car arrives home. Marta gets out of the car and stumbles in the front door. The camera does a fast zoom-in to the doorframe, revealing two newspapers and two cartons of milk, implying that Marta has been away for a few nights. We pick up on Marta in her house as she removes her curly wig, pours herself a drink (the ubiquitous J&B whiskey) and retires upstairs. As this is a *giallo* and made well into the *filone*, we expect Marta to meet some kind of sex-crazed killer in her house. But instead, the audience is presented with the character's name printed on the screen. The film then cuts to a different location: a young girl holding her school books walks down a road, and again we are told via on-screen titles that this is Françoise Pigaut (Carol Andre).

If we had missed the opening "butterfly" credits, we would have thought these were the names of the actors in the film. It is a typical sort of presentation of opening credits. But we have already had a full opening credit sequence to this film complete with the actors' names. Now we are presented with another piece of footage of another young woman, and this time we are told that she is Sarah Marchi (Wendy D'Olive). The fourth, however, breaks this pattern: a woman is shown having a massage and manicure while speaking on the telephone. The soundtrack throughout has been Gianni Ferrio's instrumental score, which makes sense, as the introductions to Marta, Françoise, and Sarah needed no diegetic sound. But with this fourth repetition, the woman is *speaking*, yet the Ferrio score still plays. We cannot hear what the conversation is about. And, most remarkably, although the woman being massaged and manicured is named, Maria (Ida Galli), she is given a subtitle under her name, "mother of Sarah." Thus, we have been presented with not the actors' names, but the characters they will be playing in the film, along with, occasionally, their relationships to others. Five other characters are introduced in this way. When the Ferrio score finishes, we join the film narrative itself, a full six and a half minutes into the film's running time.

From a narrative perspective, that is, as prosaic cinema, we are given in perhaps the most pedestrian way possible a dramatis personae for the film, including the characters' relationships to each other. But because none of these little introductory sequences contain narrative information relevant to the mystery itself, we need to read these images as reflections of the relevant character traits and roles, that is, that Marta is a playgirl, Françoise and Sarah are students, that Sarah's mother is a pampered bourgeoisie, or that Giorgio (Helmut Berger) is a concert pianist. While these character attributes may not be entirely relevant to the film narrative, they are to be read by the audience as a kind of mnemonic device, and we are asked to associate them with each character. Furthermore, it is not a common feature in any film to be given a dramatis personae. What both these opening sequences indicate, despite being unique examples within the *giallo* film, is that the opening of the film is the invitation to play the mystery game with these filmmakers.

Enzo Castellari's *Cold Eyes of Fear* begins with a figure wearing black gloves, stalking a young woman as she gets ready for bed. The camera takes the typical POV killer-cam perspective, as we voyeuristically watch her undress. The gloved figure strikes, beginning to rape the young woman, before she submits and becomes a willing victim to her assault. This opening sequence is turned around when it is revealed that what we have been watching is, in fact, a stage play. The same dynamic opens Riccardo Freda's *The Wailing*, where the initial murder sequence is revealed to be a rehearsal for a *giallo* film Michael (Stefano Patrizi) is acting in. Michele Soavi's *Stagefright* has a similar rehearsal opening but is more heavily stylized into a surreal, psycho-killer-themed dance number. I have already mentioned Mario Bava's *Bay of Blood*, wherein the first killer, wearing the typical black gloves, is almost immediately murdered by the film's real killer, again intentionally misleading its genre-savvy audience. Umberto Lenzi's *Spasmo* begins with a body found in the woods, only to reveal that this body is in fact a wooden dummy. And Mario Bava's *Five Dolls for an August Moon* opens with a "murder game" being played.

What all of these "false openings" require is a linear following of the narrative flow as it happens. We need to accept the on-screen information as it is presented to us, for there is no time for reflection within vernacular cinema. We cannot go back and figure out something that we might have missed. The image, or in Pasolini's schema, im-sign, stands in for reality as we understand and receive it, but this is not necessarily contained within a narrative world that follows our laws of anticipated continuity. Each im-sign, whether in the opening credits or the action as it begins to unfold, must be understandable on its own terms and not refer back, or forward, within the diegesis. We *must* accept the information as we are given it because we have no choice within vernacular cinema. If murders turn out to be a game, bodies turn out to be dummies, black-gloved killers turn out to be black-gloved victims, then the illogic of such narrative devices cannot be dwelled upon. Perhaps this is one of those aspects of the *giallo* that turns movie reviewers off—they are not trained to just accept narrative information as it comes to them. The *terza visione* audience does, and these are *their* films.

The Return of Orality in a Cinema of Poetry

I now want to return to Walter Ong's ideas of orality that I first introduced in chapter 2. To reiterate those points, Ong's "psychodynamics of orality," those cognitive processes storytellers and their audiences need when writing is completely unknown within a society, function in many of the formal features and stylistic devices of vernacular cinema noted in this chapter. But in addition to this quasi-Ongian approach to vernacular film, I am also arguing that those moments when the quasi-orality is most evident are also moments when these films are at their most "poetic" (in Pasolini's sense).

Take for example the use of POV shots, or as I have called it here, killer-cam. While, as I argued above, this kind of subjective camera work moves toward Pasolini's theorization of a "free indirect discourse" within cinema, the formal properties of handheld camerawork—jerky and shaky images, disrupting the continuity of the visual style in the film—cause us to notice the rupture of continuity conventions. Changing the style of filmmaking, even temporarily, creates a cognitive enigma for those watching the film: What is going on here? Moving into the subjective position of the killer him- or herself, keyed by the change in camerawork, is a visual equivalent of changing speakers or narrators in a story. But as is often the case in these moments in *gialli*, we are denied an establishing shot to determine whose perspective we are now taking (for to do so would be to reveal the identity of the film's killer). This is the equivalent, in literature, of changing narrators but without the information of who is now speaking. To have included the establishing shot of the killer before visually going into the killer's subjective perspective, would have been "direct discourse"—a cinematographic equivalent of "So Marta picked up the knife and began stalking Giacomo" in a novel. By denying that establishing shot and by denying early identification of the killer cinematically (whether the identity of the killer is predictable or not is beyond the scope of this current argument), we are closer to a cinema of poetry's "free indirect discourse." Such "free indirect discourse" is, of course, chirocentric, as it implies a literary model, and yet there are equivalents within orality. Imagine an oral storyteller who, in order to distinguish between various characters, changes his voice accordingly. The audience should pick up on the change in voice, and while it may be unclear at first who is actually speaking, without the narrator giving this information out directly ("and so Achilles said . . ."), the "tradition" of who is speaking, based on particular inflections or other oral artistry, should establish the characters without the prosaic direction. In an oral context, one does not necessarily need the direct discourse of being told who is saying what, as such information is inferred. Likewise, when we are presented with subjective POV cinematography, we infer meaning from that sequence based on the actions in the sequence itself as well as the tradition of POV camerawork being killer-cam in similar *gialli* we may have seen. Therefore, that shift to killer-cam is read by vernacular audiences without the literary models of direct discourse into a kind of poetic "free indirect discourse." And when those POV sequences are even further displaced from our own experience, as Argento does with bug-cam or Fulci with cat-cam, because of the establishment of the tradition of POV shots in cinema, we can read those moments unproblematically and, ideally, appreciate the filmmaker's artistry in playing with the convention. But what is most significant here, at least in terms of vernacular cinema's relationship to orality, is that while those conventions can be played with, they cannot be completely violated (at least within vernacular cinema contexts), as the result would be overly complicated for the vernacular audience.

Pasolini's im-signs, those images that break the continuity of the diegesis and are connotative in themselves, can, at least within the *giallo* films, also act as quasi-orality. The old saying that a picture is worth a thousand words, while certainly trite, is nonetheless true. When we are presented with an abstracted image of an extreme close-up, for example, we absorb tremendous amounts of information within the frame itself, but focused in such a way as to have multiple and simultaneous meanings and connotations. These images do not necessarily need to be retained, although good (that is, powerful) im-signs often are, but must have some kind of immediate affect. Ong noted that within primary orality cultures, narratives needed to be visceral and immediate. They were not to savor; they needed to be felt (1982: 45–46). Consider again the image of Betty with the needles under her eyes from Argento's *Opera*: we *feel* the discomfort, partially through empathy, but also recognizing our own watching of Betty *forced* to watch. We *want* to watch (or why else are we watching *Opera*?), Betty does not. We are struck by the contradictory verisimilitude of the image and its seeming artificiality, both how "realistic" it looks in terms of makeup and image composition but also how "sick" the very concept is, that some adult person needed to *think* this up, and the image *must* be fake, for what actor would subject themselves to such treatment? Actually, the pro-filmic construction in some of the shots is evident: actor Christina Marsillach has very high cheekbones, and in a few of the shots we can see that the needles and tape are not on her lower eye-lid but on her cheekbones, a safer position for the actor. But that pro-filmic safety, for us and for the actor, is less secure in other shots, where the tape appears to be on her eyelids. Are those trickles of blood running down the needles stage blood, or an on-set accident? We assume the former, but how sure are we? All these conflicting thoughts occur in the space of a second or two as the image flashes across the screen. This is the power of the im-sign; but what Pasolini did not take into account, or if he did, he never made it clear, was that the connotative power of the im-sign is not purely intellectual and distanced, but also visceral and empathetic.

Finally, those false openings, which demand of the audience that all information presented, *as it is presented*, is accepted as true, are particularly oral-like. Without the chirocentric ability to "go back over" something in order to test its validity, every new piece of information must build on the previous, slowly and with repetition. The dummy, for example, that is mistaken for a body in Lenzi's *Spasmo*, might just as easily have been a lousy special effect. Watching vernacular films, we have to accept the narrative information as we get it. Vernacular cinema audiences, whether in the *terza visione* theaters or among European horror movie fans, know the conventions of the various *filone* well enough that when they see the black-gloved killer stalking a beautiful woman, particularly if sutured into a kind of "free indirect discourse" through a POV sequence, they can expect this to be the film's central killer.

When these sequences turn out to be games or rehearsals or even bizarre stage shows in a seedy London "gentleman's club," they are playing with the *narrative* conventions (as a false opening), but not with the *cinematic* conventions; while on-screen, they have to be understood as true.

Conclusions

Stephen Thrower noted,

> To me, there is something strangely offensive about the idea of screen violence "justified by the plot," or "redeemed by context." All art, it could be argued as we reach the late, late twentieth century, is gratuitous. There is only apologetic or unapologetic gratuitousness in the depiction of violence. Even then, we can be tricked into adopting a hierarchical system of judgement by prioritising the film of "high moral seriousness" to the detriment of other, less didactic films. (1999: 153)

Thrower continued:

> The notion of there being a justified violence in art is one that rests on very shaky ground: ground that horror fans nonetheless often end up occupying, because we have allowed the terms of the argument to be defined by those who wish to censor artistic endeavour. We seem to find ourselves talking about this or that film's "responsible" use of violence, there in the film to further a psychological or social "point" that the "responsible" filmmaker is alleged to be making. As soon as we enter this discourse though, we are immediately on the defensive, with the onus upon us to "justify" a sequence of film on the criteria that many of us do not share. (154)

The *giallo's* excesses of style, whether in narrative structure; extreme close-ups and fast zooms; subjective POV sequences; or even, bringing chapter 8 in here, the grandiose set pieces of sex, violence, and gore, need to be seen bracketed off from the prosaic narrative flow of the film. Michael Grant noted that these breaks in the continuity style of classical filmmaking "exhibit an order of self-interrogation that has many features in common with the literature of modernism" (2000: 63). Such cinematic "modernism," in the Pasolini sense, creates moments of cinematic poetry that need to be seen on their own terms. But to return to some of the commentary on Pasolini's article, both de Lauretis and Deleuze see "cinema of poetry" as inherently ontological: that the *giallo*, as cinema of poetry, challenges the very ontology of cinema itself by challenging the individual spectators to question their own pleasures in watching these films, and thereby questioning the very pleasures of cinema. "Shock" cinema shocks us for a reason. We may deconstruct these shocking sequences and images for their technical composition or their use of special effects, but we do this specifically because the film's verisimilitude has been ruptured. These shocking sequences call attention to themselves through a kind of Brechtian *verfrumdungseffekt*, wherein we are jolted out of our cinematic complacency to think not only about "how" such a sequence is made, but "why." Christopher Frayling noted similar cinematic techniques and usages in the spaghetti western:

> The first strategy is a Brechtian one—"laying bare the device," stimulating the audience to question the visual conventions being used, reminding the audience that it is watching a film, and so on. . . . The second strategy takes the form of an extreme stylisation which is intended to be at odds with the (accepted) reproduction of the world in its immediate appearance, or with the everyday experience of the viewer. (1998: xxiii)

These sequences, in the *giallo*, are interesting not just because of their shock value, but because they demand we think about the very ontology of the cinema and our pleasures of watching such images. This dynamic is not only applicable to the *giallo*, but I think applies to any shocking sequence in a film. In *Opera*, Argento dares his audience to "watch" while demanding that Betty do the same, but he also punishes both Betty and the audience for daring to close their eyes, a point made by Linda Ruth Williams (2002: 13–17). Pasolini's "Cinema of Poetry" allows us to see these ruptures in a film's verisimilitude as ontological acts.

Pasolini's forty-year-old essay, "Il cinema di poesia," throws new light on the analysis of exploitation cinema, showing the *giallo* as poetical, as well as vernacular, cinema. But as anyone who has read the doggerel written on the inside of a public toilet or a greeting card can attest, identifying something as poetry is no guarantee of *quality*. Some *giallo* are very good, *artistic*, poetical cinema compositions (Argento's *Deep Red* or *Opera* for example, or Mario Bava's *Blood and Black Lace* or *Bay of Blood*); however, the vast majority are not. As *vernacular* poetry, these films may be poetic, but that is not to say they are necessarily very good poetry.

CHAPTER TEN

~

From *Giallo* to Slasher

I began this book by noting that I started studying the *giallo* as a way into studying the slasher film. In order to discuss a particular *filone*, if you will, of the late 1970s and early 1980s slasher movies, those films I had initially referred to as "Scooby-Doo" movies (2003a), I became more convinced they had strong ties to the Italian *giallo* of the early 1970s. In order to try and talk about these movies as North American *gialli* (most of the films in question are Canadian), I needed to find a few defining articles on the *giallo* in order to apply them to the slasher films I wanted to study. That no such scholarship existed in English was the reason for beginning this project.

By way of a conclusion to this book, I now would like to look at those films I had wanted to look at from the beginning, certain slasher films from the early 1980s, focusing on what these movies took from the *giallo*. But, as this study developed, I also noted how Italian horror cinema was influenced by the slasher films themselves, so I will also look at some later Italian *gialli* to see how they are, in turn, influenced by the slasher movies.

First, however, I want to keep to the early 1970s and examine Sergio Martino's *Torso*. This film encompasses many of the attributes of the *giallo*, thereby acting as a typical example of the genre for a conclusion to the book, but also I want to suggest that Martino's film is a prototypical slasher movie.

Torso: Typical *Giallo* and Prototypical Slasher

Torso, Sergio Martino's 1973 *giallo* film, features most of the standard tropes and narrative devices that are typical in the genre. In Jonathan Rosenbaum's review of the film from the British *Monthly Film Bulletin* he noted (and this is worth reiterating) that this particular film "supplies us with everything it thinks we need" (1975: 132). While Rosenbaum's review is one of the few (semi-) positive reviews on the films under consideration here, his affection for the film is based primarily on the assumption that Martino's film aims to please its audience. And as a *giallo*, pleasing the audience requires being sufficiently grounded within the *filone* to act as a landmark for the *terza visione* and European horror fan audience. For example, while the English-language title, *Torso*, is suitably exploitive, the film's Italian title keeps to the tradition of baroque and bizarre names, *I Corpi presentano trace di violenza carnale*,[1] literally "The Body Presents Signs of Sexual Violence." This sort of titling keeps within the tradition of films such as *The Case of the Bloody Iris*, whose Italian title, *Perche quelle stran gocce di sangue sul corpo di Jennifer?* translates literally as "What Are Those Drops of Blood Doing on Jennifer's Body?"[2] So seeing a film like *Violenza carnale*, as it was abbreviated throughout Europe, clearly keys the kind of film it is.

While the second half of the film takes place mostly within the grounds of an isolated villa (rare, but not completely unique within *gialli* cinema), the first part takes place very definitely within the urban spaces of an Italian city. The dramatis personae of the film are stock characters from the *giallo*: Jane (Suzy Kendall), an American studying art history in Italy; Daniela (Tina Aumont), the rich and beautiful co-ed who is being stalked by Stefano (Roberto Bisacco), an obsessed lover with violent sexual tendencies; Gianni Tomasso (Ernesto Colli), a creepy peddler who sold the killer an incriminating scarf and later resorts to blackmail; and Roberto (Luc Merenda), the "hunky" doctor who saves the day. The killer himself wears black leather driving gloves and a balaclava (although this one is white). This list of suspects includes Stefano (whom everyone believes is the killer in the film), the two motorcycle-driving students who take Carol (Christina Airoldi) to a party on the outskirts of town, and possibly even creepy Gianni, until he tries to blackmail the killer. Savvy fans of the genre might pick up on the very minor character of Daniela's father as a suspect, who suggests she and her girlfriends go to the isolated family villa in order to escape the murderer-on-the loose, but this turns out to be a red herring. For most of the film, however, Stefano is the prime suspect—he is definitely stalking Daniela, owns a scarf similar to the one the police are looking for in connection with an earlier murder, and has known Daniela since they were children.

Ultimately, the killer turns out to be the girls' art history professor, Franz (John Richardson), who had been romancing Jane. Franz had been traumatized as a child when he witnessed his brother fall to his death trying to rescue a little girl's doll. Since the girl had promised to lift her dress for Franz's brother in exchange for getting the doll, Franz has since equated (hetero)sexuality with the death of his brother and views all women as "dolls." Although much is made of that psychosexual explanation in Franz's background, the real reason for the murders is that Franz participated in a ménage-a-trois that opened the film, and the two women involved, Carol and Flo (Patrizia Adiutori), were the first to be murdered, as they were blackmailing him with pornographic pictures taken at the time. But Daniela saw Franz follow Carol just before she was murdered, and although she could not recall who she saw follow her friend, she did recall the scarf he was wearing. Daniela was killed because she was a potential witness; their friends, Katia and Ursula, were killed because they happened to be in the wrong place at the wrong time (the isolated villa where Daniela was to be killed).

Missing from the preceding is of course the central role of the amateur detective; while not all *gialli* have amateur detectives (the *poliziotto* and suspense-*gialli* do not), different characters take on different *parts* of the amateur detective role. While Jane is not the film's amateur detective, she is the one to put the incriminating pieces together to accuse Stefano and races off to warn Daniela at the villa. Although Dr. Roberto is the one who ultimately kills Franz, he is only brought to play in the final act of the film, worried why no one answered the door, when he knew for certain Jane could not have walked out of there (she had broken her ankle the previous day and he had taped it up for her). In the urban sequences of the first half of the film, the police do seem to be on the ball under the leadership of Inspector Martino (Luciano De Ambrosis), but once the action moves to the villa, the police disappear from the narrative.

From a strictly narrative perspective, Martino and co-screenwriter Ernesto Gastaldi have fashioned a highly typical *giallo* narrative.[3] Of course, Martino is able to include various set pieces—both sexual (the opening ménage-a-trois, Ursula and Katia's lesbian sequence) and suspense (Carol being stalked in the marsh, Gianni being run down). But what marks *Torso* as a different kind of *giallo* is the almost twenty-three-minute suspense sequence with which Martino concludes the film, as Jane wakes up to discover her friends murdered and the killer still present, and a game of cat and mouse begins between potential victim and killer. And this sequence, in particular, is what marks *Torso* as a *prototypical* slasher film.

By the second half of the film, once Daniela and her friends go off to the villa, *Torso* shifts gears. As is typical of the *giallo*, the murders in the first half of the film are on-screen—Flo, Carol, and Gianni. But when the killer comes calling at the villa, Stefano, Ursula, Katia, and Daniela are murdered off-camera and at once. We are thus denied any of the traditional pleasures of this kind of cinema. Jane wakes up the next morning, comes downstairs, and finds the bodies strewn across the floor. She hides and witnesses Franz, who is unaware Jane is in the house, cutting the bodies down with a hacksaw for burial. When Franz and Jane begin to play cat and mouse about the house, Jane's role begins to form into what Carol Clover identified as the "Final Girl" of the slasher tradition (1992: 35–41). In this cat and mouse game, while never engaging in full physical struggle, Jane is attempting to outwit Franz—another aspect of the Final Girl role. Although the Final Girl is often responsible for killing the monster/killer in slasher movies, Jane, as prototype of this character role, still needs the traditional *giallo* hero to arrive at the eleventh hour for the final punch-up that will ultimately send Franz off a cliff to his death.

As a prototype of the slasher film, *Torso* introduces several of the tropes and devices that became ubiquitous in these films by the end of the decade. We have the isolated location; beautiful girl students; a prototype of the Final Girl role in Jane, who, in a protracted sequence that takes up most of the final third of the film, does battle with the killer; and the discovery of all the bodies in one location.

What we do *not* have is equally significant; although not surprising, since this is a *giallo*, not a slasher film. Typical of the *giallo*, the events in *Torso* take place over several nights, perhaps as much as a week in narrative time. The action of slasher films, on the other hand, tends to get compressed into a single night or a couple of nights at best. Extending the action across several days enables an investigation to occur, as opposed to how a slasher film is structured, where the only goal seems to be survival until the sun comes up. This is perhaps the main difference between the *giallo* and the slasher: while the former focuses on the investigation, the latter focuses on survival. Another difference is that while Jane does come across the bodies in the villa, the killer does not collect the corpses and stash them in such a way as to fall out and frighten the Final Girl when she opens various cupboards or doors. The logic of Jane coming across the bodies in the villa may be prototypical, but it is also more logical as a narrative device. Also, as I have already noted, Jane as Final Girl does not physically fight the killer and needs the male hero to actually throw the punches and ensure the killer is killed. Finally, *giallo* killers do not come back from the dead the way slasher monsters do.

The *Giallo* Influence on the Slasher Film

In "The Terror Tale," I attempted to divide the slasher film into three different categories, what I would now characterize as *filone*, appropriating the term from the Italian. These *filone* were "the terror tale," in which the killer was *always* the killer and the action was motivated largely by trying to avoid this monster (e.g., *Halloween* [John Carpenter, 1978], *Friday the 13th* [Sean S. Cunningham, 1980], and *The Burning* [Tony Maylam, 1981]); second were "psycho-character studies," where the film was concerned with understanding the motivations behind serial killers (e.g., *Maniac* [William Lustig, 1980], *Fade to Black* [Vernon Zimmerman, 1980], and *Henry—Portrait of a Serial Killer* [John McNaughton, 1986]); and finally what I would now refer to as "North American *gialli*."[4]

Stephen Thrower noted, "Many [slasher films] were just mediocre, tarted-up thrillers interspersed with a fashionable quota of gory deaths" (1999: 221). Is this a fair comment? What have certain slasher movies taken from the *giallo*? Or to phrase the question slightly differently and more in keeping with the idea of the *filone* that permeates this book, what aspects of the slasher film are *sullo stesso filone* from the *giallo*—in the tradition of the *giallo*? As this last *filone* of the slasher film was the most prolific, if not the best received, and in keeping with the spirit of the *filone*, I now want to discuss how these films situate themselves in both the *giallo* and slasher traditions.

Time and space do not allow me to explore a full study here of the reception of the slasher films upon their release in the late 1970s and early 1980s; such a subject is entirely worthy of a separate study. But as a superficial and tentative position, we can say that like the *giallo*, the slasher films are vernacular. These films were cheaply and quickly made in the wake of more successful (but no less frugally made) movies like *Halloween* (John Carpenter, 1978) and *Friday the 13th* (Sean S. Cunningham, 1980). Literally dozens of these movies were produced in the four years between 1979 and 1983. As Vera Dika noted in her study of what she calls the stalker film, the major studios, in the wake of mainstream horror films such as *Rosemary's Baby* (Roman Polanski, 1968), *The Exorcist* (William Friedkin, 1973), and *The Omen* (Richard Donner, 1976), had experienced a number of big-budget horror failures (1990: 9).[5] For most of the slasher/stalker films Dika cited, the distribution pattern was the same: these were small, low-budget films (often Canadian, but Dika does not cite that), that major studios picked up cheaply in distribution deals, which therefore led to massive box-office profits, even if the film was only a moderate success because the overhead was so low (Dika 1990: 15).[6] These slasher films played the downtown cinemas, the grind-house circuits, and, of course, the drive-in cinemas; these being as close as North America gets to an equivalent of the *terza visione* audience. Dika noted that, much like Wagstaff's *terza* audience, "the [slasher film] audience does not merely 'root' for the 'home team' (the hero) in silence; instead, it behaves boisterously. It cheers, hoots, and encourages the events on screen, and it does so as a group" (Dika 1990: 17). The slasher film, as vernacular cinema, was never intended to be watched as a unified whole, as a holistic narrative to be contemplated, but only to give its audience enough shocks to justify the admission price. Therefore, like the *giallo*, we can see the slasher film as another kind of vernacular cinema.

One of the larger differences between *gialli* and slasher films is the often urban settings of most *gialli* films, while slasher films tend to be set in isolated, often rural (or at least quiet suburban) settings. Smaller towns and villages, if not the stereotypical isolated summer camp, tend to be the norm. Some *gialli* may focus their action on isolated communities or locations (lighthouses, villas, fashion houses), but by and large these films take place in cities. Slasher movies isolate their locations as a rule, although there are occasional exceptions: *Night School* (Ken Hughes, 1981) and *Graduation Day* (Herb Freed, 1981) are both slasher films, and both are urban based. While some slasher movies may restrict all the murders to school property, as in *Prom Night* (Paul Lynch, 1980), or a moving train, as in *Terror Train* (Roger Spottiswood, 1980), the vast majority will restrict only their final act to a set location, after establishing a larger locale. For example, before *My Bloody Valentine* (George Mihalka, 1981) spends its third act down the mine, the first two-thirds of the movie explore the small community of Valentine Bluffs. Films like *My Bloody Valentine* give a vague nod to the *giallo*, which, as in *Torso*, only move to the isolated locale in the second half of the film.

One reason for the slasher film's preference for isolated locales, beyond simple budgetary restraint, has to do with time scale. As I stated above, most slasher movies take place over a single twenty-four-hour period, or a few days at best. *Giallo* movies tend to take place over several days, if not weeks. The condensed narrative time line of the slasher makes for a restricted setting too. If the killer is *somewhere in the house*, then the characters stand a better chance of meeting him (occasionally her); whereas if the killer is *somewhere in the city*, then the characters stand a better chance of avoiding him or her. Because the ultimate focus of slasher films is inherently different from the *giallo*, concentrating on the chase and avoidance of the killer over the span of a few hours rather than the puzzle aspect, there is no need to incorporate the relative spatial safety of an entire city to allow for a spatial and temporal reprieve in order to reflect on the murders and figure out who is responsible for them.

When I coined the phrase "Scooby-Doo" movies to refer to a *filone* of the slasher genre, I was responding to a certain narrative tradition where the killer spends most of his or her time interacting with the other characters "normally" (i.e., not killing them). In *Halloween*, conversely, anyone who meets Michael Myers is likely to be killed on the spot, but Alex (Michael Tough) in *Prom Night* and Axel (Neil Affleck) in *My Bloody Valentine*, are not suspected of being the killer—either by the other characters or by the film audience. Both these movies include an off-screen prime suspect (they are talked about, not shown), Leonard Merch in *Prom Night* and Harry Warden in *Valentine*, killers (or suspected killers) who are known and feared by the communities, who have recently escaped from an institution, and who the police are currently searching for. This narrative *filone* echoes the hunt for the likewise escaped Myers in *Halloween*. The difference here, and *Prom Night*'s and *Valentine*'s difference from the "terror tale," is that Myers *is* continuing to kill, whereas the escapee is a red herring in the later two films. Axel takes on the persona of the escapee Warden during his murder spree, and Alex is punishing those he feels are responsible for his sister's death. In the "Scooby-Doo," or North American *gialli* slasher movies, none of the *giallo* killers is continuously killing, like Michael. The narrative game is more about *who* the killer is.

In a *gialli*-like variation of the slasher film, *Terror Train*, while we suspect from the outset that the killer is Kenny Hampson (Derek McKinnon), seeking revenge for a prank gone wrong three years earlier, because the New Year's Eve party on the titular train is a masquerade party, both games of *where* the killer is and *who* the killer is are played out due to the narrative logic of having Kenny frequently change costume. So this is a case where the audience has suspicions, but unlike *Prom Night* or *Valentine*, the suspicions are correct.

In the non-*giallo*-like slasher movies, however, suspects are unnecessary. Suspects are rarely necessary in any slasher film, as there is no real investigation or mystery to be solved. Everyone knows that the killer is Michael, or Jason, or Cropsy. We know who the killers are in the "psycho-character study" movies because they are the films' protagonists. But in the North American *gialli*, when part of the film's plot is the mystery element of *who* the killer is, we need some suspects. And most of these dramatis personae come right out of the *giallo*. There will inevitably be a minor character who is coded as somehow "creepy." Sykes (Robert Silverman) in *Prom Night* is an example; he is the school's janitor, who, it is rumored, peeks in the girls' locker room. Alfred (Jack Blum), in *Happy Birthday to Me* (J. Lee Thompson, 1981), Virginia's friend, who likes experimenting with latex masks and gruesome prosthetic heads, is another. I have already noted the escaped psycho scenario. *Prom Night* also features the local bad boy, Lou (David Mucci), as a suspect, although his inclusion seems to be "in the tradition of" Billy Nolan (John Travolta) in *Carrie* (Brian de Palma, 1976). Other suspects are vengeful fathers; both Raymond Hammon (Leslie Nielsen) in *Prom Night* and Hal

Wainwright (Lawrence Dane) in *Happy Birthday to Me* could be the killer seeking to avenge the wrongs done to their respective daughters. Of course, in *Terror Train*, almost every one present *could* be a suspect, as no one knows what costume Kenny is wearing at any one time.

The *giallo*'s amateur detective becomes the Final Girl in the slasher film. It is worth quoting Carol Clover's definition of this role in full:

> [The Final Girl is] the one character of stature who does live to tell the tale . . . . She is introduced at the beginning and is the only character to be developed in any psychological detail. We understand immediately from the attention paid it that hers is the main story line. She is intelligent, watchful, level-headed; the first character to sense something is amiss and the only one to deduce from the accumulating evidence the pattern and extent of the threat; the only one, in other words, whose perspective approaches our own privileged understanding of the situation. (1992: 44)

In the *giallo*, the amateur detective role mirrors "our own privileged understanding of the situation," as it is these characters who lead us through the solving of the mystery. But come the slasher film, that role disappears. Due to some of the reasons noted above—specifically the compression of narrative time and the focus of locale—there is little chance for investigation in the slasher movie. And yet, Clover overstates her point: of the four North American *gialli* I am dealing with in any depth here—*Prom Night*, *Terror Train*, *My Bloody Valentine*, and *Happy Birthday to Me*—only Alana (Jamie Lee Curtis) could remotely be considered a Final Girl role in the tradition of *Halloween*'s Laurie Strode (Jamie Lee Curtis) or *Friday the 13th*'s Alice (Adrienne King). More *giallo*-like, it is the police who shoot dead *Prom Night*'s Alex; Axel's love rival, TJ (Paul Kelman), collapses the mine around the killer while saving the damsel Sarah (Lori Hallier); and while Alana holds her own against Kenny, it is the train conductor, Carne (Ben Johnson), who pushes the killer out of the carriage and into the icy river. In the more *giallo*-inflected slasher movies, despite the absence of an amateur detective figure, it is still the men who often save the day, even if, like the police, they arrive deus ex machina.

Both slasher movies and *gialli* share the narrative device of connecting the current spate of murders to some kind of past trauma suffered by the killer. Dika calls this, for the slasher movies, "the past event" (1990: 59), and it was an essential element to her study. This notion of the past event also permeates the *giallo*, and we have seen throughout how *gialli* killers are compelled to murder by some past trauma. Like the *giallo*, many of the slasher movies recreate these past traumas, often as prologues and precredit sequences, in the films. *Prom Night*, for example, opens with the fatal accident of Robin Hammond (Tammy Bourne) and *Terror Train*, with the prank that sent Kenny Hampson to the asylum. *My Bloody Valentine* utilizes a two-pronged recreation of the past event: on the one hand when the story of Harry Warden's rampage is first related, and again when Axel relates seeing his father murdered by Warden. The film, however, does not open with these past events; they are related later in the film when the story becomes relevant. While some *gialli* open with the past event—*Who Saw Her Die?* opens with the murder of a young girl in a precredit sequence—most are gradually retold throughout the film as the amateur detective discovers more and more about the case. While *Deep Red* opens with a recreation of the past event, it is not until toward the end of the film when we understand its true significance and how, due to the low-angle perspective in which Argento films this opening sequence, which effectively masks what really happened, we have been misled all the way through the film.

The slasher film that reveals the most narrative indebtedness to the *giallo* is J. Lee Thompson's *Happy Birthday to Me*. On the surface, several school friends of Virginia (Melissa Sue Anderson) are being killed in some creative and bizarre ways (one is decapitated by having his scarf thrown into the moving wheel of a motorcycle, another by having barbells dropped on his neck, a third—most famously as this image graced the film's poster—is skewered in the mouth with a shish-kabob), echoing some of the bizarre murders in the *giallo*. We know almost from the outset of the film that Virginia is new to Crawford Academy, although we quickly learn she has recently *returned* to the school after being away for several years. Virginia is still under the care of a psychiatrist, Dr. Faraday (Glenn Ford), and she has undergone a radical new treatment for brain injuries, where the brain tissue is encouraged to regrow under high-radiation treatment. Halfway through the film, we actually *see* Virginia commit one, two, and finally three of the murders. But the *giallo*-like twist is still to come: the denouement of the film, a macabre birthday party where all the guests are the dead bodies of her murdered friends. Here the final guest is revealed to be Virginia herself, as the murderous Virginia removes an elaborate rubber mask, revealing herself to be Ann Thomerson (Tracey Bregman), Virginia's best friend. Just prior to this final sequence, Virginia finally understands the past event that has been repressed in her mind and was the cause of both her mother's death and the injury she sustained. Once Ann is revealed to be the film's actual killer, we get even more narrative about the past trauma. Past trauma piles on past trauma in a truly baroque plot worthy of Ernesto Gastaldi.

Birthday also takes advantage of the tradition of the *giallo* killer's black driving gloves, as does *Prom Night* before it, in which Alex also uses the black balaclava. The killer in *Night School* wears a motorcycle helmet to cover his face and is in cycle leathers when killing, including his own pair of black gloves. Axel, in *My Bloody Valentine*, dressed as the killer miner, Harry Warden, wears full coal-mining gear—light helmet, gas mask, black coveralls, and thick black work gloves. The black-gloved killers of the *giallo* seem merely to have moved across the Atlantic Ocean toward the end of the 1970s and into the 1980s.

But as I noted at the very beginning of this book, Italian vernacular cinema tends to take its lead from previous successful, often American, films. The tradition of the *filone* tends to work *from* America *to* Italy. With the popularity of the slasher film, this trend seems somewhat reversed: the Italian vernacular cinema influencing the North American. The veins of influence of the *filone* run both ways. However, in the majority of cases, Italian filmmakers are influenced by American models, and influence from Italy on Americans is still not the norm. With the success of the North American slasher film, it was inevitable, then, that Italy would begin to produce its own slasher films.

The Italian Slasher

Notwithstanding the influence American cinema has on Italian filmmakers, it must be said that the Italian slasher movie is a rarity. The similarity between the slasher movie and the *giallo* is so marked that to interpret the North American *filone* into an Italian context would be to end up with a kind of vernacular cinema that was too much like the older form of *giallo*. To do an Italian slasher movie would have risked being seen as too old fashioned and therefore not an appropriate investment. After the dominance of the *giallo* in the 1970s, other *filone* emerged, often disappearing as quickly as they began: the Nazi Sexploitation *filone* (see Koven 2004), the cannibal *filone*, the zombie *filone*, the killer nun movies, the Emmanuelle movies, the post-Apocalypse movies, and so on. The slasher movie never really seemed to grab Italian vernacular audiences, at least not in such a way as to warrant emulation.

Stagefright was the low-budget directorial debut of Argento protégé Michele Soavi, produced by Italian vernacular cinema icon, Joe D'Amato. Having worked so closely with Argento since *Tenebre* in 1982, one might have expected a more traditional thriller for an inaugural production. But Soavi chose to make a slasher movie, rather than a straightforward *giallo*.

The film begins as a stereotypical *giallo*: a serial killer stalking skid row for prostitutes to kill. But Soavi turns this around, revealing this opening as a stage production of a *giallo*/slasher narrative called "The Night Owl." We have seen this device before with Castellari's 1971 *Cold Eyes of Fear*, and something similar in Riccardo Freda's 1980 *The Wailing*; so we are in very familiar *giallo* territory with this opening sequence. We are introduced to a number of characters who are likely to be a potential murderer: Peter (David Brandon), the dictatorial director of the play who will not allow anything to compromise his art; Mark (Martin Phillips), the much put-upon stage manager who might be seeking revenge; or even Alicia (Barbra Cupisti), the actress fired because she sought medical attention for her twisted ankle and left the theater without permission. But added to the mix is an escaped psychopathic killer, Irving Wallace (Clain Parker), who murders the costume mistress, Betty (Ulrike Schwerk). As a result of Betty's murder, Peter looks even more likely to be the killer, as he realizes how good real murders will be for the show's box office. Or perhaps the film's real killer will turn out to be Ferarri (Piero Vida), the unscrupulous investor, who also sees potential revenue from the press that such a series of murders could generate. With such a cast of potential killers, plus an escaped psycho on the loose, *Stagefright* falls very much within the narrative pattern of the slasher-*gialli*, such as *Prom Night* or *My Bloody Valentine*, using the escaped killer as a red herring the way the Canadian slasher movies did. Soavi appears to be very aware of the genre sophistication of this audience, for each of the elements is introduced one at a time, pointing to their obviousness as plot devices.

However, what turns *Stagefright* around is that this particular slasher film is an "Old Skool" terror tale: Irving Wallace really *is* the killer on the loose, killing the entire cast and crew, whom Peter had locked inside the theater for the night to ensure they rehearsed. Like Michael Myers or Jason Voorhees, Wallace is always killing, never mixing "normally" with the other characters as in the *giallo*. Again, unlike the *giallo*, the story of the film takes place in a single night, which denies any chance of an investigation and pushes the narrative to one of aiming to survive. Instead of any amateur detective role, Alicia emerges as the Final Girl, engaging in physical battle with Wallace several times. Like most good slasher movie killers, Wallace is not easy to kill. Alicia throws him from the theater's catwalk and sets him on fire, but it is the theater caretaker, Willy (James Sampson), who finally shoots Wallace in the head while delivering a lecture to Alicia about how a gun cannot work unless she first takes the safety off.

Stagefright is the exception that proves the rule: while Italian vernacular filmmakers may have had a remarkable influence on the development of the slasher film in the late 1970s and early 1980s, the times had changed with the new decade. While clearly Italian vernacular cinema is still influenced by American antecedents, Soavi's film demonstrates that when the tradition of influences is so similar, emulation can quickly become redundancy. And the Italian *giallo* film gave way to the North American slasher film. While a few *giallo* films were made in the 1980s, mostly by Dario Argento himself (*Tenebre*, *Phenomena*, and *Opera*), only Lamberto Bava, Mario Bava's son, was really making *gialli* anymore, with two films, *A Blade in the Dark* (1983) and *Delirium: Photos of Gioia* (*Le Foto di Gioia*) (1987). Beyond the 1990s and into the new century, Dario Argento is still producing *giallo* films: *Trauma* (1993), *The Stendhal Syndrome* (1996), *Sleepless* (2001), *The Card Player* (*Il Cartaio*) (2004), and *Do You Like Hitchcock?* (*Ti piace Hitchcock?*) (2005).

Sporadically, other filmmakers try to produce these old-fashioned-style thrillers, with varying degrees of success, either in Italy or beyond. The best of the contemporary *gialli*, *Occhi di cristallo* (Eros Puglielli, 2004), which I was lucky enough to catch at Edinburgh's "Dead by Dawn" film festival in 2005, while available on DVD in Italian, does not offer English subtitles or an English soundtrack. It seems that with the exception of new films by internationally recognized masters of the genre, such as Argento, these thrillers seem to be made exclusively for the local, vernacular audiences. And maybe that is as it should be.

Notes

1. The tradition of bizarre titles for these films comes from the literary *giallo* tradition. The film titles are intended to echo the novels of writers like Ellery Queen, Edgar Wallace, and Fredric Brown.

2. Early in the *filone* there was a temporary vogue for "animal names" in the wake of Argento's *The Bird with the Crystal Plumage*: *Cat O' Nine Tails*, *Four Flies on Grey Velvet*, *Il gatto dagli occhi di giada* (the Italian title for *The Cat's Victims*, which translates literally as "The Cat with Jade Eyes"), *The Black Belly of the Tarantula*, *The Iguana with the Tongue of Fire*, *A Lizard in a Woman's Skin*, *Don't Torture a Duckling*, *Gatti rossi in un libirinto di verto* (the Italian title for *Eyeball*, which translates literally as "Red Cats in a Glass Maze"), and the list goes on. As Maitland McDonagh noted, in the 1970s, these films were "glutting the market with thrillers whose outlandish titles were the only interesting things about them" (1994: 96). More details are provided in the filmography.

3. Gastaldi is possibly the most prolific of *giallo* screenwriters. In addition to *Torso*, he wrote *The Forbidden Photos of a Lady Above Suspicion*, *Next!*, *The Case of the Scorpion's Tail* (*La Coda dello scorpione*) (Sergio Martino, 1971), *Death Walks at Midnight*, *All the Colors of the Dark*, *Your Vice is a Locked Door and Only I Have the Key* (*Tuo vizio è una stanza chiusa e solo io ne ho la chiave*) (Sergio Martino, 1972), and *The Case of the Bloody Iris*. Looking over Gastaldi's filmography he was the screenwriter of choice for both Sergio Martino and Luciano Ercoli. He was also a highly prolific screenwriter for the spaghetti westerns.

4. In point of fact, most of these "North American *gialli*" are Canadian.

5. Dika included as one of her examples *The Fan* (Edward Bianchi, 1981), which starred Lauren Bacall, Maureen Stapleton, and James Garner. This is not the place to quibble with Dika; however, it is worth noting that she got the date of the film's release wrong by two or three years (she cited 1979), and while on the one hand this can be seen as an irrelevancy, *The Fan*, I would argue, is a big-budget, Hollywood attempt to cash in on the slasher/stalker films.

6. For a thorough and quite detailed analysis of the financing, distribution, and ultimate success of the *Friday the 13th* movies, see Grove (2005).

~

Filmography

Antonioni, Michelangelo. *The Red Desert* [*Il Deserto rosso*]. Screenplay by Michelangelo Antonioni and Tonino Guerra. 1964. 120 min.

Argento, Dario. *The Bird with the Crystal Plumage* [*L'uccello dale piume di Cristallo*]. Screenplay by Dario Argento, based on the novel "The Screaming Mimi" by Fredric Brown. 1970. 96 min.

———. *The Card Player* [*Il Cartaio*]. Screenplay by Dario Argento and Franco Ferrini. 2004. 103 min.

———. *The Cat O' Nine Tails* [*Il Gatto a nove code*]. Screenplay by Dario Argento, Luigi Collo, and Dardano Sacchetti. 1971. 112 min.

———. *Deep Red* [*Profondo rosso*]. Screenplay by Dario Argento and Bernardino Zapponi. 1975. 120 min.

———. *Do You Like Hitchcock?* [*Ti piace Hitchcock?*]. Screenplay by Dario Argento and Franco Ferrini. 2005. 93 min.

———. *Four Flies on Grey Velvet* [*4 mosche di velluto grigio*]. Screenplay by Dario Argento, Luigi Cozzi, and Mario Foglietti. 1971. 104 min.

———. *Opera*. Screenplay by Dario Argento and Franco Ferrini. 1987. 107 min.

———. *Phenomena*. Screenplay by Dario Argento and Franco Ferrini. 1985. 110 min.

———. *Sleepless* [*Non ho sonno*]. Screenplay by Dario Argento, Franco Ferrini, and Carlo Lucarelli. 2001. 117 min.

———. *The Stendhal Syndrome* [*La Sindrome di Stendhal*]. Screenplay by Dario Argento and Franco Ferrini, based on the novel by Graziella Magherini. 1996. 113 min.

———. *Tenebre*. Screenplay by Dario Argento. 1982. 101 min.

———. *Trauma*. Screenplay by Dario Argento and T. E. D. Klein. 1993. 105 min.

Avati, Pupi. *The House with Laughing Windows* [*La Casa dale finestre che ridono*]. Screenplay by Pupi Avati, Antonio Avati, Gianni Cavina, and Maurizio Costanzo. 1976. 110 min.

Bava, Lamberto. *A Blade in the Dark* [*La casa con la scala nel buio*]. Screenplay by Dardano Sacchetti and Elisa Briganti. 1983. 108 min.

———. *Delirium: Photos of Gioia* [*Le Foto di Gioia*]. Screenplay by Gianfranco Clerici, Luciano Martino, and Daniele Stroppa. 1987. 97 min.

Bava, Mario. *Bay of Blood* [*Reazione a catena*]. Screenplay by Mario Bava, Franco Barberi, Fillipo Ottoni, Dardano Sacchetti, and Giuseppe Zaccariello. 1971. 84 min.

———. *Blood and Black Lace* [*Sei donne per l'assassino*]. Screenplay by Mario Bava, Giuseppe Barilla, and Marcello Fondato. 1964. 84 min.

———. *Five Dolls for an August Moon* [*Cinque bambole per la luna d'agosto*]. Screenplay by Mario di Nardo. 1970. 88 min.

———. *The Girl Who Knew Too Much* [*La Ragazza che sapeva troppo*]. Screenplay by Mario Bava, Enzo Corbucci, Ennio De Concini, Eliana De Sabata, Mino Guerrini, and Franco Prosperi. 1962. 86 min.

———. *Hatchet for the Honeymoon* [*Il Rosso sego della follia*]. Screenplay by Mario Bava, Santiago Moncada, and Mario Musy. 1969. 88 min.

———. *Kill, Baby . . . Kill!* [*Operazione paura*]. Screenplay by Mario Bava, Roberto Natale, and Romano Miglorini. 1966. 83 min.

Bazzoni, Luigi. *The Fifth Cord* [*Giornata nera per l'ariete*]. Screenplay by Luigi Bazzoni, Mario di Nardo, and Mario Fanelli, based on the novel by David McDonald Devine. 1971. 88 min.

Benigni, Roberto. *Il Mostro*. Screenplay by Roberto Benigni, Michel Blanc, and Vincenzo Cerami. 1994. 112 min.

Bergman, Ingmar. *The Virgin Spring* [*Jungfrukällan*]. Screenplay by Ulla Isaksson. 1960. 89 min.

Bergonzelli, Sergio. *In the Folds of the Flesh* [*Nelle pieghe della carne*]. Screenplay by Sergio Bergonzelli, Mario Caiano, and Fabio de Agostini. 1970. 88 min.

Bianchi, Edward. *The Fan*. Screenplay by Priscilla Chapman and John Hartwell, based on the novel by Bob Randall. 1981. 95 min.

Bido, Antonio. *The Bloodstained Shadow* [*Solamente nero*]. Screenplay by Antonio Bido, Marisa Andalo, and Domenico Malan. 1978. 95 min.

———. *The Cat's Victims* [*Il gatto dagli occhi di giada*]. Screenplay by Antonio Bido, Roberto Natale, Vittorio Schiraldi, and Aldo Serio. 1977. 95 min.

Boorman, John. *Deliverance*. Screenplay by James Dickey, based on his novel. 1972. 109 min.

Carnimeo, Giuliano. *The Case of the Bloody Iris* [*Perche quelle stran gocce di sangue sul corpo di Jennifer?*]. Screenplay by Ernesto Gastaldi. 1971. 94 min.

Carpenter, John. *Halloween*. Screenplay by John Carpenter and Debra Hill. 1978. 91 min.

Castellari, Enzo. *Cold Eyes of Fear* [*Gli occhi fredda della paura*]. Screenplay by Leo Anchóriz, Tito Carpi, and Enzo G. Castellari. 1971. 91 min.

Cavara, Paolo. *The Black Belly of the Tarantula* [*La Tarantula dal ventre nero*]. Screenplay by Marcello Danon and Lucile Laks. 1972. 89 min.

Clark, Bob. *Porky's*. Screenplay by Bob Clark. 1982. 94 min.

Cozzi, Luigi. *Killer Must Kill Again* [*L'Assassino è costretto ad uccidere ancora*]. Screenplay by Adriano Bolzoni, Luigi Cozzi, and Daniele Del Giudice. 1975. 86 min.

Craven, Wes. *Last House on the Left*. Screenplay by Wes Craven. 1972. 91 min.

———. *New Nightmare*. Screenplay by Wes Craven. 1994. 112 min.

———. *A Nightmare on Elm Street*. Screenplay by Wes Craven. 1984. 91 min.

Crispino, Armando. *Autopsy* [*Macchie solari*]. Screenplay by Armando Crispino and Lucio Battistrada. 1973. 100 min.

Cunningham, Sean S. *Friday the 13th*. Screenplay by Victor Miller. 1980. 95 min.

Dallamano, Massimo. *A Black Veil for Lisa* [*La Morte non ha sesso*]. Screenplay by Giuseppe Belli, Massimo Dallamano, Peter Kintzel, Audrey Nohra, Vitalino Petrilli, and Vittoriano Petrilli. 1968. 95 min.

———. *Solange* [*Cosa avente fatto a Solange?*]. Screenplay by Massimo Dallamano and Bruno Di Geronimo, based on a novel by Edgar Wallace. 1972. 102 min.

———. *What Have They Done to Our Daughters?* [*La Polizia chiede aiuto*]. Screenplay by Massimo Dallamano and Ettore Sanzò. 1974. 96 min.

Demme, Jonathan. *The Silence of the Lambs*. Screenplay by Ted Tally, based on the novel by Thomas Harris. 1991. 118 min.

De Palma, Brian. *Carrie*. Screenplay by Lawrence D. Cohen, based on the novel by Stephen King. 1976. 98 min.

Donner, Richard. *The Omen*. Screenplay by David Seltzer, based on his novel. 1976. 111 min.

Elorrieta, José María. *Feast of Satan* [*Las Amantes del diablo*]. Screenplay by José María Elorrieta, Miguel Madrid, José Luis Navarro, and Esparaco Santoni. 1971. 90 min.

Ercoli, Luciano. *Death Walks at Midnight* [*La Morte accarezza a mezzanotte*]. Screenplay by Ernesto Gastaldi and Mahnahén Velasco. 1972. 103 min.

———. *The Forbidden Photos of a Lady Above Suspicion* [*Le Foto proibite di una signora per bene*]. Screenplay by Ernesto Gastaldi and Mahnahén Velasco. 1970. 93 min.

Fellini, Federico. *La Dolce Vita*. Screenplay by Federico Fellini, Ennio Flaino, Tullio Pinelli, and Brunello Rondi. 1960. 174 min.

———. *8½*. Screenplay by Federico Fellini, Ennio Flaino, Tullio Pinelli, and Brunello Rondi. 1963. 138 min.

Fincher, David. *Alien³* Screenplay by David Giler, Walter Hill, and Larry Ferguson. 1992. 114 min.

———. *Se7en*. Screenplay by Andrew Keven Walker. 1995. 127 min.

Findlay, Michael, Roberta Findlay, and Horacio Fredriksson. *Snuff*. Screenplay by Michael Findlay, Roberta Findlay, and A. Bochin. 1976. 76 min.

Francisci, Pietro. *Hercules* [*Le Fatiche di Ercole*]. Screenplay by Pietro Francisci, Ennio De Concini, and Gaio Frattini. 1958. 98 min.

Franju, Georges. *Les Yeux sans visage*. Screenplay by Pierre Boileau, Thomas Narcejac, Jean Redon, and Claude Sautet, based on the novel by Jean Redon. 1959. 88 min.

Freda, Riccardo. *The Wailing* [*L'Obsessione che uccide*]. Screenplay by Antonio Cesare Corti, Riccardo Freda, and Fabio Piccioni. 1980. 92 min.

Freda, Riccardo (as Willy Pareto). *The Iguana with the Tongue of Fire* [*L'iguana dalla lingua di fuoco*]. Screenplay by Riccardo Freda and Sandro Continenza. 1971. 90 min.

Freed, Herb. *Graduation Day*. Screenplay by Herb Freed and Anne Marisse. 1981. 85 min.

Friedkin, William. *The Exorcist*. Screenplay by William Peter Blatty, based on his novel. 1973. 122 min.

Fulci, Lucio. *The Beyond* [*E tu vivrai nel terror—L'aldilà*]. Screenplay by Dardano Sacchetti, Giorgio Mariuzzo, and Lucio Fulci. 1981. 87 min.

———. *The Black Cat* [*Il Gatto nero*]. Screenplay by Lucio Fulci, Biagio Proietti, and Sergio Salvati, based on the story by Edgar Allan Poe. 1981. 92 min.

———. *Don't Torture a Duckling* [*Non si sevizia un paperino*]. Screenplay by Lucio Fulci, Roberto Gianviti, and Gianfranco Clerici. 1972. 102 min.

———. *A Lizard in a Woman's Skin* [*Una Lucertola con la pelle di donna*]. Screenplay by Lucio Fulci, Roberto Gianviti, José Luis Martínez Mollá, and André Tranché. 1971. 96 min.

———. *One on Top of the Other* [*Una sull'altra*]. Screenplay by Lucio Fulci, Roberto Gianviti, and José Luis Martínez Mollá. 1969. 99 min.

———. *The New York Ripper* [*Lo Squartatore di New York*]. Screenplay by Lucio Fulci, Gianfranco Clerici, Dardano Sacchetti, and Vincenzo Mannino. 1982. 93 min.

———. *Zombie* [*Zombi 2*]. Screenplay by Elisa Briganti and Dardano Sacchetti. 1979. 91 min.

Hardy, Robin. *The Wicker Man*. Screenplay by Anthony Shaffer. 1974. 100 min.

Hitchcock, Alfred. *The Birds*. Screenplay by Evan Hunter. 1963. 119 min.

Hughes, Ken. *Night School*. Screenplay by Ruth Avergon. 1981. 88 min.

Lado, Aldo. *Night Train Murders* [*L'Ultimo treno della notte*]. Screenplay by Roberto Infascelli, Renato Izzo, Aldo Lado, and Ettore Sanzò. 1975. 94 min.

———. *The Short Night of Glass Dolls* [*Malastrana*]. Screenplay by Aldo Lado. 1971. 91 min.

———. *Who Saw Her Die?* [*Chi l'ha vista morire?*]. Screenplay by Francesco Barilli, Massimo D'Avak, Aldo Lado, and Ruediger von Spiess. 1972. 94 min.

Lenzi, Umberto. *Eyeball* [*Gatti rossi in un libirinto di verto*]. Screenplay by Umberto Lenzi and Félix Tusell. 1975. 97 min.

———. *Paranoia*. Screenplay by Marcello Coscia, Bruno Di Geronimo, and Rafael Romero Marchent. 1969. 94 min.

———. *Seven Blood Stained Orchids* [*Sette orchidee macchiate di rosso*]. Screenplay by Umberto Lenzi and Roberto Gianviti, based on the novel of Edgar Wallace. 1971. 88 min.

———. *Spasmo*. Screenplay by Pino Boller, Massimo Franciosa, Umberto Lenzi, and Luisa Montagnana. 1974. 94 min.

Leone. Sergio. *Once Upon a Time in the West* [*C'era una volta il West*]. Screenplay by Dario Argento, Bernardo Bertolucci, Sergio Leone, and Sergio Donati. 1968. 165 min.

Lustig, William. *Maniac*. Screenplay by C. A. Rosenberg and Joe Spinell. 1980. 87 min.

Lynch, Paul. *Prom Night*. Screenplay by William Gray. 1980. 87 min.

Martino, Sergio. *All the Colors of the Dark* [*Tutti I colori del buio*]. Screenplay by Ernesto Gastaldi, Santiago Moncada, and Sauro Scavolini. 1972. 88 min.

———. *The Case of the Scorpion's Tail* [*La Coda dello scorpione*]. Screenplay by Vittorio Caronia, Ernesto Gastaldi, and Eduardo Manzanos Brochero. 1971. 90 min.

———. *Next!* [*Lo Strano vizio della Signora Wardh*]. Screenplay by Sauro Scavolini, Ernesto Gastaldi, and Eduardo Manzanos Brochero. 1970. 92 min.

———. *Torso* [*I Corpi presentano tracce di violenza carnale*]. Screenplay by Sergio Martino and Ernesto Gastaldi. 1973. 89 min.

———. *Your Vice Is a Locked Door and Only I Have the Key* [*Tuo vizio è una stanza chiusa e solo io ne ho la chiave*]. Screenplay by Adriano Bolzoni, Ernesto Gastaldi, Luciano Martino, and Sauro Scavolini, based on the short story "The Black Cat" by Edgar Allan Poe. 1972. 96 min.

Maylam, Tony. *The Burning*. Screenplay by Peter Lawrence and Bob Weinstein. 1981. 91 min.

McNaughton, John. *Henry—Portrait of a Serial Killer*. Screenplay by John McNaughton and Richard Fire. 1986. 83 min.

Mihalka, George. *My Bloody Valentine*. Screenplay by John Beaird. 1981. 91 min.

Miner, Steve. *Friday the 13th Part 3*. Screenplay by Martin Kitrosser and Carol Watson. 1982. 95 min.

Mogherini, Flavio. *The Pyjama Girl Case* [*La Ragazza dal pigiama giallo*]. Screenplay by Flavio Mogherini and Rafael Sánchez Campoy. 1977. 98 min.

Pasolini, Pier Paolo. *Salo, or 120 Days of Sodom* [*Salò o le 120 giornatt di Sodoma*]. Screenplay by Pier Paolo Pasolini and Sergio Citti, based on the novel by the Marquis de Sade. 1975. 115 min.

Peckinpah, Sam. *The Wild Bunch*. Screenplay by Walon Green and Sam Peckinpah. 1969. 145 min.

Polanski, Roman. *Rosemary's Baby*. Screenplay by Roman Polanski, based on the novel by Ira Levin. 1968. 136 min.

Pollock, George. *Murder, She Said*. Screenplay by David Pursall and Jack Seddon, based on the novel *4:50 from Paddington* by Agatha Christie. 1961. 87 min.

Polselli, Renato (as Ralph Brown). *Delirium* [*Delirio caldo*]. Screenplay by Renato Polselli. 1972. 90 min.

Pradeaux, Maurizio. *Death Steps in the Dark* [*Passi di morte perduti nel buio*]. Screenplay by Maurizio Pradeaux and Arpad DeRiso. 1977. 90 min.

Puglielli, Eros. *Occhi di cristallo*. Screenplay by Gabrella Blasi, Franco Ferrini, and Eros Puglielli, based on the novel *L'impagliatore* by Luca Di Fulvio. 2004. 95 min.

Ratti, Fillippo Walter. *Crazy Desires of a Murderer* [*I Vizi morbosi di una governante*]. Screenplay by Ambrogio Molteni. 1974. 88 min.

Roland, Jürgen. *The Green Archer* [*Der Grüne Bogenschütze*]. Screenplay by Wolfgang Menge and Wolfgang Schnitzler, based on the novel by Edgar Wallace. 1961. 95 min.

Romero. George A. *Dawn of the Dead*. Screenplay by Geroge A. Romero. 1978. 139 min.

Scavolini, Romano. *Nightmare*. Screenplay by Romano Scavolini. 1981. 97 min.

Schwarz, John Alan. *Faces of Death.* Screenplay by John Alan Schwartz. 1978. 105 min.

Soavi, Michele. *Dario Argento's World of Horror* [*Il Mondo dell'orrore di Dario Argento*]. Screenplay by Michele Soavi. 1985. 76 min.

———. *Stagefright* [*Deliria*]. Screenplay by George Eastman and Sheila Goldberg. 1987. 90 min.

Spottiswood, Roger. *Terror Train.* Screenplay by T. Y. Drake. 1980. 97 min.

Tessari, Duccio. *The Bloodstained Butterfly* [*Una Farfalla con le ali insanguinate*]. Screenplay by Duccio Tessari and Gianfranco Clerici. 1971. 92 min.

Thompson, J. Lee. *Happy Birthday to Me.* Screenplay by John C. W. Saxton, Peter Jobin, and Timothy Bond. 1981. 110 min.

Valerii, Tonino. *My Dear Killer* [*Mio caro assassino*]. Screenplay by Franco Bucceri, José Gutiérrez Maesso, Roberto Leoni, and Tonino Valerii. 1971. 98 min.

Visconti, Luchino. *Ossessione.* Screenplay by Luchino Visconti, Mario Alicata, and Giuseppe De Santis, based on the novel *The Postman Always Rings Twice* by James M. Caine. 1943. 140 min.

Vohrer. Alfred. *Dead Eyes of London* [*Die Toten Augen von London*]. Screenplay by Egon Eis, based on the novel by Edgar Wallace. 1961. 98 min.

Zimmermann, Vernon. *Fade to Black.* Screenplay by Vernon Zimmermann. 1980. 105 min.

~

Bibliography

Agnelli, Tiziano, Umberto Bartocci, and Adriano Rosellini. 1998. "Nascita, Morte E Resurrezione: Del Libro Giallo In Italia—Breve Storia E Catalogo Orientativo Delle Principali Collane Edite In Italia Dal 1903 Al 1948," http://www.foglio-giallo.it/index.html.

Barber, Chris. 2003. "Discovering the Esoteric Argento." In *Eyeball Compendium: Writings on Sex and Horror in the Cinema from the Pages of Eyeball Magazine, 1989–2003*, edited by Stephen Thrower. Godalming, UK: FAB Press, 85–89.

Bazin, André. 1999 [1950–55]. "The Evolution of the Language of Cinema." In *Film Theory and Criticism: Introductory Readings*, 5th ed., edited by Leo Braudy and Marshall Cohen, 43–56. Oxford: Oxford University Press.

Bertellini, Giorgio. "*Profondo Rosso/Deep Red*." In *The Cinema of Italy*, edited by Giorgio Bertellini. London: Wallflower Press, 2004, 213–22.

Bondanella, Peter. 2001. *Italian Cinema: From Neorealism to the Present*, 3rd edition. New York: Continuum.

Bordwell, David, Janet Staiger, and Kristin Thompson. 1985. *The Classical Hollywood Cinema: Film Style and Mode of Production to 1960*. London: Routledge.

Brown, Allan. 2000. *Inside the Wicker Man: The Morbid Ingenuities*. London: Sidgwick and Jackson.

Canova, Gianni. 1996. "Argento, Dario." In *The Companion to Italian Cinema*, edited by Geoffrey Nowell-Smith, with James Hay and Gianni Volpi. London: BFI, 17.

Cawelti, John G. 1976. *Adventure, Mystery, and Romance: Formula Stories as Art and Popular Culture*. Chicago: University of Chicago Press.

Christie, Agatha. 1997. *Miss Marple Omnibus*. London: HarperCollins.

———. [1939], 2003. *And Then There Were None*. London: HarperCollins.

———. [1936] 2004. *The A.B.C. Murders*. London: Berkley Publishing Group.

———. [1936] 2001. *Death on the Nile*. London: HarperCollins.

———. [1926] 2004. *The Murder of Roger Ackroyd*. London: Berkley Publishing Group.

———. [1934] 2001. *Murder on the Orient Express*. London: HarperCollins.

Clover, Carol. 1992. *Men, Women and Chainsaws: Gender in the Modern Horror Film*. London: BFI.

Combs, Richard. 1971. "Cat O' Nine Tails." *Monthly Film Bulletin* (July): 120.

———. 1973. "Erotic Blue." *Monthly Film Bulletin* (April): 81.

———. 1972. "Forbidden Photos of a Lady Above Suspicion." *Monthly Film Bulletin* (June): 112.

Cook, Pam. 1985. "The Art of Exploitation or How to Get into the Movies." *Monthly Film Bulletin* 52: 367–69.

Cozzi, Luigi. 2002. Foreword in *The Haunted World of Mario Bava* by Troy Howarth. Godalming, UK: FAB Press, 5–6.

Creed, Barbara. 1993. *The Monstrous-Feminine: Film, Feminism, Psychoanalysis*. London: Routledge.

de Lauretis, Teresa. 1980. "Re-Reading Pasolini's Essays on Cinema." *Italian Quarterly* 82.3: 159–66.

Derry, Charles. 1988. *The Suspense Thriller: Films in the Shadow of Alfred Hitchcock*. Jefferson: McFarland.

Dika, Vera. 1990. *Games of Terror: Halloween, Friday the 13th, and the Films of the Stalker Cycle*. London: Fairleigh Dickinson University Press.

Dunant, Sarah. 2000. "Body Language: A Study of Death and Gender in Crime Fiction." In *The Art of Detective Fiction*, edited by Warren Chernaik, Martin Swales, and Robert Vilain, 10–20. London: Macmillan.

Dyer, Richard, and Ginette Vincendeau, eds. 1992. *Popular European Cinema*. London: Routledge.

Eleftheriotis, Dimitris. 2001. *Popular Cinemas of Europe: Studies of Texts, Contexts and Frameworks*. London: Continuum Press, 69.

Fofi, Goffredo. 1996a. "Bava, Mario." In *The Companion to Italian Cinema*, edited by Geoffrey Nowell-Smith with James Hay and Gianni Volpi, 19. London: BFI.

———. 1996b. "Freda, Riccardo." In *The Companion to Italian Cinema*, edited by Geoffrey Nowell-Smith with James Hay and Gianni Volpi, 54. London: BFI.

Frayling, Christopher. 1998. *Spaghetti Westerns: Cowboys and Europeans from Karl May to Sergio Leone*. London: I. B. Tauris.

Freeland, Cynthia A. 2000. *The Naked and the Undead: Evil and the Appeal of Horror*. Boulder, CO: Westview Press.

Frisby, David. 1994. "The *Flâneur* in Social Theory." In *The Flâneur*, edited by Keith Tester, 81–110. London: Routledge.

———. 2000a. "Threatening Glances: Voyeurism, Eye-Violation and the Camera: From *Peeping Tom* to *Opera*." In *Art of Darkness: The Cinema of Dario Argento*, edited by Chris Gallant, 11–19. Guildford, UK: FAB Press.

Georges, Robert A. 1971. "The General Concept of Legend: Some Assumptions to Be Reexamined and Reassessed." In *American Folk Legend: A Symposium*, edited by Wayland D. Hand, 1–19. Berkeley: University of California Press.

Grainger, Julian. 2000. "*Deep Red*." In *Art of Darkness: The Cinema of Dario Argento*, edited by Chris Gallant, 115–25. Guildford, UK: FAB Press.

Grant, Michael. 2000. "Fulci's Waste Land: Cinema, Horror and the Dreams of Modernism." In *Unruly Pleasures: The Cult Film and its Critics*, edited by Xavier Mendik and Graeme Harper, 61–71. Guildford, UK: FAB Press.

———. 2003. "The 'Real' and the Abominations of Hell: Carl-Theodor Dreyer's *Vampyr* (1931) and Lucio Fulci's *E tu vivrai nel terrore—L'aldilà* (*The Beyond*, 1981)." *Kinoeye: New Perspectives on European Film* 3.2: http://www.kinoeye.org/03/02/grant02.php.

Greene, Naomi. 1990. *Pier Paolo Pasolini: Cinema as Heresy*. Princeton, NJ: Princeton University Press.

Grove, David. 2005. *Making Friday the 13th: The Legend of Camp Blood*. Godalming, UK: FAB Press.

Guins, Ray. 1996. "Tortured Looks: Dario Argento and Visual Displeasure." In *Necronomicon Book One*, edited by Andy Black, 141–53. London: Creation Books.

Hall, Stuart. 1980. "Encoding/Decoding." In *Culture, Media, Language: Working Papers in Cultural Studies, 1972–1979*, edited by Stuart Hall, Dorothy Hobson, Andrew Lowe, and Paul Willis, 128–38. London: Hutchinson.

Hanke, Ken. 2003. "The 'Lost' Horror Film Series: The Edgar Wallace *Krimis*." In *Fear without Frontiers: Horror Cinema across the Globe*, edited by Steven Jay Schneider, 111–23. Godalming, UK: FAB Press.

Hawkins, Joan. 2000. *Cutting Edge: Art-Horror and the Horrific Avant-Garde*. Minneapolis: University of Minnesota Press.

Hay, James, and Geoffrey Nowell-Smith. 1996. "Italy: An Historical Overview." In *The Companion to Italian Cinema*, edited by Geoffrey Nowell-Smith with James Hay and Gianni Volpi, 1–8. London: BFI.

Howarth, Troy. 2002. *The Haunted World of Mario Bava*. Godalming, UK: FAB Press.

Hunt, Leon. 2000. "A (Sadistic) Night at the *Opera*: Notes on the Italian Horror Film." In *The Horror Reader*, edited by Ken Gelder, 324–35. London: Routledge.

Hutchings, Peter. 2003. "The Argento Effect." In *Defining Cult Movies: The Cultural Politics of Oppositional Taste*, edited by Mark Jancovich, Antonio Lázaro Reboll, Julian Stringer, and Andy Willis, 127–41. Manchester: Manchester University Press.

Koven, Mikel J. 2002. "Filming Legends: A Revised Typology" *Contemporary Legend* n.s. 5: 114–35.

———. 2004. "'The Film You Are About to See Is Based on Documented Fact': Italian Nazi Sexploitation Cinema." In *Alternative Europe: Eurotrash and Exploitation Cinema from 1945*, edited by Ernest Mathijs and Xavier Mendik, 19–31. London: Wallflower Press.

———. 2003a. "The Terror Tale: Urban Legends and the Slasher Film." *Scope: An On-Line Journal of Film Studies* (April): http://www.nottingham.ac.uk/film/journal/articles/tale-of-terror.htm.

———. 2003b. "Traditional Narrative, Popular Aesthetics, *Weekend at Bernie's*, and Vernacular Cinema." In *Of Corpse: Death and Humor in Folklore and Popular Culture*, edited by Peter Narváez, 294–310. Logan: Utah State University Press.

Lagny, Michèle. 1992. "Popular Taste: The peplum." In *Popular European Cinema*, edited by Richard Dyer and Ginette Vincendeau, 163–80. London: Routledge.

Landis, Bill, and Michelle Clifford. 1994. *Sleazoid Express: A Mind-Twisting Tour through the Grindhouse Cinema of Times Square!* New York: Simon & Schuster.

Landy, Marcia. 2000. *Italian Film*. Cambridge: Cambridge University Press.

Leprohon, Pierre. 1972. *The Italian Cinema*. Translated by Roger Greaves and Oliver Stallybrass. London: Secker and Warburg.

Liehm, Mira. 1984. *Passion and Defiance: Film in Italy from 1942 to the Present*. Berkeley: University of California Press.

MacKinnon, Richard. 1995. Introduction to Special Issue: Vernacular Architecture. *Canadian Folklore Canadien* 17.2: 5–7.

Marcus, Laura. 2000. "Oedipus Express: Trains, Trauma and Detective Fiction." In *The Art of Detective Fiction*, edited by Warren Chernaik, Martin Swales, and Robert Vilain, 201–21. London: Macmillan.

McDonagh, Maitland. 1994. *Broken Mirrors/Broken Minds: The Dark Dreams of Dario Argento*. New York: Citadel Press.

McGillivray, David. 1973. "Evil Fingers." *Monthly Film Bulletin* (November): 227.

Mendik, Xavier. 1996. "Detection and Transgression: The Investigative Drive of the Giallo." In *Necronomicon Book One*, edited by Andy Black, 35–54. London: Creation Books.

———. 2000. "A (Repeated) Time to Die: The Investigation of Primal Trauma in the Films of Dario Argento." In *Crime Scenes: Detective Narratives in European Culture since 1945*, edited by Anne Mullen and Emer O'Beirne, 25–36. Amsterdam: Rodopi Press.

———. 2000. *Tenebre/Tenebrae*. Trowbridge, UK: Flicks Books.

Mikkelson, Barbara. 1999. "Just Dying to Get Out." *Urban Legend Reference Pages*. http://www.snopes.com/horrors/gruesome/buried.htm [accessed: 3-30-2004].

Milne, Tom. 1972. "Five Dolls for an August Moon." *Monthly Film Bulletin* (August): 156–57.

Monthly Film Bulletin. 1965. "The Evil Eye." 32 (April): 58.

Monthly Film Bulletin. 1969. "A Black Veil for Lisa." (November): 241–42.

Monthly Film Bulletin. 1970. "The Gallery Murders." (November): 233–34

Monthly Film Bulletin. 1970. "Orgasmo."(January): 15.

Morandini, Morando. 1996. "Italy: Auteurs and After." In *The Oxford History of World Cinema*, edited by Geoffrey Nowell-Smith, 586–96. Oxford: Oxford University Press.

Morse, L. A. 1989. *Video Trash & Treasures*. Toronto: HarperCollins, 233.

Mulvey, Laura. 1999 [1975]. "Visual Pleasure and Narrative Cinema." In *Film Theory and Criticism: Introductory Reading*, edited by Leo Braudy and Marshall Cohen, 833–44. Oxford: Oxford University Press.

Nayar, Sheila J. 2005. "Dis-Orientalizing Bollywood: Incorporating Indian Popular Cinema into a Survey Film Course." *New Review of Film and Television Studies* 3.1: 59–74.

——. 2003. "Dreams, Dharma and Mrs. *Doubtfire*." *Journal of Popular Film & Television* 31.2: 73–82.

——. 2004. "Invisible Representation: The Oral Contours of a National Popular Cinema." *Film Quarterly* 57.3: 13–23.

——. 1997. "The Values of Fantasy: Indian Popular Cinema through Western Scripts." *Journal of Popular Culture* 31.1: 73–90.

Neale, Steve. 2000. *Genre and Hollywood*. London: Routledge.

Needham, Gary. 2003. "Playing with Genre: Defining the Italian *Giallo*." In *Fear without Frontiers: Horror Cinema across the Globe*, edited by Steven Jay Schneider, 135–44. Godalming, UK: FAB Press.

Nerenberg, Ellen. 2001. "Monstrous Murder: Serial Killers and Detectives in Contemporary Italian Fiction." In *Monsters in the Italian Literary Imagination*, edited by Keala Jewell, 65–88. Detroit, MI: Wayne State University Press.

Newman, Kim. 1988. *Nightmare Movies: A Critical History of the Horror Film, 1968–88*. London: Bloomsbury.

——. 1986a. "Thirty Years in Another Town: The History of Italian Exploitation." *Monthly Film Bulletin* 53: 20–24.

——. 1986b. "Thirty Years in Another Town: The History of Italian Exploitation II." *Monthly Film Bulletin* 53: 51–55.

——. 1986c. "Thirty Years in Another Town: The History of Italian Exploitation III." *Monthly Film Bulletin* 53: 88–91.

Ong, Walter J. 1982. *Orality and Literacy: The Technologizing of the Word*. London: Routledge.

Oring, Elliot. 1986. "Folk Narratives." In *Folk Groups and Folklore Genres: An Introduction*, edited by Elliot Oring, 121–45. Logan: Utah State University Press.

——. 1990. "Legend, Truth, and News." *Southern Folklore* 47.2: 163–77.

Palmerini, Luca, and Gaetano Mistretta. 1996. *Spaghetti Nightmares: Italian Fantasy-Horrors as Seen through the Eyes of Their Protagonists*. Key West, FL: Fantasma Books.

Pasolini, Pier Paolo. 1976. "The Cinema of Poetry," trans. Marianne de Vettimo and Jacques Bontemps. In *Movies and Methods Vol. 1*, edited by Bill Nichols. Berkeley: University of California Press, 542–58.

Pirie, David. 1973. "The Black Belly of the Tarantula." *Monthly Film Bulletin* (March): 56.

——1972. "Four Flies on Grey Velvet." *Monthly Film Bulletin* (September): 196.

P. J. D. 1966. "Blood and Black Lace." *Monthly Film Bulletin* 33 (February): 18.

Pratt, J. 1996. "Catholic Culture." In *Italian Cultural Studies: An Introduction*, edited by D. Forgacs and R. Lumley, 129–43. Oxford: Oxford University Press.

Priestman, Martin. 1998. *Crime Fiction: From Poe to the Present*. Plymouth, UK: Northcote House Publishing Ltd.

Primiano, Leonard Norman. 1995. "Vernacular Religion and the Search for Method in Religious Folklife." Special Issue: Reflexivity and the Study of Belief *Western Folklore* 54: 37–56.

Raisbeck, John. 1973. "A Lizard in a Woman's Skin." *Monthly Film Bulletin* (July): 150.

Reich, Jacqueline. 2001. "The Mother of All Horror: Witches, Gender, and the Films of Dario Argento." In *Monsters in the Italian Literary Imagination*, edited by Keala Jewell, 89–105. Detroit, MI: Wayne State University Press.

Rose, S., L. Kamin, and R. C. Lewontin. 1984. *Not in Our Genes: Biology, Ideology and Human Nature*. London: Penguin Books.

Rosenbaum, Jonathan. 1975. "Torso." *Monthly Film Bulletin* (June): 132.

Schmid, David. 2000. "The Locus of Disruption: Serial Murder and Generic Conventions in Detective Fiction." In *The Art of Detective Fiction*, edited by Warren Chernaik, Martin Swales, and Robert Vilain, 75–89. London: Macmillan.

Shields, Rob. 1994. "Fancy Footwork: Walter Benjamin's Notes on Flânerie." In *The Flâneur*, edited by Keith Tester, 61–80. London: Routledge.

Smith, Paul. 1990. "AIDS—Don't Die of Ignorance: Exploring the Cultural Complex." In *A Nest of Vipers: Perspectives on Contemporary Legend V*, edited by Gillian Bennett and Paul Smith, 113–42. Sheffield, UK: Sheffield Academic Press.

Sorlin, Pierre. 1996. *Italian National Cinema: 1896–1996*. London: Routledge.

Sotto, Agustin L. 1987. "Notes on the Filipino Action Film." *East-West Film Journal* 1.2: 1–14.

Strick, Philip. 1983. "Tenebre." *Monthly Film Bulletin* (May): 139.

Tester, Keith. 1994. Introduction to *The Flâneur*, edited by Keith Tester, 1–21. London: Routledge.

Thompson, Kirsten, and David Bordwell. 2003. *Film History: An Introduction*, 2nd edition. London: McGraw-Hill.

Thompson, Stith. 1955–1958. *Motif-Index of Folk-Literature: A Classification of Narrative Elements in Folktales, Ballads, Myths, Fables, Mediaeval Romances, Exempla, Fabliaux, Jest-Books, and Local Legends*. Six volumes. Bloomington: Indiana University Press.

Thrower, Stephen. 1999. *Beyond Terror: The Films of Lucio Fulci*. Godalming, UK: FAB Press.

Todorov, Tzvetan. 1990. *Genres in Discourse*. Catherine Potter trans. Cambridge: Cambridge University Press.

Totaro, Donato. 2003. "The Italian Zombie Film: From Derivation to Reinvention." In *Fear without Frontiers: Horror Cinema across the Globe*, edited by Steven Jay Schneider, 161–73. Godalming, UK: FAB Press.

Volpi, Gianni. 1996. "Italian Horror Film." In *The Companion to Italian Cinema*, edited by Geoffrey Nowell-Smith, with James Hay and Gianni Volpi, 63–65. London: BFI.

Wagstaff, Christopher. 1996. "Cinema." In *Italian Cultural Studies: An Introduction*, edited by David Forgacs and Robert Lumley, 216–32. Oxford: Oxford University Press.

————. 1992. "A Forkful of Westerns: Industry, Audiences and the Italian Western." In *Popular European Cinema*, edited by Richard Dyer and Ginette Vincendeau, 245–61. London: Routledge.

Willett, Ralph. 1996. *The Naked City: Urban Crime Fiction in the USA*. Manchester, UK: Manchester University Press.

Williams, Linda. 1989. *Hard Core: Power, Pleasure and the "Frenzy of the Visible."* Berkeley: University of California Press.

————. 1999. "Film Bodies: Gender, Genre, and Excess." In *Film Theory and Criticism: Introductory Readings*, 5th ed., edited by Leo Braudy and Marshall Cohen, 701–15. Oxford: Oxford University Press.

Williams, Linda Ruth. 2002 [1994]. "An Eye for an Eye." In *Science Fiction/Horror: A Sight and Sound Reader*, edited by Kim Newman, 13–17. London: BFI.

Williams, Raymond. 1976. *Keywords: A Vocabulary of Culture and Society*. London: Flamingo.

Wood, Robin. 1979. "An Introduction to the American Horror Film." In *American Nightmare: Essays on the Horror Film*, edited by A. Britton, R. Lippe, T. Williams, and R. Wood, 7–28. Toronto: Festival of Festivals.

Index

~

About the Author

Mikel J. Koven is lecturer in film and television studies at the University of Wales, Aberystwyth. He has published extensively in the areas of folklore and film in such journals as *Ethnologies, Culture & Tradition, Contemporary Legend, Journal of American Folklore, Literature/Film Quarterly,* and *Scope.* He is coeditor of a special issue of *Western Folklore* on folklore and film and coeditor of *Filmic Folklore* (forthcoming). Koven is also a contributor in Steffan Hanke's collection *Caligari's Grandchildren* (Scarecrow, forthcoming).